Interpreting Interpretation

Interpreting Interpretation

Textual Hermeneutics as an Ascetic Discipline

William Elford Rogers

The Pennsylvania State University Press
University Park, Pennsylvania

"Self-Portrait in a Convex Mirror," copyright © 1974 by John Ashbery, from *Self-Portrait in a Convex Mirror* by John Ashbery. Used by permission of Viking Penguin, a division of Penguin Books USA Inc.

Robert Frost, "For Once, Then, Something." From *The Poetry of Robert Frost*, edited by Edward Connery Lathem. Copyright 1923, © 1969 by Holt, Rinehart and Winston. Copyright 1951 by Robert Frost. Reprinted by permission of Henry Holt and Company, Inc.

Library of Congress Cataloging-in-Publication Data

Rogers, William Elford.
   Interpreting interpretation : textual hermeneutics as an ascetic discipline / William Elford Rogers.
      p.   cm.
   Includes bibliographical references and index.
   ISBN 0-271-01059-2 (cloth : acid-free paper) — ISBN 0-271-01061-4 (pbk.)
   1. Discourse analysis. 2. Hermeneutics. 3. Semiotics.
4. Criticism. I. Title.
P302.R565   1994
401'.41—dc20   92-41210
                                                                       CIP

Copyright © 1994 The Pennsylvania State University
All rights reserved
Printed in the United States of America

Published by The Pennsylvania State University Press,
Barbara Building, Suite C, University Park, PA 16802-1003

It is the policy of The Pennsylvania State University Press to use acid-free paper for the first printing of all clothbound books. Publications on uncoated stock satisfy the minimum requirements of American National Standard for Information Sciences—Permanence of Paper for Printed Library Materials, ANSI Z39.48–1984.

Contents

Acknowledgments   vii

Abbreviations   ix

Introduction   1

1   Doing Without Entities   5

2   The Well and the Mirror   45

3   The Arts of War   99

4   Terminus at the Real   139

5   The Corpse in the Iron Lung   179

Bibliography   233

Index   237

Acknowledgments

Much of this book was written during my tenure as a Dana Foundation Fellow in the Southeastern Humanities Consortium Project at Emory University. I thank the Charles A. Dana Foundation and Emory University for their support of this project and of my research.

I thank my dean, John H. Crabtree, Jr., for nominating me to participate in this project, and Furman University for granting me sabbatical leave. I am also grateful to the Research and Professional Growth Committee of Furman University for financial support.

For interesting and helpful discussions I am indebted to Robert Detweiler, the director of the Dana project and the leader of the Dana Fellows' seminar at Emory; and to the other members of that seminar in 1989–90: John Bullard, Lucas Carpenter, Howard Carter, Nancy Corson Carter, William Garland, Jorge Gonzalez, and Gray Kochhar-Lindgren.

Parts of Chapter 2 appeared in *Furman Studies* 32 (1986) under the title "Mysteries in Frost," and an earlier version of Chapter 4 appeared in *Religion and Literature* 18 (1986) under the title "Ricoeur and the Privileging of Texts: Scripture and Literature." Support from the National Endowment for the Humanities made the writing of both of these earlier essays possible.

"Mysteries in Frost," *Furman Studies* 32 (1986): 53–64. Reprint permission granted by *Furman Studies*, Furman University, Greenville, S.C.

"Ricoeur and the Privileging of Texts: Scripture and Literature," *Religion and Literature* 18.1 (1986): 1–25. Reprint permission granted by *Religion and Literature*, University of Notre Dame, Notre Dame, Ind.

Abbreviations

B   Peirce, Charles S. *Philosophical Writings of Peirce.* Ed. Justus Buchler. New York: Dover Publications, 1955.

CIS   Rorty, Richard. *Contingency, Irony, and Solidarity.* Cambridge: Cambridge University Press, 1989.

ConP   Rorty, Richard. *Consequences of Pragmatism (Essays: 1972–1980).* Minneapolis: University of Minnesota Press, 1982.

CP   Peirce, Charles S. *Collected Papers of Charles Sanders Peirce.* 6 vols. Ed. Charles Hartshorne and Paul Weiss. Cambridge: Harvard University Press, 1931–35.

DE   Dewey, John. *Democracy and Education: An Introduction to the Philosophy of Education.* New York: Macmillan, 1916.

EBI   Ricoeur, Paul. *Essays on Biblical Interpretation.* Ed. Lewis S. Mudge. Philadelphia: Fortress Press, 1980.

EE   Dewey, John. *Experience and Education.* New York: Macmillan, 1938.

HHS   Ricoeur, Paul. *Hermeneutics and the Human Sciences.* Ed. and trans. John B. Thompson. Cambridge and Paris: Cambridge University Press and Éditions de la Maison des Sciences de L'Homme, 1981.

IT   Ricoeur, Paul. *Interpretation Theory: Discourse and the Surplus of Meaning.* Fort Worth: Texas Christian University Press, 1976.

PI   Wittgenstein, Ludwig. *Philosophical Investigations.* 3d ed. Trans. G.E.M. Anscombe. New York: Macmillan, 1958.

PMN   Rorty, Richard. *Philosophy and the Mirror of Nature.* Princeton: Princeton University Press, 1979.

SS   Peirce, Charles S., and Victoria Lady Welby. *Semiotic and Significs: The Correspondence Between Charles S. Peirce and Victoria Lady Welby.* Ed. Charles S. Hardwick. Bloomington: Indiana University Press, 1977.

W   Peirce, Charles S. *Charles S. Peirce: Selected Writings (Values in a Universe of Chance).* Ed. Philip P. Wiener. New York: Dover Publications, 1966.

How far the perspectival character of existence extends or whether it has any other character at all, whether an existence without interpretation, without 'meaning' would not become 'meaninglessness', whether on the other hand all existence is not an *interpreting* existence—this, as is only reasonable, cannot be determined even by the most assiduous and painfully conscientious analysis and self-examination of the intellect: since in the course of this analysis the human intellect cannot avoid viewing itself in its perspectival forms and *only* in them. We cannot see round our own corner. . . . The world has rather once again become for us 'infinite': insofar as we cannot reject the possibility that it *contains in itself infinite interpretations.*
—Friedrich Nietzsche, *The Gay Science*, 1887, section 374; trans. R. J. Hollingdale

The singular family resemblance between all Indian, Greek, and German philosophizing is easy enough to explain. Where there exists a language affinity it is quite impossible, thanks to the common philosophy of grammar—I mean thanks to unconscious domination and directing by similar grammatical functions—to avoid eveything being prepared in advance for a similar evolution and succession of philosophical systems: just as the road seems to be barred to certain other possibilities of world interpretation.
—Nietzsche, *Beyond Good and Evil*, 1886, section 20; trans. R. J. Hollingdale

We do not obtain the conception of Being, in the sense implied in the copula, by observing that all the things which we can think of have something in common, for there is no such thing to be observed. We get it by reflecting upon signs—words or thoughts; we observe that different predicates may be attached to the same subject, and that each makes some conception applicable to the subject; then we imagine that a subject has something true of it merely because a predicate (no matter what) is attached to it—and that we call Being. The conception of being is, therefore, a conception about a sign—a thought, or word. . . . But it is nothing new to say that metaphysical conceptions are primarily and at bottom thoughts about words, or thoughts about thoughts; it is the doctrine of Aristotle (whose categories are parts of speech) and of Kant (whose categories are the characters of different kinds of propositions).
—Charles Sanders Peirce, "Some Consequences of Four Incapacities," 1868; reprinted in *W*.

Introduction

This book is about literary education. It began in vague dissatisfaction with the way I was teaching my students about poetry. I could not even explain that dissatisfaction coherently, and I slowly became aware that my colleagues also lacked a compelling account of what we were all pretending to do.

Just to say that we impart "knowledge" and "appreciation" of poems seems to me hopelessly vague. When I tried to unpack these ideas by asking about the practical effects of this knowledge or appreciation (the pragmatist's question), the supposed effects often seemed illusory, or too trivial to justify the effort. I do not know how to demonstrate that studying literature makes a person a better citizen, or that poetry is a better recreation than pushpin.

To say that we are teaching our students "a way to think" sounds more promising. But it needs an explanation of how studying literature does that. Such an explanation requires something that looks like a theory. In many arts, perhaps even the art of teaching, the absence of theory is not necessarily fatal to practice. But in American colleges and universities, the dominant model of discourse is still the rational model of the Enlightenment. That model is no doubt outdated, and maybe American colleges and universities were never run on rational principles anyway. Nevertheless, no professor of literature today wants to say that we do not know what we are doing. In our field, the absence of theory is a scandal.

In fact, there are plenty of theories. Lately, it has become obvious that the problem of accounting for practice is not confined to the educational backwaters of small, private liberal-arts colleges such as the one where I teach. Books such as *Cultural Literacy* (1987) by E. D. Hirsch, Jr., and *The Closing of the American Mind* (also 1987) by Allan Bloom and various reports of public and private agencies and foundations have rocked boats even outside the academy. It is not just that a new generation with minds made sodden by television goes blank when confronted with the verbal intensity of poems. The problem is general to the humanities. What the humanities share as disciplines is the reading, writing, speaking, and hearing of interpretive statements about texts. The value of those activities is in question.

A great deal of the debate has fluttered around the issue of the canon, that list of texts that "should" be interpreted. This question is extremely important, and, like all important political questions, extremely difficult. But I think it is a mistake to let the debate over the canon distract from the more fundamental question of what it means to interpret a text. The problems of what is variously called pluralism, relativism, or even nihilism cannot be solved by agreeing on the canon, just as if everybody would know what to do with a text once it gets in the canon. In this book I shall have very little to say about canon and a great deal to say about interpretation. The central problem, as I see it, is to give an account of textual interpretation that will acknowledge the crucial insights of structuralism and poststructuralism, and yet will leave teachers of the humanities something to do besides dropping precious and enigmatic interpretations before uncomprehending students. Why this is a problem, and why I think it is central, should become clear in the essays that follow.

In Chapter 1, I talk about the notion of interpretation itself and the strangeness of trying to construct a theory of interpretation—that means, an interpretation of interpretation. To cope with that strangeness, I develop the notion of an "interpretive system." Interpretation can interpret itself only from within the boundaries of some particular interpretive system. I argue that the broad interpretive system called textual hermeneutics, properly conceived, best suits my purposes. From the perspective of textual hermeneutics, the world looks like a text. That principle rigorously applied allows an articulation of the relations between language, philosophy, and interpretation itself. I follow Charles Sanders Peirce, whose theory of signs led him to identify human thought with semiosis and to conclude that "Man is a sign." (Peirce preferred the spelling *semeiosis*. On the general question of terminology, see Max Fisch, "Peirce's General Theory of Signs," in Fisch, 321–22.)

INTRODUCTION

The choices I make in Chapter 1 determine everything that follows. First, I choose textual hermeneutics as the system from within which to articulate a theory of interpretive systems. Then, I choose to identify textual hermeneutics with a Peircean semiotic, which ultimately implies a Peircean brand of ontological and epistemological realism. Philosophical realism was scientifically unfashionable in Peirce's day, and is scientifically unfashionable now. Nevertheless, taking up this stance has, to my mind, decisive advantages in addressing the problems that motivate this book.

In Chapter 2, I try to exemplify the notion of "interpretive system" by applying that notion to the interpretation of two poems, one by Robert Frost and one by John Ashbery. Though I discuss only poetic texts, my hypothesis is that similar structures of interpretation could be found with other kinds of texts—for example, novels, plays, philosophical works, historical narratives, myths, scriptural texts, and so on.

Chapter 3 forms a sort of keystone by connecting the notion of "interpretive system" with the notion of "ascetic discipline." In order to do that, I consider the Oriental martial arts—particularly taekwondo, a Korean martial art—as interpretive systems. I use the discussion of the martial arts to assess some of the consequences of Wittgenstein's "private-language argument." I conclude that the vocabulary of Peirce's semiotic is more satisfactory than Wittgenstein's vocabulary for talking about ascetic disciplines. Then I propose conceiving textual hermeneutics as an ascetic discipline.

In Chapter 4, I attempt to explain more fully what it means to consider textual hermeneutics as an ascetic discipline, by distinguishing the interpretation of "privileged" or canonical texts from that of nonprivileged texts. My tactic is to pursue the distinction in the works of Paul Ricoeur between "scripture" and "literature." In certain of Ricoeur's writings, scripture can be taken as exemplary of privileged texts, as opposed to "mere" literature. My argument is that the theory of interpretive systems allows one to articulate this difference, whereas Ricoeur's hermeneutic ultimately fails to articulate it. Furthermore, once this difference is articulated, it exemplifies what is distinctive about practicing textual hermeneutics as an ascetic discipline.

In Chapter 5, I take up explicitly the question of what it means to "teach a text." In a pragmatic account, a conception means what its practical effects are conceived to be. Therefore, to talk about the practical effects in literary education of a theory of interpretive systems is another way of talking about what the notion of "interpretive system" means. I consider textual hermeneutics in a Peircean way as an ascetic discipline, and contrast the implications of that theory for education with the implications of the pragmatism of John Dewey and of Richard Rorty. I try to find in Peirce's semiotic a way out of the bind in which Dewey and Rorty leave teachers of the humanities—namely, the bind of being unable to give a cogent account of practice, of being unable to say what it means to teach the humanities by reading, writing, speaking, and hearing interpretive statements about texts.

In all of these essays, I think of myself as depending on the thought of Charles Sanders Peirce, but I am no Peirce scholar. For one thing, Peirce was a laboratory scientist by vocation, and I am illiterate in natural science. For another thing, I lack the necessary detailed knowledge of the chronological development of Peirce's thought. For yet another, I am not competent in either formal or mathematical logic, both of which are essential to a full understanding of Peirce. I have more or less plundered Peirce's writings, taking something from here and something from there, combining and bending according to my own purposes. Whether these juxtapositions and adaptations constitute a defensible use of Peirce's thought will have to be decided after the next generation of Peirce scholars has come to terms with Peirce himself. Like Whitman, Peirce was large and contained multitudes. No doubt he sometimes contradicted himself. He traveled habitually in realms of thought beyond my ken. I can only hope that the records of his journey that seem comprehensible and useful to a teacher of literature are not just a jumble of incoherent fragments torn from the larger whole.

When I began thinking about these questions, I jokingly told my friends that I was working on a book that would rescue Western civilization. What that meant, of course, was only that I was trying to make some sense out of the part of Western civilization that obsesses me—namely, the interpretation of the texts I read as privileged. I will be happy enough if I provide a vocabulary for talking about what people are doing in colleges and universities when they read, write, speak, and hear interpretive statements about texts. But this vocabulary has to be one that acknowledges the very great difficulty of talking about that in the face of postmodern anxieties about—or embracing of—pluralism, relativism, or nihilism. What emerges from these essays is not curriculum, but method—and method conceived in a way that is perhaps unusual. I argue, finally, that the humanities teach not texts, but interpretive systems.

1

Doing Without Entities

1. Interpretation: Heidegger, Derrida, Nietzsche

What is interpretation?

Even the shape of such a question is puzzling. Is it a question like What is language? or What is philosophy? Such questions seem to ask for a definition and a critique. They want an answer of the shape "Language is . . ." or "Philosophy is . . .," where what comes next does not mention language or philosophy. Language or philosophy is to be understood, and so evaluated, in terms of something other than, outside of, language or philosophy. This is not like asking, What is a platypus? There are many things other than platypuses in terms of which to tell about platypuses. But how can I tell about language without speaking, or how can I think about philosophy without philosophizing? Questions about language and philosophy fold in on themselves. The something "outside" language or philosophy appears to be a kind of impossible Archimedean standpoint.

Heidegger thinks his way into language by following the thread of his aphorism "Language speaks." He responds to the speaking of language by listening to what is spoken "purely" in the "masterful poem." Heidegger's reflecting, recalling thought (*andenkendes Denken*) is often like a digging down through deposited layers of language used—used up—as a tool (say, the biologist's definition of *platypus*). Heidegger wants to come to a core where language appears as what it originally is: the "house of Being." For humans language lets beings appear as what they are—the tree *as* a tree and not, perhaps, as raw material for a pulp mill, the cow *as* a cow and not as undeveloped shoes and steaks. So this statement "Language is the house of Being" should not be heard as even a metaphorical definition, though it has the shape of one. Being is not a category, like the category "mammal" or the category "quadruped." It is not even the category that includes all beings. Especially, it is not a category within which another category, "language," can be put. Instead, Heidegger means that for humans, Being is correlative with language. The house in the metaphor is not one of many interchangeable units of a modern apartment building, but a Bavarian farmhouse that shapes and is shaped by the lives of the peasants who dwell in it. Language is lighted up when, in speaking, it lights up Being.

In one way, Heidegger's path is like learning to move. One learns to move not by discussing mechanics, but by watching movement and by moving. To move well, as in the dance or in the martial arts, often means that one must first peel away layers of habitual movements that have been barely adequate for daily work. To move well, one thinks of the movement not as something merely instrumental for doing the work, but instead as something at the behest of which the work happens. Heidegger tries to think of language in accordance with its own nature and from the inside, because there is no other way.

Jacques Derrida wants to critique philosophy. That seems to require finding a standpoint outside philosophy. But everything that is not philosophy, that is nonphilosophical—what Derrida sometimes calls the "empirical"—seems still to belong to philosophy as its subject matter. Philosophy is omnivorous; it takes Being for its subject matter. Philosophers claim the right to philosophize about anything. Since he has to use the very words and philosophical structures he critiques, Derrida follows the devious paths of deconstruction. The strategies are by now well known: for example, writing "under erasure," at once affirming and denying the terms of metaphysics; reading written texts as determined, in ways their authors would never have dreamed, by the greater, unwritten, historical text into which books are woven; distorting the marginal passages in a text until the text collapses under its own incoherence, like a cell whose wall disintegrates when attacked by a virus; reversing the traditional polarities of Western thought—most notably, elevating absence over presence and writing over speech. All of the strategies depend in one way or another on what Derrida calls the irreducible polysemy of the linguistic sign. It is not just possible but necessary that each word mean more than one thing. Derrida learns of this necessity from Saussure, by pushing the insights of structuralism further than Saussure wanted to go.

Deconstruction is guerrilla warfare. It depends on surprise and on being able to choose its own ground. Texts are attacked at just the points where no historical author or audience would have seen any need to defend them. A fish in water, like the guerrilla among the people, the deconstructionist swims in the academy, indistinguishable from the other academicians. Only by first belonging to philosophy can the deconstructionist do the work of deconstruction. There must be a structure to deconstruct.

Heidegger's and Derrida's questions have the same shape. Both are asking *about* something to which everything, including their own asking, seems to belong. This word *about* already holds their problem within its etymological suggestion of an *outside*. How can one speak *about* something if there is nothing around and *about* it, if there is nothing that it as yet is not but is *about* to be? How can one philosophize *about* what belongs to philosophy if there is nothing outside of that belonging?

There is another way that the structure of Derrida's thought is like Heidegger's. By *Language* Heidegger does not mean any single natural language—not even Greek or German. After all, he needs both. In fact, sometimes his etymologizing carries him all the way back to Indo-European, the hypothetical ancestor language in which every word begins with an asterisk to show that it is unattested (absent). Similarly, Derrida is talking not about the philosophy of Plato or of Aristotle or of Kant, but about the idea of philosophy that covers what any particular philosopher might say. One could perhaps think here in Saussure's terms. Maybe Language as such stands to the natural languages, and philosophy to the particular philosophies, as the phoneme stands to its allophones, or as *langue* stands to *parole*. Language as such can perhaps be thought of as the unheard, unseen structure of differences that makes the natural languages possible; philosophy as such can perhaps be thought of as the enabling structure of differences attested only in particular philosophical systems.

And Heidegger's and Derrida's questions push each thinker toward what sounds like a new language: Heidegger's etymologizing, in which words take on resonances that let them enter into strange combinations and new harmonies; Derrida's punning, in which words begin to skid and fly out of their contexts. But here is a difference. These paths toward a new language go in opposite directions. Heidegger's way is centripetal. By putting many different words together, he makes the single word do more than it has done before—not because it means many different things, but because its fragments have been glued back together, so to speak, and it has been given back the lost fullness of its core. Derrida's way is centrifugal. By making a central word mean different and contradictory things, he wants to shake ("solicit") the structures dependent on that word by scattering its meanings ("dissemination").

Sometimes Heidegger's etymologizing seems just a bothersome tic, and Derrida's punning an irritating display of cleverness. Nevertheless, their different strategies are symptoms of a deep difference in their problems. Heidegger's problem, stated as abstractly as possible, is to think how something can be the same as its other—how, that is, Language can be correlative with Being. Derrida's problem, on the contrary, is to think how something can be different from its "proper," from what belongs to it—how the relation of "belonging" is not enough to assimilate the nonphilosophical to philosophy.

In two different ways, Nietzsche's thought is the background to both Heidegger's and Derrida's problems, which brings me back to the question of interpretation. If Heidegger's thinking about Language and Derrida's thinking about philosophy are to be instructive for thinking about interpretation, their thought must be seen against the background of such passages from Nietzsche as the ones that stand as epigraphs to this book. Taken together, those passages on the one hand suggest the deep ties between language, philosophy, and interpretation. These seem, almost, three names for the same thing considered under different aspects, like the three Persons of the Trinity. And on the other hand, the passages argue implicitly that whatever problems there are in getting outside, in talking *about*, language and philosophy, arise a fortiori in talking about interpretation. If Nietzsche's thought is taken as a clue, it would seem, in the first place, that interpretation would have to interpret itself, just as language has to speak of speaking and only of speaking, and as philosophy has to think of thought and only of thought. Language speaks; thought thinks; interpretation interprets.

But in the second place, it would seem that trying to think and speak about interpretation would meet at once with both Heidegger's problem and Derrida's problem. Interpretation is a kind of middle. This is not to say that language and philosophy are just particular categories that can be put under the universal category of interpretation. But the passages from Nietzsche imply that interpretation has to face two ways at once. It has to think something as being the same as its other, and it has to think how something can be different from what it properly belongs to. As in the passage from *Beyond Good and Evil*, if "world interpretation" is *only* grammar, in the sense of being determined by Indo-European grammatical categories, then how is it possible to think of philosophical systems as *interpreting* a world? How does grammar assimilate the nonlinguistic to itself? How is the grammatical system the same as or correlative with a world? In Heidegger's terms, how do Language and Being belong to each other? If, however, the world for humans is only an infinite container of interpretations, as in the passage from *The Gay Science*, then how is it possible to think and speak of the world as different from the particular interpretations it belongs to? Interpretation, then, has the problem of at once interpreting sameness in difference and difference in sameness.

I put the problem this way for two reasons. First, I want to profit, if possible, from following Heidegger's and Derrida's reflections on problems that, seen from this angle, have a similar structure. I will say more about this soon. Second, putting the problem this way gets me closer to the decisive step of this book, which is to interpret interpretation by thinking about *signs* and, in particular, by thinking through the semiotic of Charles Sanders Peirce. It is precisely the sign that for human consciousness has the structure of sameness and difference that characterizes interpretation. For consciousness, the sign is the same as, belongs inseparably to, what it signifies; and yet its being as sign depends on its difference from the signified. The sign, like interpretation, mediates. This much has seemed obvious since, at least, St. Augustine's *De doctrina christiana*. What is perhaps not so obvious at once—but what should be more obvious after a thoughtful detour through Heidegger, Derrida, and Nietzsche—is that I have gotten nowhere if I merely bring in "sign" as a category from outside interpretation in order to talk *about* interpretation. Moreover, it could be seriously misleading to think of "sign" itself this way. The sign has the structure of sameness and difference; the sign mediates. But if everything is interpretation, as from within interpretation it must appear to be, then what is the same as or different from what? What is mediated? Only more interpretations. This needs careful thought, and I am counting on Peirce as a guide.

Meanwhile, I have been edging toward the hypothesis that the question What is interpretation? has something of the same shape as the questions What is language? and What is philosophy? It might be instructive now to lay out in summary what is to be inferred by this hypothesis from Heidegger's and Derrida's reflections.

First, interpretation interprets itself. That means that if the idea of the sign is used to interpret interpretation, then "sign" must be thought of not as a category including interpretation, but as correlative with interpretation. That is, semiosis is already interpretation. Just as it is not very helpful in the long run to try to define language or philosophy in terms of categories presumably drawn from outside themselves, so it is a mistake to think of the terms in which one talks about interpretation as other than interpretive.

Second, it is always necessary to choose a particular way of interpreting. This particular way of interpreting is not interpretation as such, but is made possible by interpretation. Maybe any particular way of interpreting is made possible precisely by the differential structure within which it stands with respect to other ways of interpreting. Heidegger chooses German, and occasionally Greek, as the particular natural language to speak about Language. Derrida chooses structuralism as the particular philosophical system from within which to deconstruct philosophy. The particular choice is obviously crucial. Presumably, reasons of various kinds, theoretical or historical, could be given for it. Later, I will give reasons for my own choice.

Third, to interpret interpretation, a particular way of interpreting must be self-transcending. It must, in a way, contain its other. Heidegger's German sounds strange. His prose sometimes treads a blurred path between the semantically well formed and the unintelligible. Criticizing Heidegger for inaccurate etymologies or deficient Greek would be beside the point. Heidegger is shaping a new language, and presumably he writes in German because that natural language has remarkable resources that already gesture toward something linguistically other. Derrida adopts the vocabulary of structuralism because Saussure's insights, pushed far enough, undermine the "scientific" linguistics Saussure aimed at. Poststructuralism is the "taking up" (*Aufhebung*) of structuralism, in much the same way that Heidegger's prose is the "taking up" of the German language.

Aufhebung is "taking up" as my elementary-school teacher would "take up" my pencil when I amused myself by noisily rolling it down the writing surface of my desk. The teacher would then return the pencil when it was time to write. This use of *take up* holds both senses of *aufheben*: "cancel" and "preserve." The shape of the pencil makes it handy as a toy and as a tool. It holds in its shape the necessity and purpose of its own taking up. Two other English idioms echo in the term. There is the idiom by which someone "takes up" someone else on something, as Derrida "takes up" Saussure on Saussure's own assumptions. And in a way Heidegger "takes up" the German language and Derrida "takes up" Saussure's work as unfinished tasks, or even as one "takes up" a burden or an avocation. A particular way of interpreting that is to be useful for thinking about interpretation must hold in itself the capacity for its own taking up. It must put itself forward to be taken up. That capacity of any particular way of interpreting would presumably be one of the reasons for choosing it.

Finally, as I have said, interpretation must address the problem of sameness and difference. One of the constantly nagging issues of this book will be the relation of interpretation, language, and philosophy. My constant hope is that Peirce's idea of the sign will in some way help to thread that labyrinth.

2. Peirce's Semiotic

It is time to explore Peirce's idea of the sign. I quote here some definitions of *sign*, from various places in Peirce's writings, with comments on how his idea of the sign seems to provide what is needed to talk about interpretation from within. First, "a sign is something, A, which denotes some fact or object, B, to some interpretant thought, C" (*CP*, 1.347). Peirce's word *interpretant* is what is interesting here. Besides hinting that semiosis essentially involves interpretation (or something like it), naming the interpretant is a decisive turn in thinking about signs. Augustine thought of a sign as something that stands for something else. Saussure thought of a sign as the unity of signifier and signified; structuralism is shot through with binary oppositions such as this basic one. The unity of signifier and signified is an objective fact for the scientific intelligence that studies *langue*. In other words, Augustine and Saussure have in common that for them the sign relation is dyadic. A stands for B. For Peirce the sign relation is triadic: A stands for B to C. There are three elements in the relation, not two. The third element is the interpretant, the thought that interprets the sign.

Naming the interpretant uncovers a whole new field of questioning: what quality, force, or rule connects the sign to its object for the interpretant thought? What makes anybody think of a rose—not only the concept, but even the particular rose one thinks of—when one hears the word *rose*? For Saussure the connection of signified with signifier is the unquestioned (*arbitraire*) principle of *langue*, understood from the outside as an ultimate fact. The question opened up by Peirce's idea of the interpretant is a questioning of semiosis by itself, from inside. Peirce himself engaged in a seemingly endless classifying of signs, which he thought of as pioneering work in this territory. Each of his categories of signs represents a subspecies of the basic triadic relation, a different way of relating sign, object, and interpretant with one another. But each category is also a *rule*; that is, it is itself a sign that stands for its instances to Peirce's thought in his reflection on signs. For Saussure, science questions language. For Peirce, semiosis questions itself.

Another of Peirce's definitions:

> A sign, or *representamen*, is something which stands to somebody for something in some respect or capacity. It addresses somebody, that is, creates in the mind of that person an equivalent sign, or perhaps a more developed sign. That sign which it creates I call the *interpretant* of the first sign. The sign stands for something, its *object*. It stands for its object, not in all respects, but in reference to a sort of idea, which I have sometimes called the *ground* of the representamen. (*CP*, 2.228)

This definition stresses the triadic nature of the sign relation. There is also some hint here of how Peirce's semiotic might have to face the problem of sameness and difference. First, the definition brings in the notion of the "ground." The sign is different from the object in that it does not stand for it "in all respects"; but it is the same as the object for the interpretant thought in that there is some respect in which it can stand for (even stand in for) the object. For example, a red rose is not like my love in all respects, but it has some capacity—call it "blushing"—which is identical to a capacity she has. More important, however, is Peirce's notion that the sign relation is self-replicating. The interpretant of the first sign (which is "equivalent to" or a "more developed" version of the first sign) then becomes a sign for the next interpretant, and so on.

I bring in here one more definition of *sign* that makes this same point more strongly: "Sign—Anything which determines something else (its *interpretant*) to refer to an object to which itself refers (its *object*) in the same way, the interpretant in turn becoming a sign, and so on *ad infinitum*" (*CP*, 2.303). The first interpretant is for the next interpretant the same as the first sign: it is "equivalent to" the first sign or includes it; and it refers to the same object "in the same way." Elsewhere (*CP*, 2.230), Peirce explains the process more fully. Every sign has "some explanation or argument or other context, showing how—upon what system or for what reason—the Sign represents the Object. . . . Now the Sign and the Explanation together make up another Sign," which will also have its explanation, and so the "already enlarged Sign will make up a still larger Sign." One can even imagine, even though such a thing might not exist, a "Sign of itself, containing its own explanation, and those of all its significant parts; and according to this explanation, each such part has some other part as its Object." Thus interpretation interprets itself. The interpretant, at first counting as something different from the sign that determines it, then becomes identical with that sign for the infinite chain of interpretants in which it is a link. This infinite replication of signs, this operation of sameness and difference, is for Peirce the fundamental nature of consciousness.

So far, then, I have meant to make two points about Peirce's idea of the sign. First, Peirce's sign is self-referential: it brings about its own signing by subsequent signs. One might say, taking the cue from Peirce's term *interpretant*, that the nature of the sign is to interpret itself in interpreting its object. The three elements of one sign relation (object, sign, and interpretant) are taken up together as a single sign for the next interpretant, that triadic relation is taken up as a single element for the next, and so on, endlessly. If one were to diagram the process, the result would be a kind of self-similar fractal surface. This is the first point that makes Peirce's semiotic seem helpful in thinking questions such as What is interpretation? once it seems that there is no Archimedean standpoint outside interpretation.

Second, Peirce's idea of the sign characteristically involves the problematic of sameness and difference. It is not necessary to think that Peirce "solves" the problem of sameness in difference and difference in sameness, but only that his reflection on signs has this characteristic, a characteristic that seems necessary for any reflection on interpretation that takes Nietzsche's, Heidegger's, and Derrida's thought into account.

But besides these two points, there are two more things to be learned from Heidegger's and Derrida's reflections: that it is always necessary to choose a particular way of interpreting, and that the particular way of interpreting chosen must have the capacity to transcend itself, to be taken up as the German language is taken up in Heidegger's philosophical discourse or as structuralism is taken up in poststructuralism. It may be a little tricky to show how Peirce's semiotic points toward the particular way of interpreting that I will choose. That argument might already involve a decisive turning away from Peirce's own chief concerns, a taking up of Peirce's semiotic into something else. Once this step is taken, however, it may not be so tricky, but it will still be complicated, to show how the particular way of interpreting I choose has as an essential characteristic the capacity to transcend itself.

By way of getting at these difficult questions, I want to consider more fully one important implication of Peirce's idea of the sign. As a logician, Peirce would have seen at once that his apparently simple definition of *sign* involves an infinite regression. An interpretant cannot be an interpretant unless it becomes a sign for the next interpretant, which cannot be an interpretant unless *it* becomes a sign for the next interpretant, which cannot be an interpretant unless . . . , and so on. At this rate, there never actually is a sign, if a sign is considered as an event in space-time. As Peirce says of the sign relation, "this relation cannot consist in any actual event that ever can have occurred . . ."; and, "For the same reason the interpretant cannot be a definite individual object" (*CP*, 1.542). For most purposes, of course, it is all right to talk of the sign as virtual, as having the *capacity* to produce an interpretant thought, and this is the line Peirce often takes.

But Peirce, who once thought it necessary to defend himself against the charge of "triadomany" (the insane obsession with threes), could of course not content himself with only one infinite regression where he could find two more. There is another infinite regression in the direction of the object, since any representation of the object one has in mind must be the interpretant of some previous representation. In two seminal papers that attempt to overthrow Cartesianism, Peirce argues that humans think only with signs and that all cognitions are therefore determined by previous cognitions: "Questions Concerning Certain Faculties Claimed for Man" and "Some Consequences of Four Incapacities," which appeared in *The Journal of Speculative Philosophy* for 1868 (*W*, 15–72). In the first of those papers Peirce compares the object of representation to the limit of an infinite mathematical series, as in a later statement: "an endless series of representations, each representing the one behind it, may be conceived to have an absolute object at its limit" (*CP*, 1.339).

Finally, like the object and the interpretant, the sign itself may be thought of as being involved in an infinite regress. Peirce calls the sign a "vehicle conveying into the mind something from without"; he calls "that which it conveys, its meaning" (*CP*, 1.339). The statement is a little cloudy. I think Peirce means something like this. Say that you are a skillful tracker, and you observe some marks on the ground that indicate to you that a two-hundred-pound man in cowboy boots has passed this way recently. Then the man is conceived as the object, the marks are conceived as the sign, and your visual imagination of the man is conceived as the interpretant. (I say "conceived as" and not "actually is" for the reasons given above: until the infinite chain of significations is complete, there are no actual signs or interpretants.)

Now suppose I ask you what the marks mean. You might answer me with an English sentence: "A two-hundred-pound man in cowboy boots passed this way recently." That sentence would tell what the sign conveys. It would be a translation, as it were, from the sign system of your visual imagination into the sign system of the English language. In fact, at one place Peirce says that the commonly accepted definition of *meaning* is "the translation of a sign into another system of signs" (*CP*, 4.127). Your English sentence is itself a representation. In fact, the only way you can convey your visual imagination to me is by representing it to me: "The meaning of a representation can be nothing but a representation. In fact, it is nothing but the representation itself conceived as stripped of irrelevant clothing" (*CP*, 1.339). That is, you did not give me a detailed description of your imagining, nor did you tell me all of the private associations in the midst of which you arrived at your conclusion. You gave me the bottom line. But the English sentence, too, contains elements that could be thought of as irrelevant to the representation of what it represents—for example, its sound or its syntax, since I could represent the same state of affairs differently in English, or in French or German. Peirce concludes that the "clothing" of the representation "never can be completely stripped off; it is only changed for something more diaphanous. So there is an infinite regression here" (*CP*, 1.339), an infinite regression into other systems of signs into which the original representation may be "translated" when one asks for its "meaning."

The all-important point in all of this talk about infinite regressions is that Peirce's idea of the sign keeps the sign and the interpretant from being identified with actual events or definite objects, even though Peirce himself often talks as if they could be. Even the object exists for consciousness only as a kind of limit of an infinite series of signs.

Whether and how the object "really exists" for Peirce apart from consciousness is another, and a complicated, question. Peirce claimed to be a "scholastic realist." In *Peirce, Semeiotic, and Pragmatism*, Max Fisch has an essay whose title suggests the danger of making any categorical statements about Peirce's realism: "Peirce's Progress from Nominalism toward Realism" (Fisch, 184–200). Fisch distinguishes five different stages in this progress, some of the stages themselves being complex. In *Peirce*, Christopher Hookway discusses how Peirce's realism connects with his belief in the validity of scientific inquiry (151–80), his pragmatism (234–61), and his metaphysics (262–88). What Peirce's realism might mean for my idea of textual hermeneutics will emerge later, and mostly by implication. But to think of textual hermeneutics as a Peircean theory of signs would mean, among other things, to answer questions about being and knowing as a philosophical realist like Peirce might answer them. Meanwhile, my immediate point is that by the nature of the sign relation, all three elements of the relation are themselves relations, not links in an infinite chain but the empty places in semiotic space that the links may occupy and that therefore make the chain possible.

In his writings on logic Peirce sometimes speaks of relations in terms of chemical valences, or potentials for entering into certain types of bonding. His idea of sign seems in a peculiar way to be trying to do without entities and, in effect, to make do with relations. In the first of his two papers against Cartesianism, for example, Peirce writes, "all the cognitive faculties we know of are relative, and consequently their products are relations. But the cognition of a relation is determined by previous cognitions. No cognition not determined by a previous cognition, then, can be known" (*W*, 37). It might seem strange to think of relations as somehow prior for thought, and to think of entities as those things which *are* only insofar as they stand in relations, but I think this is what Peirce's semiotic asks. Whatever is taken into the chain of signification is ipso facto a relation, and humans think only in signs. In other words, Peirce in his own way articulates the dependence of signification on the absence of the signified.

This line of thought provides a clue of sorts. Derrida arrives at his conclusions about the absence of the signified by reflecting on the work of Saussure. Derrida pushes Saussure's own idea that language is "arbitrary" and "differential," where these are two sides of the same coin. Language is arbitrary because the meaning of the linguistic sign depends only on the structure of differences within which the sign is embedded, and not on any particular sort of correspondence between words and things. If Saussure is right about at least this much, then the strangeness of Peirce's relational semiotic is only the strangeness of the most familiar, intimate, and everyday experience. It is the strangeness of language—where words can be thought of as individual entities only because they stand in differential relations with the other words; where the pursuit of linguistic meaning involves, if not an infinite regress, at least an endless circling through all the words of the language, with the size of the circle limited only by the "size" of the language, itself an ill-defined concept. Language, what is closest to human beings, is all relations.

Peirce himself often speaks of words as only one subclass of signs. But sometimes he seems to recognize explicitly that words are not self-subsistent individual entities: "the word 'fast,' which is a Sign, is not imaginable, since it is not *this word itself* that can be set down on paper or pronounced, but only *an instance* of it, and since it is the very same word when it is written as it is when it is pronounced, but it is one word when it means 'rapidly' and quite another when it means 'immovable,' and a third where it refers to abstinence" (*CP*, 2.230; written in 1910). And toward the end of his refutation of Descartes, Peirce writes, "there is no element whatever of man's consciousness which has not something corresponding to it in the word. . . . [M]y language is the sum total of myself; for the man is the thought" (*W*, 71). Here Peirce seems to bring together language, thinking, and interpretation under the heading of the "word."

In such passages, Peirce seems not far from the poststructuralists, though he never seems tempted to the paths of deconstruction. Neither

Peirce nor Saussure would deny that there is *some* sort of connection between words and things. For Saussure, words are connected to things through the concept, which is the "signified" in the sign relation. For Peirce, words are conventional signs—and to that extent he can agree with Saussure about the "arbitrary" nature of language—but the goal of scientific inquiry is to make the conventional signs represent reality accurately. (That means, of course, in Peirce's sense of "represent" and Peirce's sense of "reality.") Human thought for Peirce is not doomed by language never to touch anything outside linguistic conventions. But poststructuralist thought, whose challenges I am concerned to meet, is a taking up of structuralism, which bases itself on linguistics. And Peirce also talks about human consciousness in linguistic terms. What I have been moving toward, then, is an argument for linguistic interpretation as the particular way of interpreting, the particular interpretive system (to anticipate an important concept) in terms of which to interpret interpretation.

In short, the argument goes something like this. If Peirce's idea of the sign is to be helpful at all, it should offer a thread through the labyrinth of thinking about interpretation. Peirce's reflections lead to the conclusion that human thought is through and through relational, and that entities exist for human consciousness only insofar as they stand in semiotic relations. But the insight of structuralism is precisely that language, that which human beings know most intimately, is through and through relational. At all times human beings have in front of them, behind them, over them, under them, and on all sides the relational structures of their language. If semiosis according to Peirce seems strange just because it possesses the very same characteristic as language, it makes sense to try to think of semiosis by thinking of linguistic interpretation of some sort. If Peirce's semiotic has such deep affinities with structuralist and poststructuralist notions of language, why not assimilate his semiotic entirely to the linguistic, the territory that seems strangest to reflect on precisely because it is where human beings are most at home?

This move also has the advantage of bringing Peirce squarely into contemporary discussions about language, thought, and interpretation. It is clear, however, that this move would be in some ways alien to Peirce's own inclinations. He was a logician and a laboratory scientist, and his interest was primarily in finding out the truth. Truth for Peirce is that which science (understood, to be sure, as he understands it) aims at finding out. Logic properly speaking is a normative science. Peirce would have wanted his thought to be of interest primarily to historians of logic and philosophers of science. And so it is, to some degree. But to think of Peirce's semiotic primarily from the standpoint of linguistic interpretation represents a contemporary "taking up" of his thought by disciplines he himself was not particularly interested in. Peirce had a classical education, and he had some interest in linguistics insofar as he believed that linguistic categories lie behind the categories of logic. But he seems to have troubled himself little about what today would be called literary criticism and literary theory. And yet, those disciplines, along with the social sciences that root themselves in structural linguistics, are the disciplines that most often invoke his thought as still viable for contemporary discussion.

This is a historical, if not strictly philosophical, argument for taking linguistic interpretation as the particular interpretive system from within which to think about interpretation as such. Under the hypothesis that Peirce's semiotic can offer a guiding thread, his semiotic seems most thinkable nowadays from the standpoint of linguistic interpretation of some sort.

But of what sort? I have argued that any particular interpretive system that interprets interpretation will have the capacity to transcend itself. A set of instructions for breaking a simple code, for example, though it could be described as a rule of linguistic interpretation, seems not obviously to possess this capacity. A list of discrete "steps" in interpreting a poem that a teacher might distribute to an introductory class also would seem to be a relatively fixed, self-enclosed system. An open-ended system is needed, one in which reference is always made not just to the subject matter being interpreted, but to the process of interpreting itself. Working toward such a system is a major task of this book, and a task that by its nature continues beyond the boundaries of this or any future book.

3. *Textual Hermeneutics as Interpretation*

It seems important to make at least one choice at the outset. Is speech prior, or is writing prior? Orality, or literacy? Is the paradigm to be the interpretation of the spoken word, or textual hermeneutics? This is Derrida's problematic. The opposition is not so simple as the difference between the ear and the eye, because spoken communication normally involves visible gestures, and readers "hear" or subvocalize texts. But the experiences of speech and writing have seemed very different, at least since Augustine learned from Ambrose how to read silently. So it is not enough just to mention linguistic interpretation, as if that were obviously some single essence.

I will come down on the side of textual hermeneutics—understood as I understand it, of course, since there are at least as many notions of textual hermeneutics as there are schools of criticism. I think Derrida is right about one crucial point. The problem of absence in presence and presence in absence—the problem of the sign—is more obvious, easier to think, when one is dealing with writing (which implies the absence of the author) than when one is dealing with speech (which implies the presence of the speaker). In this sense (and this sense only, for the moment), writing is "prior to" speech.

It follows that self-reference (reflexivity) is more obvious in textual hermeneutics than it is in interpreting most situations of "living speech." The point in textual hermeneutics seems to be to articulate a "meaning" in some shape different from that of the text being interpreted. The interpretation often takes the shape of a new text. The whole enterprise involves a necessary assumption that the text I am producing, my interpretation of Milton, is itself susceptible to the same process of interpretation. Like Milton's poem, it can be cut loose from the situation of its production. If I can articulate the meaning of Milton's text, then meaning is no more tied to my text than it is to Milton's—whatever notion of "meaning" I might have. Milton's absence from his text implies my potential absence from my own. What can be done to Milton's writing can also be done to mine. In situations of speech, however, people say, "You had to be there." The interpretation of speech only sometimes consists in articulating a meaning. Instead, it usually takes the shape of behavior or dialogic response. You speak, and I nod; I do what you want me to; I ask *whether* you meant such-and-such; I answer you. When newscasters "interpret" one of the president's speeches, they treat the speech as if it were a written text, and normally in fact work from a written text.

When Derrida tries to reverse the traditional polarity of speech and writing by showing how the structures that make writing possible also ground speech, he is trying not to overthrow speech but to think beyond the opposition. Debates about which is really prior, writing or speech, miss the point. The point is, again, to criticize philosophy from within philosophy, using the oppositions that philosophy provides. I think one need not follow the ways of deconstruction in order to interpret interpretation. But if one wants to enter the field in which language, philosophy, and interpretation are talked about, one must address the issues posed by deconstruction.

Deconstruction is upsetting because the issues it raises are important, even when its practice seems merely naughty or perverse. The locus of these issues is textual hermeneutics. The crisis of the humanities, if there is a crisis, is occurring in the debates about textual interpretation. If the humanities have a place of their own, and are not to be absorbed by formal logic or the natural sciences, then that place must be established somewhere in the neighborhood of textual hermeneutics, the discipline distinctive of the humanities. That is another reason, and perhaps the decisive one, for choosing textual hermeneutics as the particular interpretive system from within which to think about interpretation.

What does the world look like, then, from the perspective of textual hermeneutics? Clearly, it looks like a text. A text can be thought of as a weaving of signs. That means that for consciousness it exists only virtually, until somebody writes or reads it; that is, until it is taken as sign into some particular chain of signification. But in Peirce's philosophy the same kind of thing can be said about material objects, facts, events, sensations, and even emotions. And just as the world seems to exert a reactive force on our cognitions, which Peirce describes under his category of "Secondness," so there seems to be something in texts that constrains interpretation to some degree. On this particular point there seems to be no difference between the world according to Peirce and the text according to hermeneutics. In textual hermeneutics, certain "parts" of the text are selected as being "significant," and this always happens against a background of other "parts" that are ignored as irrelevant for interpretation. For example, in interpreting prose texts I normally do not look for meter or rhyme, whereas in interpreting poetic texts these features might take on great importance. The "irrelevant" features of the text remain, as it were, blank. Only those features that are taken into the sign relation actually become *features* for the interpreter.

In one of the passages I have quoted above, Peirce talks about the explanation that necessarily belongs to every sign. There is "some explanation or argument or other context, showing how—upon what system or for what reason—the Sign represents the Object" (*CP*, 2.230). In textual interpretation the interpretive statement is a sign of— that is, stands for—the text. The passage from Peirce suggests that there is some explicit or implicit set of interconnected rules (the interconnectedness is implied in Peirce's word "system") for moving from the significant features of the text to the interpretive statement. I can "argue for" or "support" my interpretation, in other words, by explaining the principles on which I have connected the features of the text to the features of my interpretive statement. This system of rules or principles is what I am calling an *interpretive system*. To apply an interpretive system means precisely to take something into the chain of signification, to take it as a sign, or as a *word* in the broad sense that Peirce uses when he says that the word or sign a person uses *is* the person.

To apply an interpretive system means to make something into a word. One could even say that it means to take up (*aufheben*) something as a word. But words are relations. After all this laborious circling, then, I seem to be led to something like a starting point. For all the reasons I have given, it seems appropriate to interpret interpretation from within the interpretive system of textual hermeneutics. What does an interpretive system look like from the standpoint of textual hermeneutics itself? *An interpretive system is a structure of relations such that each relation determines its relata also to be relations.* It is a system for making things into words.

The implications of this notion of "interpretive system" are the subject of the rest of this book. But it is important to recall here why this statement about interpretive systems does not imply a definition of interpretation as such, in the normal sense of definition. Why not? What keeps me from presenting a "definition" of the following shape: "Interpretation is the use of an interpretive system, where an interpretive system is . . . ," and so on? This statement would have the grammatical shape of a definition, but it could be proposed only in an entirely different spirit. The statement would not be a definition of interpretation in terms of categories drawn from outside interpretation. It is not like saying, for example, "A platypus is a mammal that lays eggs." Unlike the definition of platypus, the "definition" of interpretation would be an instance of what it defines.

A definition connects the definiendum with the definiens by means of the copula, thus making the definiens a sign of the definiendum, and vice versa. That is, a definition asserts that definiendum and definiens stand for each other. The rules governing definition, then, have been used to make definiendum and definiens signs of each other. This could be put yet another way: definiendum and definiens have been made into words precisely by being brought into relation with each other. That is usually more obvious from the side of the definiendum, where something that is not a word for somebody (that is, has no meaning for somebody) is made into a word by becoming a relation, a place in the semantic field. Clearly, though, the definition equally makes the definiens into a semantic place by bringing it into relation with the definiendum. The relation of defining is reciprocal. So when interpretation is "defined" as I have suggested, the statement is self-referential.

What is being defined is what underwrites the possibility of definition, and so if I try to use the definition to understand the nature of interpretation "from the outside," I wander in a useless circle. In order to define at all, I must have already understood interpretation—as defined—from the inside.

As for defining, what can be done is to define one interpretive system from the standpoint of another, as one natural language can be defined in terms of another, or as one philosophical system can be defined in terms of another, or (what I am doing here) Peirce's semiotic can be defined in terms of textual hermeneutics. Heidegger believes that humans can respond to Language only in the working of a particular language; Derrida believes that a critique of philosophy as such is possible only at the boundaries where particular philosophical systems break down. Similarly, interpretation as such can be encountered only in the working and the failure to work of particular interpretive systems.

I want to stress once again where the definition of *interpretive system* points, as a guide for further inquiry. If one accepts the insights of structuralism into the differential nature of language, it is not surprising that textual hermeneutics sees everything as relations, since words are relations. But to stress with Peirce that there is a background, an argument or explanation for connecting one sign with another, implies a whole field of inquiry. Peirce saw this discipline as a branch of logic broadly considered. He called it "methodeutic" or "pure rhetoric": "Its task is to ascertain the laws by which in every scientific intelligence one sign gives birth to another, and especially one thought brings forth another" (*CP*, 2.229). I would substitute "hermeneutic intelligence"; but I think it might not seem necessary to do so if *scientific* today meant what Peirce meant by it. *Science* in the commonly accepted sense today, and in Peirce's day, implies methodological nominalism. Peirce thought, however, that only philosophical realism could make sense of the scientific endeavor. I am arguing that talking from the perspective of textual hermeneutics means talking in some sense like a philosophical realist.

There is, then, a theory of interpretive systems, even though there is no theory of interpretation as such. This is like saying that linguists have theories of languages, without having a theory of language as such, or that systematic philosophers have theories of philosophical systems, without having a theory of philosophy. There are many theories of interpretive systems, each one articulated from within the boundaries of some particular interpretive system, and each one susceptible to being articulated in terms of some other system. I have chosen textual hermeneutics as the interpretive system from which to look at other interpretive systems. This means to see how human activities construe the world as a text, and to pay attention to the systems of relations that determine experiences to be significant—that is, that make experiences into something resembling words or take them up as though into language.

4. Peirce's Doctrine of the Categories

In the rest of this chapter, I want to return to a question implied at the beginning: What is the relation between language, philosophy, and interpretation? But that question is much too big. I want to creep up on it by asking a more specific question, more directly related to the concerns of this book: What does philosophy look like from the perspective of textual hermeneutics? Even that question is too big, and so I want to restrict myself further to a consideration of certain points in Peirce's philosophy. Peirce's semiotic is crucial to his philosophy, and Peirce's semiotic is after all what is being taken up here into textual hermeneutics. So it seems fair to ask, What do the central concepts of Peirce's philosophy look like from the perspective of textual hermeneutics? To ask this means to follow the thread of Peirce's own formulas: "Man is a sign" and "My language is the sum total of myself." It means asking how Being—Being according to Peirce, to be sure—can become a text to be taken into language.

I come back to the passage from Peirce's refutation of Cartesianism quoted at the beginning of this book. In one way it sounds remarkably Nietzschean before Nietzsche. "The concept of being is, therefore, a conception about a sign—a thought, or word." As Peirce says, he means by this that metaphysical thought is thought about linguistic categories: about grammatical categories (Aristotle) or about the structure of propositions (Kant). If this is so, then the place to look in any philosopher for reflections relevant to the question of language and being would be in his doctrine of categories.

In 1867 Peirce published a paper "On a New List of Categories," and his doctrine of the categories is central to his philosophical thinking from first to last. I am relying heavily here on Peirce's early works. As one of the most fruitful of his philosophical conceptions, his doctrine of the categories was constantly evolving. Hookway's discussion (80–117) is instructive. Peirce most often called his categories simply Firstness, Secondness, and Thirdness. These are phenomenological categories. That is, they are ways of categorizing the elements of whatever can be present "before the mind" as phenomenon. At the most abstract, these categories are relations: Firstness is a monadic relation, Secondness a dyadic relation, and Thirdness a triadic relation. A First is what it is apart from anything else, a Second is what stands in relation with only one other thing, and a Third is what brings two other things into relation with itself and each other.

The Third stands in general for plural relations of three or more places, because Peirce believed that any relation of more than three places could be resolved into a complexus of triadic relations. Peirce thought of logical reasoning as spatial in nature: reasoning from diagrams, or from the actual spatial relationships on the page of symbols standing for terms or individuals. Therefore, if asked why Thirdness is needed as a category but why Fourthness, Fifthness, and so on, are not, he could present as an argument the fact that it is impossible by joining single lines end to end to produce a line with more than two ends; but by proper connecting of triadic diagrams (three lines with their ends connected at one point, leaving three "tails" free) one can produce a diagram with four, five, or as many free tails as one pleases. The single line represents a dyadic relation. It connects its two ends. The triadic diagram represents the triadic relation. It symbolizes the connection of three things in one point.

These rather empty, abstract concepts of Firstness, Secondness, and Thirdness may be filled out somewhat by considering the ontological categories implied by the phenomenological ones. Peirce normally calls these ontological categories *quality* or *possibility* (a First), *fact* or *reaction* (a Second), and *law* or *general* or *habit* (a Third). Firsts are characteristics (such as the color red) that might be possessed by some existent thing, but as Firsts the qualities are not to be identified with the actual properties of any existing thing. They are only possibilities. Seconds are what resist, as Peirce often says, with "brute force," and they are always single, particular, actual things. They need not be material objects. Whatever disturbs the consciousness, which has a kind of inertia and resists changing the focus of its attention, has about it an element of Secondness. As laws, Thirds are generals that ground the ability to predict what the actual facts will be in the future. Peirce often says that Thirdness has about it a "would-be"; or, "Continuity represents thirdness almost to perfection" (*CP*, 1.337).

Peirce's many attempts to classify signs depend on his categories. Just to illustrate, it will be enough for me to discuss briefly one of those classifications. There are three elements in the sign relation: sign ground, object, and interpretant. With each of these elements Peirce associates a trichotomy.

In the first place, something can serve as a sign because of its own

Firstness, because of its own Secondness, or because of its own Thirdness. That is, it might be a sign because of some *quality* it embodies (as when a red rose reminds me of a fire engine, just because the rose is red), or because it is an actual *existing* object (as when somebody's elbow in my ribs serves as a sign of that person's presence), or because it embodies some *law* or convention (as with words, considered as part of the conventional semiotic system of the language). The first trichotomy, then, is that of Qualisigns, Sinsigns (*sin-* as in *single*, since actual events are unique), and Legisigns.

The second trichotomy is the more familiar one of *Icons, Indices,* and *Symbols.* This trichotomy classifies signs according to their relations to their objects. An Icon is related to its object through Firstness; that is, by sharing some quality with that object. An Index is related to its object through some actual physical connection (smoke as a sign of fire, for example). A Symbol is related to its object through some convention.

Peirce's third trichotomy divides signs according to how the sign determines the interpretant—that is, roughly speaking, according to how the sign is taken in thought. A sign may be taken as a sign of a First, a sign of a Second, or a sign of a Third. Here the identity of Peirce's logic and his semiotic becomes visible. Peirce, like Kant, ties his categories to the operations of logic, but he does it in a different way. Peirce associates Firstness with the *Term*, which is the name of a quality—as, for example, in the proposition "The moon is blue," the term *blue* represents a quality attributed to the moon. A device Peirce often uses is to write the term considered as a First this way: "_____ is blue." He shows by the device that the term *blue* represents a mere possibility, an empty place in a relation, something "looking for a home," as it were, among actually existent things. (Another of Peirce's names for such a sign is *Rheme.*) Secondness is associated with the *Proposition* (sometimes called the *Dicent Sign*), which asserts the actual existence of the state of affairs it describes. There is an element of "brute force" in the proposition taken as true, at least, because there is some state of affairs that "makes one" say what one says. On the other side, there is something about the proposition itself that "makes one" focus attention in a particular way on the state of affairs it represents. Thirdness, finally, is associated with the *Argument*. The valid argument form is a general rule or law. It allows one to predict that future arguments of the same form will for the most part and in the long run produce true conclusions.

There is an intimate connection, then, among metaphysics, logic, and language in Peirce's philosophy. A great deal more could be said about Peirce's categories. One can hardly read a page of his voluminous and incredibly wide-ranging works without meeting the categories in one guise or another. But my concern here is only to see how those categories look from the perspective of textual hermeneutics. A way into that is to see how the categories are connected with Peirce's idea of the sign.

Peirce sometimes, in fact, defines the sign in terms of the categories: "A *Sign*, or *Representamen*, is a First which stands in such a genuine triadic relation to a Second, called its *Object*, as to be capable of determining a Third, called its *Interpretant*, to assume the same triadic relation to its Object in which it stands itself to the same Object" (*CP*, 2.274). This definition looks very much like one I quoted before, except that the mention of the categories is added. Peirce says something similar in a letter to Lady Welby, though he uses less technical language: "A *Third* is something which brings a First into relation to a Second. A Sign is a sort of Third" (*SS*, 31).

And I need to pause here to clear up some possible confusion on two points. In the letter to Lady Welby, Peirce uses the term *Sign* to refer to the whole triadic relation, and not just to the First in question as in the preceding definition. Does he want to say that the sign is a First, or that it is a Third? This is a bothersome inconsistency in Peirce's terminology, but I think it can be cleared up if instead of *Sign* in the first of these two definitions I read *Sign ground*. The sign ground is a First, the sign relation itself a Third.

The second point is maybe more philosophically troublesome, but less central to what I am doing here. If all thought is signs, and signs are Thirds, how can Firstness and Secondness be phenomenological categories—that is, categories of what can be before the mind? There is no doubt that Peirce thought of signs as Thirds: he says, for example, that the "idea of a sign, or representation" is one of the most obvious "ideas in which Thirdness is predominant" (*CP*, 1.338–39). Even his definition of a Third in the 1867 paper on the categories sounds very much like some of his definitions of the sign: "The conception of a *third* is that of an object which is so related to two others, that one of them must be related in the same way in which the third is related to that other" (*CP*, 1.556). I think it is enough for my purposes just to say that Firsts or Seconds *as such* cannot be before the mind, since all thought is in signs; but that one can nevertheless focus attention on the Firsts and Seconds that are elements of the Thirds that are signs. (See Hookway, 95–96, on Peirce's notion of "prescindability" of one element of cognition from another.) It would work this way, then: a footprint is a sign of a man to the tracker. The print's quality of being foot-shaped, a First, is brought into relation with a Second, a particular passing of a particular man, in a Third, the habit or rule by means of which the tracker interprets the footprint. This relation thus determined is the interpretant thought, which now becomes the sign of the man in the tracker's mind.

Let me go on, and further than Peirce does, along the path he indicates. Peirce defines signs in terms of his categories. The question here, since I am trying to look at the world from the perspective of textual hermeneutics, is whether the definition can be set on its head, so to speak. Can the categories be defined in terms of linguistic signs? Nietzsche says that grammar determines the fate of thought; Peirce himself says that "metaphysical conceptions are primarily and at bottom thoughts about words." But how is this so? How does it or should it happen? How can metaphysical categories be arrived at by beginning with a reflection on linguistic categories?

Presumably, in more than one way. Aristotle, according to Peirce, accepts as normative the grammatical categories of Greek. Kant, on the contrary, begins with the structure of logical propositions. Kant believed that logic had scarcely been improved upon since Aristotle; it would follow that the structure of the proposition common to many languages implies a more universal set of categories than the grammar of any particular natural language could. But my task is to approach Peirce's categories not through English grammar or through formal logic (though Peirce himself might have been happier with the second of these approaches), but through textual hermeneutics as it has been influenced by the insights of structuralism and poststructuralism. If Peirce's categories are to be connected with textual hermeneutics as it is or may be understood today, what is the method of connection?

A helpful first step is to talk briefly about the affinities between Peirce's categories and Kant's. Peirce devoted a great deal of time to studying Kant. He says that his father, the Harvard mathematician Benjamin Peirce, guided him through Kant's first *Critique*. Peirce spent, he says, two hours a day for more than three years on this project and ended by knowing Kant's book almost by heart. Kant considered his list of categories a purification of Aristotle's, because Kant's categories are based on the sounder principle of the logical proposition. Kant has twelve categories under four headings: quantity, quality, relation, and modality. Peirce's categories, I believe, are homologous with Kant's categories of relation.

Kant's first relational category is the substance/attribute relation, which he derives from the structure of the categorical proposition—e.g., "This rock is hard." Such propositions, Kant says, assign attributes (predicates) to things (subjects) conceived as bearers of those attributes. The rock is conceived as something different from the hardness it bears as an attribute. In fact, the rock itself is conceived as a substance different from any and all of its attributes. In general, Kant argues, the possibility of constructing a categorical proposition depends on human beings' possessing the substance/attribute relation as an empty category of thought, which is filled out by particular intuitions.

Kant's second relational category is causality (the cause/effect relation), which he derives from the hypothetical proposition—e.g., "If you are deprived of food, then you will starve." Here the condition described in the antecedent of the proposition is often (though not always) asserted as the cause of the condition described in the consequent. The connecting of antecedent events with consequences, as happens in the hypothetical proposition, must depend on some category of human thought—since, as Hume had pointed out, causality itself is not directly observable in the external world.

Kant's third relational category, reciprocity (the part/whole relation), is derived from the disjunctive proposition—e.g., "Either I will win, or I will die." Here the clauses of the proposition, taken together, are conceived as exhaustively determining a whole. The conditions described thus stand in a relation of mutual interdependency (reciprocity) with respect to each other and to the whole that they determine.

Kant's argument for adopting these relations as fundamental categories of human thought is that logic finds these three types of proposition indispensable, and that the possibility of each type depends on the respective relation. Peirce was far from accepting Kant's view of logic or Kant's procedure of transcendental deduction, and so it would be a mistake to say that Peirce's categories are the same as Kant's. But there are affinities that should become clearer as I go along.

It is interesting that traditional concepts of the "thing" in Western metaphysics can also be seen as homologous with Kant's relational categories. In his essay "The Origin of the Work of Art" Heidegger summarizes three different concepts of the "thing," only to reject them all as inadequate for thinking about the "thingliness" of the work of art. All three concepts are both venerable and current, according to Heidegger. The first concept regards the thing as a substance with its accidents (traits or characteristics), and this concept Heidegger, like Kant, associates with the subject-predicate structure of the ordinary proposition (Heidegger, 22–24). The second concept regards the thing as that which is perceptible by the senses: as Heidegger says, "things move us bodily" (25). It is easy enough to see in this concept an understanding of the thing as cause of certain effects in human sense organs, and thus to connect the concept with Kant's second relational category. Finally, Heidegger mentions the concept of the thing as "formed matter" (26). It is perhaps not so easy to see how this concept is homologous with

Kant's third relational category, but it might make some sense to regard the form as the whole in terms of which each part of the material thing has its place, or to say that a reciprocal relation obtains between the form and the matter on the one hand, and on the other hand among the various material parts considered in terms of the roles they play in embodying the form.

Again, Peirce's categories are not identical with the traditional thing concepts. But perhaps they are homologous. That is, perhaps these thing concepts could be reformulated in terms of Peirce's categories. If that is so, and if Peirce's categories can themselves be articulated in linguistic terms, then a step will have been taken toward understanding what the world looks like from the perspective of textual hermeneutics—how things, in short, can be like words. From the perspective of textual hermeneutics, to see the world as text means to break down in the interpretation the opposition of words and things.

5. Saussure's Oppositions and Peirce's Categories

My method here will be to try to derive Peirce's categories from three of Saussure's crucial concepts: the relation of signifier to signified, the syntagmatic relation, and the paradigmatic relation. I do not use *derive* here in the strong or metaphysical sense. I do not mean to argue that Peirce's categories must be metaphysically grounded in Saussure's. I mean to show only that there is a projection of Peirce's categories, so to speak, in textual hermeneutics, and that one can find the principle of this projection by starting with Saussure's relations. I will not always understand those relations exactly as Saussure seems to have understood them, however. For instance, in general these relations should not be thought of as dyadic (as involving only binary oppositions), as Saussure seems to have thought of them sometimes. In the particular case of the relation of signifier with signified, Saussure's binary thinking creates difficulties that Peirce's own subtler analysis helps to resolve.

Saussure defines the linguistic sign as the unity of signifier and signified, where the signifier is the acoustic image and the signified is a concept. The acoustic image of the word *arbre* stands in French for the concept "tree." Since I am talking about textual hermeneutics, I am more concerned with the graphic image than with the acoustic, but I believe that the kinds of things I am going to say here can be said, mutatis mutandis, about both. Derrida presumably would insist on the philosophical priority of the graphic image. By Saussure's analysis, concepts also would be involved in the differential structure that constitutes *langue*. That is, concepts would be language-specific and therefore arbitrary, and that would at least pose a problem for the sort of objective scientific analysis Saussure aims at. This is a point that poststructuralists make.

But a more immediate problem is that Saussure's analysis does not seem to deal adequately with the relation between the word and what Peirce calls its "replicas," or the actual audible or visible embodiments of the word. Specifically, one might ask about "acoustic image." Is it a sound as an actual speaker or listener imagines it might be made? Is it the image in the mind of a sound that has just been in the ear? Both? Is it a rule for making or interpreting actual sounds? Peirce's analysis teases out some of these distinctions.

> We speak of writing or pronouncing the word "man"; but it is only a *replica*, or embodiment of the word, that is pronounced or written. The word itself has no existence although it has a real being, *consisting in* the fact that existents *will* conform to it. It is a general mode of succession of three sounds or representamens of sounds, which becomes a sign only in the fact that a habit, or acquired law, will cause replicas of it to be interpreted as meaning a man or men. The word and its meaning are both general rules; but the word alone of the two prescribes the qualities of its replicas in themselves. (CP, 2.292)

This passage may be compared with the one quoted earlier in which Peirce discusses the word *fast*, and with the one in which Peirce defines *meaning* as a translation from one system of signs into another. Meaning, as translatable, does not prescribe the particular qualities of the signs that have the meaning. Words do prescribe the particular qualities of the replicas that stand for the words. The replicas are in the first place signs of the occurrence of the word (not, notice, the *word itself*, but its *occurrence*). Through the word the replicas are signs of whatever the word is a sign of.

Technically, the replica is for Peirce a Rhematic Indexical Sinsign of its word (see, for example, *CP*, 2.261). That means that the replica can be a sign because it is in itself a single individual occurrence (Sinsign). It is Indexical because it has some real, existent connection with its object. That is, I have learned the word by seeing or hearing actual replicas of it in actual situations in which the thing, event, or relation referred to by the word is actually present. As Peirce puts it: "A Replica of the word 'camel' is . . . really affected, through the knowledge of camels, common to the speaker and auditor, by the real camel it denotes, even if this one is not individually known to the auditor; and it is through such real connection that the word 'camel' calls up the idea of a camel" (*CP*, 2.261). Finally, and this is the important point, the replica is a Rhematic sign because it is taken in thought as a sign of certain qualities it possesses (the qualities, namely, prescribed by the word considered as a rule) that make it suitable as a sign of an occurrence of the word.

These qualities are what Peirce elsewhere calls the sign ground. They are the phonetic or graphic features of the sounds or the letters that make those sounds or letters suitable to serve as a replica of a word. There are other "irrelevant" characteristics of the sounds or letters. The picture of my voice on the screen of the oscilloscope as I speak the word *man* is highly individual, and even slightly different from time to time. There are many ways of writing the word *man*: large letters or small, print or script, decorated or plain, various typefaces and fonts, and so on. But all of these occurrences are replicas of the word *man* because they all presumably embody some quality or qualities prescribed by the word for its replicas. (That it turns out to be very difficult to say just what those "essential" qualities are is another problem. Nevertheless, most of the time we know when we have encountered a replica of the word *man*, just as we know when we have encountered a chair or a table or a tree without being able easily to give the necessary and sufficient characteristics of chairs, tables, or trees.)

I believe that this line of thought leads back to Peirce's definition of sign as a "First which stands in such a genuine triadic relation to a Second, called its *Object*, as to be capable of determining a Third, called its *Interpretant*, to assume the same triadic relation to its Object" (*CP*, 2.274). If the First in question here is taken to mean the sign ground, as I have suggested, then this definition can be explicated in terms of replicas and words. A quality is a First; certain qualities, then, of the replica (namely, those prescribed by the rule that is the word) stand as signs of an occurrence of the word. The word itself, as a rule, is a Third, but an individual occurrence of the word in speech or writing is a Second. Seconds need not be material objects. In this case, the Second consists in the actual application of an existing rule. This is normally called a "use" of the word. So some quality (a First) of the replica stands for the occurrence (a Second) of the word. Now, the word is what it is by virtue of the conventions of the language. A word in an unknown language or alphabet is mere sound or shape, but a word in my own language "means what it means." So when I hear or read a *word* (and not a mere sound or shape), then my thought precisely becomes the rule that is the word. That is, I "think" the word itself, and that thought now stands in my mind for the individual occurrence of the word. I am thinking, to put it very precisely, that some certain characteristic of the sound or shape is a sign of an individual occurrence of the conventional sign "man," or "camel," or whatever. My interpretant thought is then a Third, which, for purposes of subsequent thought, becomes a sign of the word I have just heard or read. Now, presumably, I can go on to take the word as a sign of a concept, perhaps, and think of men or camels instead of words.

I have gone through this tedious analysis to stress two points: first, that I want to consider the signifier/signified relation not at the level at which Saussure's analysis begins, where the acoustic image signifies the concept, but at what might be called a prior level, where the replica signifies the word. Then (and this is really the crucial point), the qualities that qualify the replica as a sign of the word are, like all qualities, Firsts. It might seem strange to say so, in light of some of Peirce's statements such as "Firstness is the mode of being which consists in its subject being positively such as it is regardless of aught else" (*CP*, 1.25). But it is helpful to read Peirce's next sentence in this passage: "That can only be a possibility." Since I think in signs, which are Thirds, I can know Firstness only indirectly, as it were, through the actualization of possibilities. So if the Firstness of the replica seems to depend on the word, it depends on it only in the way that a possibility depends on a rule for its actualization.

The qualities of the replicas are Firsts. To take the replicas as signs of the word involves a couple of related presuppositions. First, there are relevant qualities of the replica and irrelevant qualities of the replica, and these may be analytically distinguished from each other—however difficult it may actually prove to be. Some characteristics of the sound or the letter are necessary for it to stand for the word, and others are not. Otherwise, it would be impossible to distinguish one word from another. Not knowing a word in a strange language means not knowing "what to listen for" in speech or "what to look for" in writing, and thus to experience the replicas of the word as mere sound or mere shape. In fact, the relevant and irrelevant qualities are never separate in any actual sound or letter—or for that matter, in any "concrete" thing, and that is just what *concrete* means.

The second presupposition is that the relevant qualities are *shared* among the many replicas of the same word. Every actual instance of the sounds meaning "man" or of the sequence of letters m, a, n has some characteristic(s) in common with all the other instances. Otherwise, the word would not be repeatable, and would therefore not be a word.

That the identical quality can be shared implies that it is not tied down to any individual, concrete replica, but has a mode of being independent of any of its actual embodiments. This mode of being is what Peirce calls "possibility," and this is the sense in which Firsts are what they are regardless of anything else. Any individual, concrete replica is in fact different in some respects from any other.

When the matter is put this way, it no longer seems so metaphysically inevitable that qualities (Firsts) have their own mode of being, that they are separable from each other, and that it is the same quality that is instantiated in different individuals. If only individual concrete entities are real (as the nominalist, for example, Peirce's philosophical nemesis, would have it), then to talk about qualities this way seems wrong. Where does the notion of quality come from, then? Whence Firstness?

From the perspective of linguistic interpretation, the assumption that replicas of words have distinguishable, repeatable qualities is necessitated precisely by the phenomenon of the word itself. If there were no Firsts, then words could not exist as they seem in fact to exist, or be understood as Peirce tries to understand them. The strongest reason human beings have to suppose that there are Firsts is precisely that Firsts are presupposed every day in the phenomenon of language. The relation that seems to obtain between words and their replicas can be explained, apparently, only under the assumption of something very like Firstness. If there are not analytically separable, repeatable qualities of sounds and letters, how can I know that the sounds or letters occurring right now are replicas of the same word that occurred yesterday? Human beings know that there is Firstness because they know that there are words and replicas of those words. From the perspective of linguistic interpretation, language itself refutes the nominalist.

Firstness from the perspective of linguistic interpretation, then, appears to be an artifact of language, to be derived in the first place from the relation between signifier and signified. Words are understood, and then Firsts are understood as precisely those sorts of things that make possible the embodiment of the word in its replicas. Peirce's definition of the sign in terms of the categories would thus be stood upon its head. From the linguistic perspective—specifically, the perspective of textual hermeneutics—the category is defined in terms of the linguistic sign. Firstness is an artifact of the word.

But having gone this far, one cannot logically stop with linguistic signs. Replicas of words are individual, concrete things. It is as individual, concrete things that they embody qualities. Therefore, other individual concrete things such as chairs, tables, and trees also must embody qualities. It becomes necessary to talk about "attributes" of "things"—to predicate. If the word is always behind or under its replica as a rule prescribing its relevant qualities, and if the qualities emerge as such in human consciousness only because of the relation between the word and its replicas, then it becomes necessary to think of a something underlying the sensible qualities of other individual things. Thus the concept of substance arises, most obviously in the shape of the categorical proposition, but even before that in the relation of signifier to signified. The tree that is green in summer, gold in autumn, and gray and stark in winter while nevertheless remaining the same tree, is thought as a substance bearing its various attributes. As Peirce says of the word, the tree itself as substance is unimaginable. It is known only through its attributes. From the perspective of textual hermeneutics, it is not just a figure but literally so to say that the tree is the word that makes possible the qualities that are its signs.

This argument is not how Peirce would have connected his category of Firstness with Kant's substance/attribute relation, or with the concept that Heidegger discusses of thing as substance. Nevertheless, the interpretive system of textual hermeneutics provides this way of articulating these connections. Peirce most often prefers to talk about the relationship between language and Being in terms of logic, and not in terms of the relation of signifier and signified. Nevertheless, textual hermeneutics provides this way of talking about the relation between language and substantial being.

For textual hermeneutics, then, linguistic signs would not be defined in terms of Firstness. Instead, the fact of the linguistic sign is what makes Firstness necessary as a category of thought. The Firstness of the signifier, of that which is closest to human beings, then becomes the paradigm of metaphysical thought about quality or possibility.

Peirce himself provides a clue about how Secondness may be derived from linguistic categories. He says in one passage that relative pronouns are *Indices* of what has gone before in a text, that inflectional endings are *Indices* of the other words in the sentence that govern the inflected words, and that possessive pronouns are *Indices* of the word denoting the thing possessed (*CP*, 2.287). *Index* here means a sign related to its object through some actual physical connection—that is, through Secondness. Strictly speaking, then, here and throughout my discussion of Secondness, *word* refers to a replica of the word. In this case, the physical connection occurs in the acoustic stream (speech) or in the physical text (writing). On reflection, it seems that Peirce's remarks could be pushed further. Every word in a spoken or written sentence or "syntagm" (a well-formed construction) is an Index of every other, by virtue of the physical connection dictated by the rules of grammar.

Saussure makes this point through his concept of the syntagmatic relation, or the syntagmatic "axis" of any instance of *parole*. The syntagmatic axis is thought of as the "horizontal" axis. It is the axis of "combination," conceived of as something like a string (a syntactic shape) along which words are strung end to end like beads. Thus a construction is thought of as being built up by successive addition of linguistic units, as a complexus of dyadic relations. Just as what is normally called a word is a rule prescribing the qualities of its replicas, so what is normally called grammar is a set of rules prescribing the modes of combining words in dyadic relations. It is not necessary to describe language this way. For generative grammarians, for example, the fundamental linguistic unit is not the word or the phoneme, but instead the sentence. Nevertheless, it remains a possibility, and an apparently quite natural procedure, to describe a sentence as a series of words laid end to end. This sort of description can go rather far, though structural grammar, like any grammar I know of, eventually runs into difficulties created by its own assumptions.

Saussure discusses the problem of dividing the acoustic stream into words and phonemes. In listening to a strange language, it is generally impossible to tell where one word leaves off and another begins. There would be a similar problem in reading a text written in a strange alphabet, an alphabet that might be phonetic or syllabic or ideographic, that might read up or down or right or left, and that might not leave clear spaces between words. With one's own language, however, there is rarely any difficulty in dividing a spoken sentence or a written text into its constituent words, even if the sentence is spoken rapidly or the text is written without spaces. It is precisely through this division that the possibility of the syntagmatic relation can be conceived and that the separate words can become indices of each other.

The syntagmatic relations among the words in a construction are dyadic; the separate words are Seconds with respect to each other, "resisting" each other precisely in their separateness. But another kind of Secondness or "brute force" operates here, as well. For the speaker or writer and the listener or reader, grammar operates as a constraint. The syntax cannot be just anything, if the construction is to be well formed—i.e., intelligible. In conceiving the syntagmatic relation, the user of the language conceives the language itself as an other, a Second. Thus, it is possible to articulate Secondness in terms of linguistic categories: Secondness is the kind of relation that exists between the words in a syntagm.

As with Firstness, however, I want to go beyond merely giving the syntagmatic relation as an *instance* of Secondness. If Peirce's categories are to be derived from linguistic categories, it is necessary to show how Secondness can be derived from the syntagmatic relation.

Speech is conceived as an event in time; writing is conceived as a construction in space that is nevertheless apprehended temporally—not as a painting is apprehended, all at once, but in linear sequence. ("Concrete poetry," for example, exists by attempting to break down this distinction.) It is as event (something that "comes forth") that speech or writing can be divided into words standing as indices of each other. What is true of one event as event must be true of all events. If a sentence as event is divisible into parts (called words) that stand in dyadic, indexical relations with each other, so must all events as such be divisible into parts standing in dyadic indexical relations. When I speak or write a sentence, the first word to some degree limits the possibilities for the second; and the further I go, the more limited the possibilities become as the syntax becomes more definite. The possibility of stringing (replicas of) words together in sentences involves the idea of determined physical connection. From the perspective of linguistic interpretation, things look this way: because human beings speak and write, they know that determined physical connection (Secondness) lurks in whatever is conceived as event. Instead of saying with the phenomenologist that syntagmata exhibit Secondness because they are events, textual hermeneutics would say that events exhibit Secondness because events are by definition whatever resembles syntagmata. For human beings the linguistic construction is the paradigmatic event.

"Determined physical connection" seems a possible description of causality. Another, perhaps more usual description of causality could be derived from the observation that speech occurs in time and that writing is normally thought of as linear. Causality could then be described as "determined temporal succession," a notion that could also be derived from the experience of language. Causality is not visible or audible; from the perspective of textual hermeneutics it arises as a concept made necessary by the fact that human beings experience syntagmata, and from there is extended to the experience of all events, even the nonlinguistic. Language gives humans ways of thinking about beings, and not just by providing labels. A thing, according to the second of the traditional thing concepts that Heidegger discusses, is whatever is capable of affecting human sense organs, whatever is capable of being the cause of certain effects. It is possible to conceive that the notion of causality and the associated thing concept would not even come up if human beings did not experience syntagmata—just as the notion of Being comes up, Peirce hints, only in considering the relation between grammatical subjects and predicates.

It remains to consider whether Peirce's category of Thirdness can be derived from linguistic categories. I want to look here at Saussure's notion of the paradigmatic relation or the paradigmatic axis. In constructing a sentence or other syntagm, the speaker or writer selects, as it were, from an available lexicon the words that may fill the slots in the syntactic structure. I might write, for example, "The man bit the dog"; or, reporting on the same state of affairs, one might write "John bit Fido," "A human bit a canine," "John nipped his dog," "He bit him," or something else. The sets of lexical items that could be substituted for each other are the paradigms: {man, John, human, he, . . .}, {bit, nipped, . . .}, {the, a, his, . . .}, {dog, Fido, canine, him, . . .}.

The alternatives are the different ways of saying "the same thing." Alternatives are virtually present in every sentence, whether the writer or reader is conscious of them or not. These alternatives hover, so to speak, over the actual words of the sentence, and so the paradigmatic axis is thought of as the "vertical" axis or the axis of "selection."

Ultimately, the whole lexicon is immanent in any particular utterance because I can construct a paradigm on any principle I want to. I can think of the sentence "The man bit the dog" in many different ways. It might be, for instance, not a report on a particular state of affairs, but an example of the normal order of the English sentence. Then any noun, pronoun, verbal nominal, or noun clause can belong to the paradigm of *man*. Or, the sentence could exemplify a particular sequence of sounds, as in a technical discussion of poetics, for example. Then, any word rhyming with *dog* might belong to its paradigm, or any word beginning with *d*, or any accented monosyllable, and so on.

The point is that the concept of a "paradigm" involves the notion of a "principle" (as Peirce would say, a "rule" or "law") in terms of which the paradigm is constructed. This principle is neither a quality nor a fact—neither a First nor a Second. It governs what "will be," in two senses. First, to the extent that a speaker or writer is conscious of the paradigm, its law will govern the selection actually made. Words mean by their differential relations with other words. The words that seem to be possible choices and yet are *not* chosen by the poet are as important as the word actually put in the poem. (The search for the mot juste.) That is the basis of the pedagogical technique in which the teacher asks questions of the form, "Why didn't the poet say _____?" From the side of the listener or reader, then, the paradigm within which a particular word is thought to fit will govern the interpretation of the word. I have said before that words can be thought of as rules prescribing Firsts (the qualities of their replicas); and grammar can be thought of as rules prescribing Seconds (the dyadic relations of words in syntagmata). Paradigms, then, can be thought of as rules prescribing Thirds—namely, meanings.

Paradigms, as laws, are themselves Thirds. But can Thirdness in general be derived from the concept of the paradigmatic relation? Obviously, I am going to say yes. A paradigm is a rule for constructing a collection, but the collection is always open-ended and virtual. Strictly speaking, not even a single member of the collection is actually present in the sentence, by the nature of the paradigmatic relation. What is called a "word" in the sentence is only a replica of the word, and it is not among replicas, but among words themselves, that the choices are made. In becoming aware of the paradigmatic axis in speech or writing, human beings are brought nearest to the differential structure of language, to the fact that words are what they are because of their similarities to and differences from other words. Since words do not subsist as independent entities that are what they are regardless of their relation with other words, there must be some relation or connection between any word and all other words, if words are to function at all.

That relation is Thirdness, the triadic relation that brings any given word into connection with any other given word through the concept of sameness or of difference. From the perspective of linguistic interpretation, then, Thirdness is precisely what is posited in order to account for the observed functioning of the paradigmatic relation. Thirdness in general is the mode of being that resembles the linguistic paradigm.

To articulate Kant's third relational category—reciprocity—in terms of textual hermeneutics would be to say that the organism of the world is a language, that each individual being is intelligible only in terms of its relations with other individual beings and with the whole world of which all beings are parts. It is perhaps clearer now, too, how the concept of the thing as formed matter is homologous with Kant's category. Matter and form are unintelligible apart from each other, just as words and their paradigms are inseparable in thinking. Kant's category of reciprocity and the concept of thing as formed matter are homologous precisely in conforming to the linguistic category of the paradigmatic relation. One way to put this, speaking within the interpretive system of textual hermeneutics, is to say that the world is a whole and has form for human beings because language is a whole and has form.

6. Language and Logic

I would like to return now briefly to the question of the relation between language and logic. The questions of metaphysics and those of logic seemed to Peirce intimately related, as the quotation at the beginning of this book suggests. Logic properly understood is, for Peirce, a general semiotic. At least, as Max Fisch argues in "Peirce's General Theory of Signs," Peirce had arrived at this formulation by 1903 (Fisch, 339). In my discussion of Peirce's phenomenological categories, I have been starting not with logical categories but with more specifically linguistic categories. How might Peirce's logic look from the perspective of textual hermeneutics? Peirce's logic is a very big subject, and I am very far from expert. I will have only a very little to say about it here.

Peirce distinguishes three kinds of inference: abduction, deduction, and induction. Not surprisingly, each of these kinds is associated with one of his categories.

Abduction (which Peirce sometimes called retroduction) is hypothesis making. I will adapt an example that Peirce himself gives. Suppose I come into a room containing several bags of black beans and one bag of white beans. All the bags are open. I see scattered on the floor some loose beans, all of which are white. I infer, "These beans came from the bag of white beans." Naturally, I might be wrong. Somebody might have brought the white beans from somewhere else, or they might have been spilled when another bag of white beans was removed from the room, and so on. In abduction I notice that something (the loose beans) has some of the same characteristics (whiteness) as something else (the beans in the bag). I hypothesize that the things therefore share all the relevant characteristics (i.e., that the loose beans share with the ones in the bag the characteristic of belonging to that particular bag).

An example of deduction would be as follows. Suppose I myself have filled a bag with white beans and put it in a room. Then I go into the room, and without looking, I take a handful of beans from the bag. Still without looking, I infer, "All these beans in my hand are white." Peirce consistently speaks of deduction as involving reasoning from diagrams. He has his own complicated system of existential graphs, but for rough understanding Venn diagrams will do. In this case, maybe, what happens in my mind is something like this: I imagine a circle containing all the white beans in the world. Then within that circle I draw a smaller circle which I imagine to contain all the beans in this bag. Then I will see that any yet smaller circle within the circle containing the bagged beans (a circle representing my handful, for example) will necessarily contain only white beans. From a general rule about the characteristics of the bagged beans, I have inferred something about the characteristics of a particular handful.

Induction involves both abduction and deduction. If I walk into a room containing many closed bags of beans, and I want to know what color the beans are, I will open a few of the bags and take some samples. If all the beans I get are white, I might hypothesize that "All the beans in these bags are white." If I am scientifically minded, however, I will not stop there. I will predict, reasoning from my hypothesis, that any sample I take from now on will be composed entirely of white beans. I will then take more samples, and the longer I go without finding beans of any other color, the surer I will be that my hypothesis is true. From studying the characteristics of samples, induction arrives at a general rule about what characteristics future samples will have.

Peirce associates abduction with Firstness. He calls it "originary" (*CP*, 2.96), where *originary* is a word of Firstness. He makes this association because in abduction the only warrant for the conclusion is a similarity between the characteristics of what is mentioned in the premises and the characteristics of what is mentioned in the conclusion. For example, all I have to go on in my inference that the loose beans are from the bag of white beans is the fact that the loose beans are white. Thus, I am reasoning from a quality.

From the perspective of linguistic interpretation, what warrants this kind of mental process? Most often, when I listen to clear speech or read a legible text, I am not aware that anything like abduction is involved. I seem to be simply perceiving the speech or the writing. Actually, Peirce argues, perceptual judgments themselves have the form of logical inference. It is just that human beings do not normally have the sense of controlling the logical process, in the case of perceptual judgments. Hookway discusses this point in his chapter on Peirce's theory of perception (see especially 160–66), and I shall return to this point in Chapter 3. But I quickly become aware of performing abductions when I listen to a speaker who mumbles, or listen to someone over a telephone with a bad connection, or try to read poor handwriting or a fragmentary text. I am constantly in the process of hypothesizing what words the sounds or letters replicate. I have to infer from the presence of *some* of the qualities of its replicas prescribed by a particular word the virtual presence of *all* of the relevant qualities. By the earlier arguments for the derivation of Firstness from the relation of signifier and signified, then, the force behind abduction is precisely the force of the listener's or reader's experience that often or at least sometimes speech is correctly heard and texts are correctly read. Peirce says, "the only hope of retroductive reasoning ever reaching the truth is that there may be some natural tendency toward an agreement between the ideas which suggest themselves to the human mind and those which are concerned in the laws of nature" (*CP*, 1.81). This is perhaps a way of saying that the process of abduction, upon which the advance of human knowledge hinges, depends upon whether the world speaks human language.

Peirce refers to deduction as "obsistent" (*CP*, 2.96), thus associating it with Secondness. That is because when the premises are represented in a diagram, as in the Venn diagrams described above, the thinker is compelled to represent the conclusion. But Peirce's existential diagrams, or the algebraic symbolism of modern formal logic, or even natural-language syllogisms, are also species of diagrams. If I say, in Aristotelian fashion,

> All S's are P's,
> All M's are S's,
> Therefore, all M's are P's,

I am diagramming the necessity of my conclusion by putting the subjects and predicates in particular places in English sentences as written on the page. From the linguistic perspective, then, by the arguments earlier deriving Secondness from the syntagmatic relation, the constraint on deduction to draw certain conclusions appears to be the constraint of grammar.

Finally, Peirce calls induction "transuasive" (*CP*, 2.96), linking it with Thirdness. In the process of inductive inquiry, I derive a general law from the observed characteristics of a sample, and I deduce from that law predictions about future samples, which might then lead me to correct my statement of the general law. How would induction look from the perspective of textual hermeneutics? In interpreting any particular word in a text, I must first hypothesize the appropriate paradigm. If, for example, I am trying to recover the historical author's thoughts, I must decide which words in the language of his day he meant to be set off against the word he in fact used, if I want to catch the nuances of his text. Having hypothesized such a paradigm and interpreted the particular word in the light of it, I can make certain predictions about other words in the text and their paradigms. For example, if near the beginning of a text I find several instances in which it seems to make sense to interpret the word *man* as referring to humankind, to men and women taken together, I would not expect to find later passages in which the author is careful to distinguish *humankind*, *man*, and *men and women*. If I do find such passages, I am led to correct my initial hypothesis. This is how induction appears in interpreting, and by the arguments deriving Thirdness from the paradigmatic relation, the force of induction is the force of the reader's conviction (or cheerful faith) that in some cases the meaning of the text has been satisfactorily arrived at.

I believe, then, that Peirce's categories of Firstness, Secondness, and Thirdness can be derived from linguistic categories. Let me stress again that when I say "derived from," I do not mean that the linguistic categories offer the only correct explanation of Peirce's phenomenology or his realist ontology, or the explanation that Peirce himself would have given. I mean only that starting with the categories of linguistic interpretation, one can deduce the necessity of Peirce's categories. That suggests not that textual hermeneutics is the only way, or even the best way, of interpreting the world, but only that there is an articulation from within textual hermeneutics of the relations among philosophy, language, and interpretation—at least, insofar as "philosophy" is identified with Peirce's philosophical system and systems translatable into Peirce's system.

So I have come full circle, back to the question of philosophy, language, and interpretation. It might be a good idea to say again briefly where I think I have been, and why I have thought it was necessary to go there.

I began by asking about interpretation, which seems, like philosophy and language itself, approachable only from inside. Since it is therefore necessary always to interpret from within some interpretive system, I asked which system seems most useful now. Following the thread of Peirce's notion of "sign," I concluded in favor of textual hermeneutics, and arrived at a definition of *interpretive system* from within the perspective of textual hermeneutics: an interpretive system is any structure of relations such that each relation determines its relata also to be relations.

There are several reasons for choosing textual hermeneutics as the interpretive system for the purposes of this book, but the decisive reason is that the crisis of the humanities in our time is the crisis of textual hermeneutics. If the crisis cannot be passed from within textual hermeneutics itself, then the humanities as disciplines should fold their tents and allow themselves to be taken up within the framework of other disciplines. For myself, I would prefer that if the humanities are to be taken up at all, they be taken up into a broader or different perspective of textual hermeneutics itself.

Having come into the interpretive system of textual hermeneutics, itself intimately bound with language, I thought it helpful to ask how philosophy would be articulated from within that system. Being a finite creature, I narrowed my inquiry to an exploration of Peirce's phenomenological and ontological categories. By that exploration I have hoped to make a few suggestions not only about how philosophy can be articulated in terms of linguistic categories, but about how the world looks when a serious attempt is made to read it as a text.

Probably no one can read or write without making some commitments that I would describe as metaphysical. At least, I have assumed here that I am free to choose an interpretive system, and that reasons can be given, and so on. But I do not mean to make any absolute metaphysical commitments to textual hermeneutics. If anyone were to ask me, "Is the world *really* a text?" I would say, "Yes, from within textual hermeneutics. From within textual hermeneutics everything is a text." If the questioner were to persist, "No, but *really*. Do you *really* think the world is a text? Or, do you think the world is *really* a text?" I would say, "I don't know." I would not want to imply that I am an agnostic on the question, but only that I am a "fallibilist" in Peirce's sense—someone who has no way of being absolutely certain that his beliefs are without error. I am, after all, arguing that in a crucial sense my way of life as a teacher of the humanities depends on thinking of the world as a text. But I might be mistaken. And so I would want to imply by my answer that the question strikes me as not completely silly.

2

The Well and the Mirror

In this chapter I want to flesh out the concept of "interpretive system" with a couple of examples of interpretive systems at work. Previously I spoke as though textual hermeneutics were a single discipline, one big coherent interpretive system. If one is talking about how things appear now, that is of course not right. Textual hermeneutics seems rather to look like a bundle of competing interpretive systems that share certain "family resemblances," to anticipate a discussion of Wittgenstein's analogy. This just means that there are many different ways to interpret texts. Each particular interpretive system is one among many hermeneutic strategies. And some methods that at one time or another have been called interpretation might not fit my idea of interpretation at all.

My idea of interpretation is Peircean. Here I argue that the particular interpretive systems I will discuss are Peircean, and therefore count as various strategies within the broad interpretive system I have been calling textual hermeneutics. This broad interpretive system, identified with Peirce's semiotic, is the one from the perspective of which these essays look at their subjects.

To look at the world and interpretation itself from the perspective of textual hermeneutics means to look at the world first from the perspective of whatever strategy, whatever particular interpretive system, one happens to use to interpret texts. For a theory of interpretive systems to be articulated in terms of textual hermeneutics, what is crucial is to understand how interpretive systems work with texts, what the relation of interpretive systems is to interpretation itself, and how this understanding is to be acquired.

In this chapter, I have several specific objectives. First, I want to show what it means to say that the study of interpretive systems is "pure" ("speculative") rhetoric or "methodeutic" in Peirce's sense, but with one twist. For Peirce, methodeutic is the study of the rules according to which a scientific intelligence connects signs; I am interested in the rules according to which a hermeneutic intelligence connects signs. As I have said before, I think this distinction might not be necessary if the word *science* were used today the way Peirce used it. The concepts that belong to interpretive systems arise retroactively, as it were, as a way of talking about what has in fact already happened in interpretation. Second, I want to show what it means to say that textual hermeneutics, properly understood, is "self-transcending." That is, although the concepts belonging to any interpretive system can be used heuristically or even programatically to produce interpretive statements, nevertheless they also point beyond themselves, raising questions that cannot be answered within the limits of the system. To locate the places where this happens reads like a deconstruction, not of the text being interpreted, but of the interpretive system itself. This kind of deconstruction is a necessary step in understanding an interpretive system. The limits of the interpretive system can be understood only by approaching them from the inside. To approach an interpretive system from the outside means to articulate it in terms of some other system, thus distorting its concepts. Third and finally, I want to show what it means to say that interpretive systems stand in a "reciprocal relation" with the texts they interpret, and that the object of study in the humanities is therefore not the texts themselves, but the interpretive systems in their interactions with those texts. What one comes to know about directly is not texts, but instead interpretive systems in their relations with texts. A corollary is that the notion of "correctness" narrowly understood depends on the particular interpretive system one is operating within. An interpretive statement can be justified or criticized only in terms of some particular interpretive system.

Since life is short, I can illustrate these points with only two examples. I have chosen two poems, one by Robert Frost and one by John Ashbery. To some people the choices will seem quirky. To others they might seem disingenuous. I choose poems because I am more comfortable working with poetry than with other kinds of texts. I choose these two poems partly, I admit, because they help me to make some of the points I want to make, but also partly just because I like them. I do not mean to suggest that the interpretation of poetry is somehow normative for interpretive practice in general. I am betting that a close look at interpretive practice in the case of other literary types, from philosophical texts to plays to newspapers, will show that similar patterns of interpretation are already occurring and that parallel interpretive problems are already arising. But my purpose here is just to put forward as clearly as I can a theory of interpretive systems. If the examples seem too limited or contrived, then all I can ask is that someone else test the theory on some other examples.

1. Frost and Roman Jakobson

For Once, Then, Something

Others taunt me with having knelt at well-curbs
Always wrong to the light, so never seeing
Deeper down in the well than where the water
Gives me back in a shining surface picture
Me myself in the summer heaven, godlike,
Looking out of a wreath of fern and cloud puffs.
Once, when trying with chin against a well-curb,
I discerned, as I thought, beyond the picture,
Through the picture, a something white, uncertain,
Something more of the depths—and then I lost it.
Water came to rebuke the too clear water.
One drop fell from a fern, and lo, a ripple
Shook whatever it was lay there at bottom,
Blurred it, blotted it out. What was that whiteness?
Truth? A pebble of quartz? For once, then, something.
                                        (Frost, 91)

"For Once, Then, Something" is about looking into the world and finding oneself there. Maybe it is also about looking into poems and finding oneself there. But the poem is also about looking into the world or poems and finding there something that is not oneself, something fundamental and mysterious, something that in its otherness might or might not be an immediate human concern. I use the word *mystery* here in something of its New Testament sense, *mysterion,* that which is known by revelation but is beyond human comprehension. There are mysteries in poems, things interpreters seem to know without being able to derive them from their interpretive systems. Because the mysteries are not consciously worked out from the interpretive system, they strike the interpreter as having the quality of revelation. My hypothesis is that any interpretive system, pushed to its boundary, gestures toward mysteries by raising questions unanswerable within the system. What results from pushing an interpretive system to its boundary is a kind of deconstruction—not of the poem, but of the interpretive system and even of the interpreter.

I want to begin with an interpretive system that regards poems as acts of communication from one human being to another. Poems need not be thought of this way. They can be thought of as hermetic discourse, or psychotherapy, or automatic writing. Nevertheless, many critics who write interpretive statements assume that some sort of communication has occurred. Even those who admit only of misreadings sometimes analyze poems as failed acts of communication. Most traditional criticism, at least, posits the communicative situation as a model for talking about poems. Some author (*addresser*) is speaking to some audience (*addressee*) on some subject (in some *context*), employing some physical *channel* and some *code* to send a *message*. These six elements in the communicative situation are of course familiar from Roman Jakobson's analysis. At the same time, I do not want to suggest that Jakobson's model is ultimate in any sense. It is just a way of talking about the problems I want to talk about.

If one thinks of Jakobson's addresser and addressee as self-subsistent Cartesian egos, the channel as some physical object, and the context as a collection of entities, then clearly the model cannot be an interpretive system. The elements of the model would correspond with entities and not with relations, whereas an interpretive system is a structure of relations. But the names Jakobson chooses suggest that he already is thinking in terms of relations. Human beings are called addressers or addressees by virtue of a relation between them; instead of "sound wave" or "telegraph wire" Jakobson says "channel," which suggests an in-between; and he calls the world a context, an interweaving of entities. The potential of Jakobson's model as an interpretive system, however, is realized only in its application to texts.

It is important to understand what I mean by "applying" the model as interpretive system. I do not mean that I decode poems, produce interpretive statements, by searching out Jakobson's six elements in the text or somehow constructing from them a machine whose input is a poem and whose output is an interpretive statement. Yet I do not mean to deny that Jakobson's model can have heuristic functions. I might be led to think up an interpretive statement that I had not thought of, by asking myself questions such as, Who is the addressee of this poem? or What is the context of this poem? But I still have to do the thinking up.

The model does not write the interpretive statement for me, and sometimes when I ask the heuristic questions, I come up empty.

To apply the model as interpretive system means, rather, something like this: I read a poem, I think I understand it, and, possibly, I write an interpretive statement. Now, if someone asks me (or I ask myself) what the connection is between my interpretive statement and the text of the poem, I explain the connection by appealing to one or more of the concepts of Jakobson's model. I say something like this: "Well, my interpretation says the opposite of what the text says, because I think the author is being ironic." When I say that, the concept of "addresser" (author) is presented as that which underwrites the connection of my interpretive statement with the poem. I can make the connection only under the assumption that there is an addresser who can adopt and communicate an ironic attitude. Or, if I say, "Gloriana stands for Queen Elizabeth, because *The Faerie Queene* is allegorical," then I am presupposing a particular historical context that underwrites my interpretation. The concepts of the interpretive system are, in Peirce's sense, methodeutic. They explain how a hermeneutic intelligence has in fact connected signs with each other. When I explain the connections, I am not giving a metaphysical justification of my interpretation. I am only articulating explicitly the presuppositions, often unconscious at the time, that underwrote it.

I have defined an interpretive system as a structure of relations such that each relation determines its relata also to be relations. Jakobson's model is a structure, in that each element can be understood only in terms of all the others. There can be no addressee without an addresser, no message without a channel (or vice versa), and so on. It is maybe not so clear how each of the elements in the model can be the name of a relation. That point is easier to see, however, if one considers certain characteristic problems of interpretation that can be associated with the elements of the model. Each of these problems involves a mystery, so to speak, that must be revealed when an interpretive statement is written. The problem gets solved—the mystery is revealed—without being comprehended. The interpretive system is not the source of the interpretive statement. It is only that the connection between the interpretive statement and the poem can be explained in terms of the interpretive system. It is crucial for the interpreter that the interpretation retain at some level the quality of unquestioned, revealed truth.

The characteristic problems of interpretation, the ones I want to illustrate with the poem by Frost, are these: (1) the problem of *voice*. The concept of the "author" (addresser) produces the correlative concepts of "implied author" and "speaker," as opposed to the actual historical person of the author. The question here is, What is the relation of the author to the voice speaking in the poem? (2) The problem of *audience*. The concept of the historical "reader" (addressee) gives rise to the correlative concepts of "implied reader" and "fictional reader." The question here is, How should the poem be taken? What is the proper relation of the reader to the poem? (3) The problem of *reference*. The fact that a poem is conceived as arising in a particular context makes one ask, What is the poem about? What is the relation of the poem to its context(s)? (4) The problem of physical *form*. Poems require a physical channel: print on the page, with a particular shape; a speech apparatus vibrating the air, with particular patterns of sound. Some physical features are thought of as significant in any particular realization of a poem, and some are not. The question is, What is the relation of the physical features of the poem to its content (message)? (5) The problem of *diction*. The words of the poem fit in a particular way into the enormously complex web of oppositions that constitutes the natural language, the code in terms of which the poem has meaning. The question arises, What is the relation of the vocabulary of the poem to "ordinary" language? And (6) the problem of *theme*. The theme of the poem, as stated by the critic, is that cultural form under which the poem is to be subsumed in order to make it intelligible to the interpretive community. Put more simply, the theme is that about the poem which enables me to bring it into meaningful relation with my life. The statement of the theme is the answer to the question of what the poem is saying to me—its *message*, in short. But the interpretation is always more or less inadequate to the poem. So the question here is, What is the relation of the poem to its interpretations?

Everybody will recognize these six problems (voice, audience, reference, form, diction, theme) as venerable and recurring problems in literary criticism. Everybody will also recognize these six concepts as indispensable for traditional literary analysis. I want to look at Frost's poem to show that these concepts themselves raise questions to which logically compelling answers cannot be given—that is, answers implied by the concepts themselves. And yet, any particular interpretive statement implies a particular answer to each of these questions.

Voice. If I say that any interpretive statement must somehow take account of the actual person who produced the poem, then I have to ask what the relation of this author is to the poem. Because drama and, especially, dramatic irony are possibilities of language, critics distinguish "author" from "implied author," and both from the "speaker." The real historical author could be as distant from the speaker as the dramatist is from the villain of the piece. Or, the author could be speaking in propria persona. Even here the Latin *persona*, "mask," implies that the self who meets the world is already a disguise, a dramatic pose. So the speaker could be completely different from the author, identical with the author, or anything in between. The black marks on the white page do not tell me what the situation is. I project, instead, a speaking voice and judge from the tone of that voice where the author "stands." How I project this stance is mysterious, because the black marks on the white page admit of many contradictory constructions.

Consider Frost's poem. I shall exaggerate to make my points, and sometimes my readings might seem deliberately perverse. But a perverse reading is not just silly. It cannot be just ignored. It sounds perverse because it challenges assumptions, and because one can continue to maintain its internal logic in the face of conventional outrage. In fact, some of the interpretations that sound, to me at least, the most outrageous can already be found in critical discussions of this poem.

One might ask, then, whether the last phrase of the poem—which is also its title—is ironic or serious. Is there a double or single perspective? I could imagine, first, that the entire poem is a dramatic monologue by a speaker who is a bit of a fool. He is too much the literalist. When others "taunt" him gently about his self-absorption, using the image of looking into wells, he takes them literally and tries to solve the problem by actually looking into wells better. Or if he is not silly, he is at least childish. He wants to put his detractors at a disadvantage by refuting them at the level of the physical image. He goes around contorting himself, absurdly "trying with chin against a well-curb." When he does see something, he loses it at once. That is, he is impervious to the point of the taunts, because of the very mind-set the "others" complain about. He himself is the bungler who shakes the drop off the fern and destroys his momentary vision. In this reading the last phrase is spoken by someone who lets others' misunderstood opinions force him into absurdity, and who takes a smug satisfaction in having proved the others wrong on a triviality. But in fact, he has proved them right. "Truth? A pebble of quartz?" It makes no difference to him what he has seen or missed, since there was "something," enough to put him one up on the others. Now, someone might say that to do this kind of thing in a poem is very unlike Frost. But that argument is neither here nor there, for Frost might have done it for once.

Or, I might imagine that Frost himself is speaking here, or at least a persona that in Frost's body of work becomes almost indistinguishable from the public man himself. Then, I could regard the last phrase of the poem as playful on the surface, but at a deeper level serious. Frost, well aware of what the "others" taunt him with, turns their image around on them. If he is capable of even a momentary sense perception that recognizes the existence of something other than himself, he is already out of the solipsist's box, and he can use the image proposed by the "others" to talk about the uncertainties in every sort of human perception. It might be true that he tends to see himself wherever he looks; but nobody else does much better, not even the "others," and Frost at least has the Socratic advantage of understanding how difficult it really is to get self-knowledge. Everybody imagines himself to see truth and pebbles of quartz, but maybe only the poet *really* sees them, however fleeting his glimpse. And whoever can glimpse the one, can glimpse the other. The last phrase of the poem then becomes an affirmation of the power of the poet and the poem to create the "momentary stay against confusion" that Frost once said he was seeking. (This definition of a poem is in Frost's essay "The Figure a Poem Makes.")

Or, growing ever more subtle, one might propose a third relation between author and speaker. Maybe Frost is gently mocking a less mature version of his genuine personality, a young poet who was capable once of being sure that his trivial experience at well-curbs translated into something of grand universal significance. Now, the mature Frost is poised indecisively, unable to make up his mind how important the whole experience was, ruefully mocking himself for ever thinking that a clear resolution could ever come from any experience. The last phrase of the poem is then at once less than ironic, and less than completely affirmative.

And so it goes. By positing various degrees of separation between author and speaker, various degrees of the author's approval or disapproval of what the speaker says, I posit many different readings. If one is inclined to grant a living author some sort of special interpretive authority, one might be able to "solve" such interpretive questions by listening carefully to the author's tone of voice in reading the poem. Or one might not. But the interpreter who believes in authors and their importance for interpretation must project a tone in order to write an interpretive statement. The interpretive decision gets made in a moment that subjectively resembles the revelation of a mystery. Even if the decision is subsequently rationalized in the process of critical debate, it does not result from consciously working out the implications of the concept of the "author." What rule is there subtle enough to select among the numberless possible relations between author and speaker in poems? The concept of the "author" enters critical discourse as a way of explaining the connections that have already been made in interpretation.

What, in fact, has become of the concept of "author" in my discussion of Frost's poem? How is it being used? That there can be a problem of voice implies at least a potential distance between "what is being said in the poem" and "what the poem means." What is being said in the poem is what is spoken there by the speaker. What the poem means is, presumably, what is said in my interpretive statement. At least, the interpretive statement is what I produce when someone asks me what the poem means. As far as my interpretation is concerned, *author* becomes precisely the name of the relation between what is said in the poem and what is meant by it. The concept of an "author" is the concept to which I appeal in order to connect my interpretive statement with what is said in the poem. The author is, as it were, the space between what is said and what is meant.

This sounds odd, because it is customary to use the term *author* to refer to the actual historical person (e.g., Robert Frost) in all of his or her temporal and spatial relations. But that is not what I mean by "author" in appealing to this concept to explain the interpretation of a particular text; nor, I think, can I mean that. I can talk only about the relation of this actual historical person to the text in question. I always mean, at most, a particular content of consciousness—Peirce might say a chain of signification—in some person (e.g., Frost) at some particular time (e.g., while Frost was composing this poem). What the speaker of the poem says is, in some perhaps very complex way, a sign of the chain of signification in the historical person's consciousness. What my interpretive statement says is presumably also a sign of that chain of signification, a translation of it into another system of signs called, in general, critical discourse. When I explain my interpretive statement, the sign which is the historical person's consciousness and to which I give the name *author* is the rule by means of which I try to connect my statement with what the speaker says in the poem. It is instructive to compare here Paul Ricoeur's discussion of the "implied author," which appears in the third volume of *Time and Narrative*: "If a work is considered as the resolution of a problem, . . . [the] singularity of the solution, replying to the singularity of the problem, can take on a proper name, that of the author" (162).

To be an author, then, means to be interpreted as constituting a particular stance toward what is written. To say that there is an author who is being ironic, for example, means precisely that interpretation hypothesizes a stance toward what the speaker says that would explain the connection between that and an interpretive statement that says the opposite.

The relation of "author" has as its relata what the "speaker" of the text says and the "theme" of the text. The theme of the text is its "message," in Jakobson's terms, and so I shall say more below about how *theme* is the name of a relation. It is worth noting here, however, that if I think of theme in intentional terms, as referring to "what the author means," then the theme constitutes a relation between the author's world and mine. To state a theme is to identify a similarity between some historical person's consciousness and my own that enables me to understand that person. Also, the speaker must be inferred entirely from what is said, and is inseparably implicated in it. That is, the speaker and what is spoken are constituted solely as a network of linguistic relations. I am constrained to think this way about the speaker and what is spoken precisely when I conceive of the poem as an artifact of an author's consciousness. To think of *author*, then, as the name of a relation between the theme and what the speaker says means thinking of these also as the names of relations.

It is important to note, finally, that I am not arguing that one has to think of any of these terms this way. One may continue to think of authors as Cartesian egos and of themes as self-subsistent Platonic forms, or whatever. Here and subsequently, I am trying only to illustrate what it means to employ the elements of Jakobson's model as an interpretive system in my sense.

Audience. Corresponding to the triad of "author," "implied author," and "speaker," there are the "reader" and the correlatives "implied reader" and "fictional reader" (as, for example, the "gentle Reader" of the traditional novel). I have to take up a stance toward a poem, placing myself in relation to it, either according to the imperatives of my own condition, or by trying to see where the poem wants me to stand. The structure of the reader's response to the poem depends upon the reader's stance.

For example, one might ask whether Frost's poem is "heard" or "overheard." Suppose, as most critics probably would, that there is very little distance between author and speaker. Then, is Frost addressing somebody in particular? Or is he invoking the conventions of meditative poetry, merely letting anybody listen to his "private thoughts"? In short, is the poem more in the mode of persuasion or more in the mode of meditation? The poem might have (does have) the surface structure of argument in either case, but the reader's affective responses would be rather different.

If the poem is taken as persuasive, it requires at first a greater tension, a skeptical distancing, between Frost and the reader. A reader would not be playing the game if the reader did not at the beginning momentarily entertain the attitude of the "others" as a possible dialectical position or at least as a straw man. In this scenario, the reader moves from genial skepticism to complete identification with Frost's point of view (whatever that is conceived to be). The structure of the emotional response is perhaps something like the structure of the response to a successful political speech or a friendly sales talk. The poem exemplifies a pattern that is basically comic, a movement from dissonance to harmony.

If, on the other hand, the poem is taken as meditation, as "overheard," then to play the game means to think Frost's thoughts and adopt his attitudes from the beginning. I need not acknowledge the validity in the taunts of the "others," except insofar as they echo self-doubts. There is no clear confrontation between two points of view, in which one view triumphs. Instead, the reader is let in on an intimate moment of self-examination. The poem becomes altogether darker, and more dubious about the capacity of the ego to comprehend itself or govern its own discourse. In this scenario, the "reader" collapses together with the "author," but the "author" himself fragments into various conflicting impulses. The structure of the emotional response is perhaps more like the structure of the response to the diary of an articulate and sensitive person at a moment of spiritual crisis. The pattern here is one of fragmentation and complexity, potentially satirical or even tragic. Why should a poet meditate upon these matters, if they do not represent a serious and unresolved problem for him? I share his anxiety from the first line. "Others taunt me" (maybe they are right); "*Once*" (only) I saw something, "as I thought" (maybe I was wrong), but "then I lost it" immediately. "What was that whiteness?" It was "something," no doubt, but was it the something that is not there or the something that is? The poem as meditation becomes at best an attempt to talk oneself into something.

There are of course other possible relations between reader and author, reader and speaker. I might take the poem as neither persuasion nor meditation, but as having the affective qualities of report, or verse epistle, or dramatic monologue, in each case implying a different stance and different emotional response of the reader. But if the reader's emotional response is conceived as an essential component of the meaning, then the reader's relation to the poem must be revealed before interpretive statements can be written. The reader's stance grounds whatever interpretive principles are brought into play, and not the other way around.

Here "audience" has come to mean just a particular stance toward the poem. As Paul Ricoeur says, "By implied reader we must then understand the role assigned to the real reader by the instructions in the text." Thus, "the real reader is the pole opposite the text in the process of interaction giving rise to the meaning of the work" (*Time and Narrative*, 3.170–71). If the problem of audience arises in the first place, that means that a reader is conscious of a potential distance between the effects the poem is "supposed" to have and the effects it in fact does have on actual historical persons. If the awareness of this distance is implicated in my interpretive statement, then clearly I am not the "audience" of the poem, because the effects it is having on me as a real historical person in all my temporal and spatial relations are not the effects it is supposed to have. The "implied audience," however, is not the audience either, since it is *my* interpretation that is in question. *Audience* in my interpretation is the name of a space, the relation between my stance toward the poem and the stance I hypothesize for somebody else whose existence is hypothetical.

Again, in Peirce's terms: the text is taken as a sign of its implied reader, and my actual responses are signs of the text. My responses, then, should be signs of the responses of the implied reader. If I am perfectly satisfied with my actual responses, or am unaware of any other possible responses, then the problem of the audience does not come up. But if not? In what sense can my personal responses be said to look through the signs of the text to the hypothetical responses of an implied reader, when I am acutely conscious of the differences between myself and this other reader? What is the connection between the two sets of responses? I must be telling myself something like this: "If I were to take such-and-such a stance toward the poem—that is, if I were to take the poem differently—then these responses that I am actually having would be transformed into a different set of responses that I think the poem is asking me to have instead. To take up that other stance would mean to become what I call the 'audience' of the poem."

Where there is a difference between actual effects and hypothetical effects, then, the concept of an audience becomes a set of transformation rules, a way of explaining how my responses could be said to stand for the responses of an implied reader. As a concept of an interpretive system, "audience" refers not to some particular group of actual historical persons, but to an interpretive stance. My point here, again, is to say something not about audiences, but about interpretive systems. My stance toward the poem is of course constituted by the relations between me and the text, and the implied reader is of course also a stance, a construct of linguistic relations. And so thinking of "audience" as an interpretive concept involves thinking also of its relata as relations.

Reference. It might seem odd to think of *author* and *audience* as names of relations. I have to think of them that way, however, if they are going to be parts of an interpretive system in my sense of the term. The point is maybe a little easier to see with the terms *reference* or *context*. *Reference* clearly names the relation between the text of the poem and what is thought of as outside that text: the world, or some selected part of it. The term *context* might at first seem to refer to some collection of entities that stands over against the text, prior to and independent of it. But in interpreting, what does and does not count as context is always implicitly recreated or at least selected by the interpretation. Once I think I understand Frost's poem, for example, I am ready to say that everything I need to know about wells is somehow given *with* the poem, though maybe not exactly *in* the poem. If there is something I need to know about wells that the poem does not actually say, at least the poem hints at what kind of research I need to do. Whatever I know or find out about wells that seems relevant is then assigned to the "context," as being given with the poem but not in it. Not everything I might know or find out about wells counts as part of the context, however. So text is a sign of context; context is what is given with the text. *Context* now appears to be the name of the relation, the rule, in terms of which interpretation has decided what is "in" the text and what is relevant to but "outside of" it. At least for anyone whose notion of texts takes into account the insights of structuralism and poststructuralism, there is no difficulty in conceiving the text as a structure of relations. And the concept of "context" itself suggests that in interpreting, the world (what is "outside" the text) exists only as a relation with what is "in" the text. "Context," then, is an interpretive concept when it means the relation between, on the one hand, a text and, on the other hand, the world construed as the reciprocal of the text.

Most critics would not be content to take the poem at the surface level, and in fact the poem itself seems to prod a reader to look for something beyond or beneath the "shining surface picture." Poems by Frost often balance playfully on the brink of allegory. They refuse to give the decisive push that would propel a reader from the concrete situation into some abstract *sententia*. But the poems also deny the comfort of thinking that the concrete situation is all they are getting at.

What is this poem about, if it is not just about looking into wells to make fools of one's friends or oneself? I have already hinted at some of the obvious possibilities. Perhaps the poem is about epistemology, the "uncertain" nature of human perception and cognition. Frost's biographer mentions the possible allusion to a skeptical saying attributed to Democritus: "Of truth we know nothing, for truth lies at the bottom of a well" (Thompson, 562). Human beings see and know by constructing a "picture," and of course the picture is always to some extent a picture of themselves. Human beings want to organize the world around themselves, want to be the Olympian Zeus created by the most sublime effort of the human imagination, "in the summer heaven godlike, / Looking out of a wreath of fern and cloud puffs." And so their pictures are self-flattering illusions. Glimpses of what is "beyond the picture, / Through the picture" are always of a "something" indefinite, "white," without distinguishing qualities ("white" as in "white noise") and "uncertain."

Indeed, with a slight change of emphasis, the poem could be seen as about the deep and potentially tragic split between the cultural world and the natural world. The "others," as naive materialists, assume that the locus of ultimate reality is the material substances of the natural world. The human world is just an illusion, a "picture" added on. The poet, by taking this view seriously, finds out how difficult it is to sustain and how unsatisfying to human beings it ultimately is. If nature, matter, is the only reality, then humans never really get to it. Nor would they know if they had: "Truth? A pebble of quartz?" A cultural abstraction of the utmost importance to human life, or an insignificant bit of natural matter? "Water came to rebuke the too clear water": water in the poem is the medium that simultaneously conceals and reveals, the surface that contains the reflections, and the depth that contains the whiteness. The very medium (the imagination? perhaps even consciousness as a kind of Derridean process of *différance*?) that permits human beings what contact they have with the natural world "rebukes" them for trying to dwell entirely in it. The human world is the place for humans. "The woods are lovely, dark, and deep, / But I have promises to keep."

Or perhaps the water in the poem is rather associated with what it so often symbolizes in Freudian interpretations of dreams and poems, namely birth. Going into the water, seeing below the surface of the water, is like going back into the amniotic fluid, a return to the womb, a search for origins. Needless to say, it makes no difference whether Frost himself was conscious of such meanings. Perhaps what occurs in the poem is an insight into the reality of the subconscious. Looking into the well is like looking deeply into oneself. At first one encounters the "godlike," controlling ego, the object of narcissism. And then one begins to suspect the existence of "Something more of the depths," something "Blurred" and "blotted," never to be encountered directly.

And of course, if poems well up from the subconscious, as poets so often say, then looking deep into a dark well is a good image for writing a poem. One could go rather far along these lines. To an extent not often appreciated by people who do not read much poetry, poets live not in the everyday world of things and events, but in the world of poems. Their significant history is literary history. That is why it is often helpful to look at poems as Harold Bloom might, to discover the possible "anxiety of influence." Could Frost be overturning a precursor poet, say, Wordsworth? Could he be writing an anti-Romantic poem, in which he argues implicitly that the "celestial light" and "clouds of glory" that Wordsworth's "Child" perceives are after all an investment the human being makes in nature and not "Intimations of Immortality" after all? In this reading of Frost's poem, the poem becomes a rejection of the Romantic enterprise, a satire on the major trope of Romantic poetry: personification, the finding of a human self in the natural world. Frost's poem accepts human limitations, as Romantic poetry in its insistence on "godlike" human infinitude is never able to do, and celebrates a victory of the Classical over the Romantic.

Now, these four interpretive statements I have just proposed are related to each other in complex ways, but it is important to see that one cannot have all of them at once. The real issue is the extent to which Frost's poem is self-referential, a poem about poetry. The first two statements suggest that the poem is about the world, about something outside itself: the epistemological problem, or the nature/culture split. The second pair of statements suggests that the poem is about itself: the production of the poem from the subconscious, or the relation of the poem to the Romantic enterprise. The poem gestures primarily to the world, or the poem gestures primarily back at itself. One cannot have both. (A third possibility, of course, also mutually exclusive, is that the relation between poem and world is reciprocal, as pervasively in the poetry of Frost's contemporary Wallace Stevens.) The interpretive decision must have been made—the mystery must be revealed—in order for interpretive statements to be written.

In any case, different interpretive statements pick and sort the elements of the world "outside" the poem in different ways. The text and the world as it appears for the interpretive statement mutually determine each other. *Context* as the name of an interpretive concept names that reciprocal relation between the text and its world.

Form. The physical "form" of a poem, insofar as it is a form, is already a rule—a relation among, say, all the poems now in the world or to come later that are sonnets. In the particular interpretation, *form* is the name of a relation between the particular poem and the set of other texts that share a similar physical structure. To pay attention to the form of a particular poem means to conceive of it as a structure of physical relations: rhymes, meters, line positions, and so on. But the collection of other texts to which the particular poem is related is now conceived also as a differential structure of relations, a little universe within the larger universe of language. In such a little universe each sonnet, say, exists as such by virtue of its similarities to and differences from all the other sonnets. This is what it means to take "form" as a concept of an interpretive system.

I shall be relatively brief in talking about the physical form of Frost's poem. That is not because there is little to say, but because there is too much. The sound of Frost's poetry is important. But sound is difficult to discuss briefly, especially for a poem that can be conceived as a battleground where Classical hendecasyllabics, blank verse, and Frost's "sound of sense" are all contending for the mastery.

Stanley Burnshaw recounts how the poem got written as the result of Frost's explanation of Latin meters to his daughter (130). Reuben Brower identifies Catullus's "Qui dono lepidum novum libellum" as one of Frost's favorites, and talks about the "metrical tour de force" by which Frost turned, as Frost said, "iambic into hendecasyllabics" (138-39). Eleven-syllable lines are not unusual in English blank verse. Hamlet's "To be or not to be" soliloquy begins with a string of them, for example. And of course the transition from Classical verse to American verse involves a change from quantitative to accentual. So a detailed analysis of sound would involve decisions about whether hendecasyllabic or blank verse gets the upper hand, and about the extent to which either pattern is reinforced or traduced by the normal rhythms of colloquial speech. Then, one would have to decide what those decisions might imply about Frost's attitudes toward Catullus, American versification, or meter in general.

I quail before the task, especially since I know of no very satisfactory way of talking about the sound of poetry. Therefore, I shall confine myself to a few remarks about the printed form of Frost's poem, its shape on the page, which of course corresponds in more or less complicated ways with its patterns of sound.

When I glance at the poem on the page, it *looks* like a sonnet. But it is unrhymed, and it has fifteen lines instead of the usual fourteen. On the other hand, the division of thought, corresponding to the syntactic divisions marked by end punctuation, in the first fourteen lines is very like that of a traditional Petrarchan sonnet turned upside down. I see a sestet (lines 1–6, the first sentence) followed by an octave in two quatrains (lines 7–10 and 11–14), where the only one-sentence line (11) conceptually ties the first of the quatrains to the second, just as the rhyme scheme in the Petrarchan sonnet ties the quatrains together.

Now, what should I make of this? Nothing, some critics would say, and that would be a reasonable response. Still, I might consider that the Petrarchan sonnet is a difficult form in English, often appearing highly wrought, more a performance than a conversation even in the works of the best poets. Maybe I am dealing here with what Jurij Lotman calls a "minus device" (Lotman, *The Structure of the Artistic Text*, 94–103). By presenting a poem that looks like a Petrarchan sonnet (or rather, an upside-down Petrarchan sonnet), Frost is calling attention to the fact that his poem is *not* a sonnet, *not* a performance, *not* a deliberate artifice. And this of course would be part of the game, for the poem itself suggests that there is no determinate thing that is not an artifice—i.e., that is not cultural. If people see anything in wells besides themselves, that something is "uncertain." And what about the extra fifteenth line? Clearly, it is the remainder, the undigested, the "something" left over that does not fit the form and that therefore is an icon of what it mentions: the truth or the pebble, whichever one will. The line *is* "something" (that is, "something more") only in relation to the sonnets that the poem is not.

Should an interpretation of Frost's poem mention Petrarchan sonnets, since the poem clearly is *not* a sonnet? I suspect that this decision would be made in practice according to whether mentioning sonnets would help a critic straddle more firmly whatever hobby horse he or she happened to be riding. But the concept of "form" itself cannot give the rule here. If I am so sure that Frost is consciously or unconsciously (notice the hedging here) invoking sonnets, why am I? That is the mystery.

Diction. It is a commonplace that Frost's poetry most often uses what rhetoric books call "common" diction—meaning, usually, words that are not distinctively formal or "poetic." Frost ostensibly adopts the notion, articulated by Wordsworth, that the poet is a "man speaking to men." It is another commonplace that part of Frost's special genius is to realize the maximum potentialities of this common diction, to make the words of ordinary language deeply resonant.

There is of course an antinomy lurking here for the critic. For precisely to the extent that one notices and draws out the resonances of Frost's words, the words cease to sound like ordinary language, and they lose the unliterary quality that made them seem "common" in the first place. The mystery here is how far one should go in drawing out the resonances. I can give no rule based on the concept of the "code" itself that tells the critic where to stop. And yet, the critic in fact stops somewhere.

To notice diction at all means to notice the relation between the language of the poem and language from somewhere else—between two subcodes of the natural language. The relation might be one of similarity or of difference. *Diction* refers not merely to the words a poet uses, but to the rule that the poet has employed for selecting those words. The concept of "diction" always relates two sets of words: the words the poet has chosen, and the words the poet has not chosen. But these sets themselves are rules (relations) determining which words do and which words do not belong to the sets. When I think of "diction" or "code" as an interpretive concept, I think of the language as broken up into discrete systems or subcodes, each system constituted by its own structure of differential relations. "Diction" or "code" then becomes a concept relating those subcodes, a concept to which I can appeal to explain why my interpretation imputes connotations in addition to the lexical meaning of the words in the poem.

Some examples: what about Frost's phrase "wrong to the light" in line 2? What is this light? Is Frost talking plainly and simply about the sunlight, or is he alluding also to Wordsworth's "celestial light" or to God as Light? If the last, then looking into wells to place oneself at the center of the universe is more than forgivable self-absorption. It is the sin of Lucifer, kneeling in self-worship. Once one begins to hear biblical echoes, it is easy to find other words and phrases to bear out the hypothesis. What about the *lo* in line 12? Is it merely the archaic but still colloquial *lo* of "Lo and behold," or is it the biblical *lo*? And the *depths* in line 10—could the word refer to the depths out of which the Psalmist cries (Psalm 130)? I have already said that Frost's well might be a Freudian well, but wells are of course important sites at several places in the Bible, too. To which biblical wells, if any, does the poem allude?

The recurring word *picture* (lines 4, 8, 9) presents another kind of conundrum. Which of the several possible contexts (connotations) of this "ordinary" word are being invoked? If the picture in question is a picture such as an artist paints, then the poet is the creator of his own illusion. If the picture is one such as appears on a photographic plate, then perhaps matter is the agent of deception. Or perhaps *picture* means to suggest also a philosophical context, and stands for representation in general.

It might also be significant that the "something" the poet sees is *white*. Apart from the suggestions of whiteness that I have already mentioned, should one think as well of *Moby-Dick* and Melville's digression on whiteness? Melville's passage is a kind of landmark in American literature, after all, in which whiteness as a symbol of innocence and purity is decisively undermined. Whiteness in the whale becomes the emblem of the monstrous, the unintelligible, the evil. Is there something positively sinister about the white object the poet glimpses? Certainly whiteness takes on such a symbolic value in a sonnet Frost published later, "Design," where a white spider camouflaged on a freakishly white flower captures an innocent moth. Richard Poirier, for example, goes this far, connecting the whiteness in the well with "Design" and with *Moby-Dick* (252).

This line of reflection might find support in the etymology of the word *quartz*. The word comes ultimately from a root meaning "to grasp" or "to hold," a root that also produces the Greek word *Siren*. The Sirens in the *Odyssey* lure men with their sweet song to death in the water. They hold out to Odysseus the promise of *knowledge*. The etymology of *quartz*, then, is like the etymology of certain other terms for substances found deep in the earth: *nickel* (from German *Nickel* = demon, dwarf) and *cobalt* (= kobold, goblin), so named by miners of copper and silver who thought the ores of these other metals to be deceptive or injurious. A Derridean excursus into etymology thus opens the possibility that whatever is "at bottom" lurks there like a demon—is, perhaps, as in Frost's "Design," part of the "design of darkness to appall."

The problem of diction subsumes the problem of intertextuality among written texts. The problem of diction is the larger, because this problem requires taking into account also the place of the words in relation to all spoken discourse. How far should one go in relating Frost's poems to other texts? The poet is still a person speaking to persons, maybe, but he is now speaking to persons who know the Bible, the works of Freud, the vocabulary of philosophical discourse, *Moby-Dick*, the *Odyssey*, and a good etymological dictionary. Somewhere along the line, one traduces the initial intuition that Frost is using "ordinary" language, "nonpoetic" diction. And yet one wants to hold onto that intuition, precisely to distinguish Frost from some other poets. The concept of "diction" itself, used as an interpretive concept, raises questions that push the critic to the boundaries of what that concept can do.

Theme. Unavoidably, I have talked about theme already. If a poem could not be related in some way to some known cultural form, I would not be able to say anything about the poem. The theme of a poem is just its relation to some known cultural form. Theme is different from context. *Context* refers to the relation between what is construed as being in the text and what is construed as being outside of it, its subject matter. *Theme*, as I use it here, refers to what the poem says about the cultural form that is construed as being both inside and outside the text. To think of theme this way means to think of the poem and the cultural form as relations between the addresser and the addressee. If Frost can pass a message to me by writing the poem, then the poem constitutes a relation between us. And if he passes a message to me, then I must know what he is talking about. Whatever he is talking about must be a cultural form at least insofar as it *can* be talked about, be taken up into language. That cultural form then also constitutes a relation between us. To think that a poem can have a theme, then, means to think that there is already some relation between the poet and me, and that there can be another one: namely, the poem.

The concept of "theme" turns out to be the crucial concept in this particular interpretive system for considerations of "correctness." To say that my interpretive statement is "correct" means that I have gotten the message right. To show that, I muster all the arguments that I can: that there is independent evidence for the author's intention, that I have taken the proper stance toward the poem, that I know what objects in the world the poem refers to, that the relevant physical features of the poem support the interpretive statement, and that I understand the nuances of the words. Whether the question of correctness can always be settled in this interpretive system is an issue that I shall not take up here. In practice, critics usually agree about some points and disagree about others. It should be obvious that I think the question of correctness cannot always be settled in favor of a message that is unitary, unambiguous, and unequivocal. But neither is there anything in the interpretive system to suggest that messages always have to be unitary, unambiguous, and unequivocal. The concept of "correctness" itself does not exclude the possibility of multiple meanings.

In the particular case of Frost's poem, I could relate it to specific, important cultural forms with well-known names. For example, I might say that Frost's "whiteness" at the bottom of the well is a metaphor for the Kantian *Ding an sich*, the thing-in-itself which human beings know (through transcendental deduction) must be there, but which they experience only through their own representations of it (only, that is, as phenomenon). Or, I might call the pebble or whatever it is an emblem of truth as *presence* (*aletheia*), an idea extremely important in the logocentric Western metaphysics that Derrida wants to deconstruct. Or, the poet's reaction to the "whiteness" might be seen as a restatement of Keats's theory of "Negative Capability," the supreme quality of the poet that allows him to exist in a state of uncertainty without having to plump for one rational conclusion or another. The message of the poem would then appear simply as the relation between the poem and the cultural form, the concept to which I would appeal in order to explain my connecting the poem with the cultural form I have chosen.

I hope I have shown that there are mysteries in Frost's poem, things an interpreter seems to know, but cannot account for knowing on the basis of a particular interpretive system. One might ask whether mysteries are so easy to find here just because Frost is, as everybody knows, a master ironist. There are two answers to make here. First, the problem of irony is itself just an alternative statement of the problem of voice, so that I would make no progress if I were to try to "explain" the mysteries by appealing to the concept of irony. Second, I believe parallel problems may be found in the work of many poets not thought of primarily as ironists, such as Milton, Wordsworth, and Robert Lowell at his most maudlin.

Have I carried out a deconstruction here? Yes, but not a deconstruction of the poem, I think. To say that I have deconstructed the poem would imply that my words are somehow more fundamental than the words of the poem, that my interpretive categories of "voice," "audience," and so on, are more real somehow than the linguistic structure that is the poem. But I do not want to claim that kind of metaphysical absoluteness for my terms. And certainly I continue to think that the poem is a far more impressive text than are my readings of it or any other readings of it that I know.

What I have done here, rather, is to deconstruct my own interpretive categories. I have shown how those categories allow me to articulate my understanding of the poem (to "say what I know about it") without ever allowing me to suppose that I *comprehend* or master the poem. And I have shown how the interpretive system itself ultimately makes me ask questions that I cannot answer within its boundaries.

2. *Ashbery and Metaphor*

Unfortunately, John Ashbery's "Self-Portrait in a Convex Mirror," the concluding poem in the collection by that name, is too long to reproduce here. My first impulse is to say that this poem is atypical of Ashbery. But I am not quite sure what I would be meaning by "atypical" here, except that to me this poem seems not quite so hermetically sealed as many of Ashbery's other poems. And even at that, some of the other poems (usually, the longer ones) in this collection seem also to aspire to a certain condition of intelligibility. The poems are difficult, but I have at least the illusion of understanding them a little bit.

In "Self-Portrait in a Convex Mirror" Ashbery seems concerned to explore the extent to which understanding is an illusion. The poem is paradoxical in sounding at once self-indulgent, at times nearly weepy, and relentlessly postmodern in insisting on the disappearance of the subject. Ashbery is reciting some of the lessons of French structuralism and poststructuralism. If one had to put a name to it (no doubt a bad idea), that might be as good a name as any for the "new preciosity / In the wind" (lines 268–69) that challenges and is challenged by the High Renaissance "argument" (291) of Parmigianino's self-portrait. The poem is paradoxical also in a way that does seem typical of Ashbery's poetry. What might be called the tone or mood seems highly coherent—in fact, almost uniformly flat for such a long poem—whereas the individual units (phrases, sentences, longer passages) from the point of view of logic are always jostling against each other. Ashbery has phrases for it: "it all boil[s] down to one / Uniform substance, a magma of interiors" (130–31), while all along "each part of the whole falls off / And cannot know it knew" (549–50). Or,

> That is the tune but there are no words.
> The words are only speculation
> (From the Latin *speculum*, mirror):
> They seek and cannot find the meaning of the music.
> (47–50)

Ashbery's mastery of this tactic, perhaps ultimately learned from Stevens, makes him a poet's poet and puts him in the odd position of being at once one of the most quotable and one of the least accessible of contemporary poets.

But my point here is that the paradoxes of this poem work to make it a kind of metapoetry, or commentary on itself—in fact, a self-portrait. The paradoxes work in much the same way as the paradox inherent in the sentence "I am lying," which calls attention to the fact that the sentence is a metastatement. A better example might be a statement such as "The jury will disregard that last remark," where the jury have to regard the remark in order to understand what they are being required to disregard. Considered as metapoetry, "Self-Portrait in a Convex Mirror" is clearest, or at least most explicit, where it is most insistent in denying the validity of traditional critical concepts. One way into the poem is to explore how it deconstructs familiar categories such as the ones that seem to be named in Jakobson's model. What Ashbery's poem deconstructs, I shall argue, is specifically the Cartesian interpretation of Jakobson's model, which regards the six elements in the model as the names of substantial entities.

As with any deconstruction, this one depends for its possibility on the structure it deconstructs. In that sense, one might still argue that Jakobson's model of communication provides a way of talking about "what the poem means." But maybe there is another moment in the interpretation of Ashbery's poem. Perhaps the deconstruction of certain traditional critical concepts is not "all" that the poem "says." Later, I shall ask what is left after the traditional concepts have been deconstructed—whether, that is, there is another interpretive system in terms of which to articulate what remains after the shards of the traditional system have been swept away.

The poem begins early to perform its disappearing trick on the subject. Both author and reader, considered as substantial Cartesian souls, waver and blur. This is the "secret" of Parmigianino's painting that is "too plain" (43): that "the soul is not a soul" (44). Human beings cannot help thinking of themselves and others as substantial souls. But there is in fact nothing behind or under the surface of the visible expressed in the painting, or the surface of the moment of consciousness considered as an epiphenomenon of experience:

> your eyes proclaim
> That everything is surface. The surface is what's
>   there
> And nothing can exist except what's there.
> (79–81)

But even here the words cannot get loose from the Cartesian picture. The "eyes proclaim," as if there were a meaning behind the eyes, a soul expressed by the surface that is the painting.

The absence of the soul, made poignant (44) by the human being's inability to think or speak of the soul as absent, has devastating consequences for poetry as traditionally conceived:

> just as there are no words for the surface,
>   that is,
> No words to say what it really is, that it is not
> Superficial but a visible core, then there is
> No way out of the problem of pathos vs. experience.
> (92–95)

These lines can be read from the perspective of poststructuralism. There can be no words for the surface, because all words belong to the surface. One cannot get outside of the surface to talk about it. All words are signifiers that imply the absence of the signified. Words mean only through their oppositions with other words, but there are no "core" words for the words meaning the surface to stand in opposition to. Words are "what's there." There is no way, then, to talk about how or why for human beings the "inner" (pathos, what I feel) is different from the "outer" (experience, what happens to me). As far as words are concerned, the surface and the core are the same. The soul is the absent signified. And yet poetry has been traditionally conceived as the expression of emotion, or even (the Romantic enterprise) as the imaginative healing of the split between desire and fact. It turns out that the project is futile. There is "No way out of the problem," because the very nature of words as signifiers keeps them from meaning what has to be meant. There is also another sense in which there is no way out of the problem: human consciousness is overwhelmed by language and cannot help thinking in terms of signifier and signified. The problem will not go away just because someone points out that the soul is not a soul. The logical paradox is the necessary destination of language-bound thought.

What replaces the absolutely simple substance of the Cartesian soul is a chaotic collection of fluid states and discrete particles of consciousness, illuminated or darkened by language:

> How many people came and stayed a certain time,
> Uttered light or dark speech that became part of you
> Like light behind windblown fog and sand,
> Filtered and influenced by it, until no part
> Remains that is surely you.
>
> (109–13)

The sense that the self is sometimes taken over by others sometimes becomes acute. In viewing Parmigianino's painting,

> the whole of me
> Is seen to be supplanted by the strict
> Otherness of the painter in his
> Other room.
>
> (237–40)

The lines at first seem to imply that Parmigianino, at least, possesses a masterful self that can absorb the viewer's self. Parmigianino, one might say, intends to communicate his being to the viewers of his painting. But it turns out that even the artist—*especially* the artist—is not the master of his own intentions: "It is the principle that makes works of art so unlike / What the artist intended" (447–48). "Creation" (458, 472) takes over the artist with its "otherness" (468, 475), and

> things
> Do get done in this way, but never the things
> We set out to accomplish and wanted so desperately
> To see come into being.
>
> (459–62)

Still, it is impossible for the viewer to conceive of the painting in any other way than as the fulfilling of a human intention: "One is forced to read / The perfectly plausible accomplishment of a purpose" (464–65). It is something inescapably read "Into" (466) the painting.

This is Ashbery's commentary on the hermeneutic that aims at the recovery of the artist's intention. The enterprise is inevitable but doomed, because the idea of the substantial Cartesian soul, which human beings cannot shake off, is a fiction.

Whatever arguments there are for the disappearance of the artist or poet apply also to the viewer or reader. The viewer keeps getting absorbed into the painting, or into the "life" (296) of the painter's "argument" (291): "we are in fact it, / If we could get back to it . . ." (298–99). But also, one of the recurring movements of the poem is a slackening of concentration or a drifting of attention away from the painting: "The balloon pops, the attention / Turns dully away" (100–101).

Even toward the end of the poem, someone is "allowing extraneous matters" to "break up" the day and "cloud the focus / Of the crystal ball" so that "Its scene drifts away" (480–82). As in one of Ashbery's metaphors, the painting "swims" in and out of the focus of consciousness:

> As I start to forget it
> It presents its stereotype again
> But it is an unfamiliar stereotype. . . .
> (207–9)

How can a stereotype be "unfamiliar"? This Ashberyism is logically paradoxical, but nevertheless precisely suggests that peculiar state of consciousness in which I think of something that I am pretty sure I have thought of before, without being able to remember where or when. There is an odd sense of simultaneous possession and dispossession. A somewhat similar moment occurs later: "A breeze like the turning of a page / Brings back your face" (311–12). Looking at the painting is like reading, but Parmigianino's face is only on alternate pages. The other pages are doodled over with the viewer's private associations, and it is not even clear that the reader is the one turning the pages. Maybe they are just turning in the "breeze," consciousness controlled by something beyond itself, as in lines 116–20. Finally, even the "fertile / Thought-associations" (483–84) do not belong to the self. They "appear no more, or rarely" (485), and they fade, "Given back to you because they are worthless" (488).

The poem pretends, at least, to perform an honest introspection. And if the reader of the poem were to perform an introspection at least as honest, what would become of the hermeneutics of response? If I am not the master of my own responses and cannot sustain the focus of my attention, and if many of my responses are consequently dull, stupid, mundane, or irrelevant to the poem, then how can I argue that my associations are not "worthless"? Finally, there is no way to separate the responses that have worth from those that do not.

So reader-response theories of interpretation go bankrupt, in the first place because the reader is not a substantial Cartesian ego before whom the text situates itself as an object. No particular stance toward a poem can be taken up when the subject who is supposed to take up the stance has disappeared. But in the second place, an honest examination of the moments of attention that make up consciousness shows that the responses that get reported are being selected according to some criterion of relevance. If people respond to poems the way Ashbery says he responds to the painting, then the only way for reader-oriented interpretations to get written is to decide which responses are normative. And that sounds like anything but straightforward reporting.

One of Ashbery's tactics in deconstructing the concepts of "addresser" (author, painter) and "addressee" (reader, viewer) is his use of personal pronouns. Ambiguous reference seems sometimes to identify, sometimes to confuse, painter with poet with reader. For example, in lines 24 and following, the poem seems to be talking about Parmigianino's alleged "soul." But the conclusion of the line of argument here seems applicable to everybody: "the soul is not a soul" (44), and "it fits / Its hollow perfectly: its room, our moment of attention" (46–47). What is one to make of this *it* and this *our*? Is it that Parmigianino's soul exists only insofar as the viewers of the painting make room for it in their attention? Or is it generally the case that what people mistake for their souls is just the sequence of moments of attention, epiphenomena of experience? Both? Does "our" refer only to viewers of the painting, or does it mean everybody?

Similarly, in lines 100 and following the poet seems to be talking about himself, as his attention drifts from the painting and he begins to think of his friends who visited him and of "what yesterday / Was like" (104–5). But then,

> A peculiar slant
> Of memory . . . intrudes on the dreaming model
> In the silence of the studio as he considers
> Lifting the pencil to the self-portrait.
> How many people came and stayed a certain time,

Uttered light or dark speech that became part
    of you. . . .
                                        (105–10)

Who is "he" in line 107? The poet has just been remembering, but of course Parmigianino painted the self-portrait. On the other hand, this painter of a self-portrait uses a pencil, and Ashbery's poem is also a self-portrait. But painters use pencils, too. Who is the "you" in line 110 (and 113–14)? Is the poet talking about Parmigianino in an apostrophe, is he instructing himself, or is he addressing the reader directly? Maybe he is talking about the human condition in general, using the *you* that is the more intimate version of the pronoun *one*. By line 120 Ashbery has modulated back into the *I*, and the *you* that seems specifically to refer to Parmigianino. But the blurring of persons has already been accomplished.

Examples of this sort could be multiplied. Ashbery plays similar tricks with the pronoun *one* (e.g., 56, 149, 545), with the nominative and objective forms *we* and *us*, and by alternating *we*, *one*, and *you* (e.g., 233–50). The sliding reference of the pronouns reinforces the argument that the Cartesian ego vanishes into its relations.

But no doubt the pronoun that is most bothersome in this poem is *it*. For example, it seems crucial in interpreting the section about "Realism," "forms," and "ideal beauty" to make some decision about what "it" in line 187 refers to:

Sydney Freedberg in his
Parmigianino says of it: "Realism in this portrait
No longer produces an objective truth, but a *bizarria*. . . ."
                                        (186–88)

What is this *it*? How is the quotation from Freedberg to be taken? I think any of the following could be plausibly argued, along with some others. "It" is the "one dream" (182), maybe the dream of a substantial soul living in time but surrounded by eternal forms. In this case, Freedberg's comment might mean that realism in art produces what looks like chaos and distortion, but in fact still expresses the forms upon which beauty depends. "It" is the act of waking from this dream and consequently attempting to live in the "slum" (186) of the postmodern sensibility. In this case Ashbery might be using Freedberg's comment to suggest that what looks like realism in Renaissance art now seems only another device for perpetuating the illusion that there are eternal forms, an illusion that postmodern human beings can see through all too clearly now that it has been lost. "It" is the "slum" itself of the postmodern sensibility, a realism that privileges distortion and disharmony, from the perspective of which Freedberg's comment might simply be wrong. The portrait does produce "an objective truth," and for exactly that reason it says to the postmodern sensibility that the forms exist only as posited opposites of the distorted real. The forms "forage in secret on our idea of distortion" (202). "It" simply refers ahead, to the portrait, in which case the point of Freedberg's comment might be to show how strangely art imitates life, how the forms in the painting are connected with its distortions as dreams are connected with lived experience.

There is a reprise of the device in the beginning of the next section of the poem: "As I start to forget it, / It presents its stereotype again" (207–8). At one level, "It" seems to refer to the portrait, but it could also refer to the dream, or to the whole train of thought of the preceding section.

Ashbery indulges in a mild orgy of vague reference in lines 297 and following, where the apparent antecedent of the first *it* is either the painter's "argument" (291), or "another life" that is "stocked there" (296):

> that it,
> Not we, are the change; that we are in fact it
> If we could get back to it, relive some of the way
> It looked, turn our faces to the globe as it sets
> And still be coming out all right:
> Nerves normal, breath normal. Since it is a metaphor
> Made to include us, we are part of it and
> Can live in it as in fact we have done. . . .
> (297–304)

The *it* after "globe" seems to refer to "globe"; on reflection, however, it might make sense to talk about the metaphorical "setting" of the globe of an argument. But the following occurrences of *it*—do they refer to the globe or to the argument? Either the globe of the earth (though it is the globe of the sun that sets) or Parmigianino's self-portrait could be referred to as a "metaphor" for the human condition (as already in lines 55ff. and 88ff.), something that "we are part of" and "Can live in . . . as in fact we have done." And of course, the portrait itself produces the illusion of a globe or a "crystal ball" (482).

The "it game" in the poem is not always played so spectacularly, but it is often played. Often enough, the bottom line is that one decides that it does not really matter much what these instances of *it* refer to. As in intimate conversations, sometimes, ambiguous reference seems not seriously to impede things. The game is a tactic in Ashbery's assault on the concept of "reference" itself. To the extent that sentences playing the game of ambiguous reference at least teeter on the brink of sense, the whole theory that sense depends on reference is shaken.

The poem is more explicit in spots. To say, for example, that "everything is surface" and that "The surface is what's there / And nothing can exist except what's there" (80–81), is to say that the only possible kind of reference is self-reference. This would be true especially for the postmodern period, when "We don't need paintings or / Doggerel written by mature poets" (414–15) to explain the paradoxical human desire to live in time and to be outside of time. The desire is too obvious, as human beings become aware of the impermanence of the self, as "one / Is always cresting into one's present" (385–86): "The explosion is so precise, so fine" (416). Perhaps there is no longer "any point" to art, if art is conceived as reflection at leisure on enduring human experience. The "leisure to / Indulge stately pastimes" (419–20) does not exist any more:

> Today has no margins, the event arrives
> Flush with its edges, is of the same substance,
> Indistinguishable.
>
> (421–23)

The work of art is an event like any other. It cannot be something that occurs in the margins of experience as commentary, but must refer, if it refers to anything, to itself.

What is left for art to accomplish is "Play" (424): "It exists, in a society specifically / Organized as a demonstration of itself" (424–25). It is hard not to hear a faintly satirical tone here, as though Ashbery is not always perfectly happy with such a society. Maybe among the "assholes" (426) who will not always play the game are included not only politicians and critics, but also, at times, mature poets.

Anyway, my point is that play is by its nature self-referential. If art exists in the postmodern world, it does not exist as a commentary or reflection on previous shared experience, but instead as self-referential, autotelic activity. To think that poetry refers beyond itself, is "about" something, is to "confuse issues" (429, 490–91). The answer to the hermeneutic question What is this talking about? is always the same.

Poems talk only about themselves, and the question is therefore not worth asking. What is "extraneous" (144, 480) to the work of art turns out to be everything that is thought of as being outside it. There is an "action of leveling" (129), which reduces everything extraneous to a "Uniform substance, a magma of interiors" (131), represented by the "silver blur" (141) at the edge of Parmigianino's convex mirror.

The physical form of Ashbery's poem looks sprawling on the page. A careful analysis might reveal pervasive rhythmical patterns. But Ashbery talks about form in general by talking about the painting, a more obviously physical "thing" than a poem is. He says of the portrait,

> I see in this [what?] only the chaos
> Of your round mirror which organizes everything
> Around the polestar of your eyes which are empty,
> Know nothing, dream but reveal nothing.
> (120–23)

The concept of "form" implies a center of a system, an organizing principle. Here the putative center is absent. The soul is not a soul, and what is organized by it might as well be called a chaos as a form. Freedberg's commentary on the painting, and Ashbery's commentary on Freedberg (186ff.), are susceptible to several different readings, but in any case one point seems to be that the idea of form itself depends on the idea of distortion: "The forms retain a strong measure of ideal beauty / As they forage in secret on our idea of distortion" (201–2). The most "extreme care in rendering" (230) exactly what the mirror shows produces, in fact, a "*bizarria*" (188). The result, as Freedberg points out, is that

> The surprise, the tension are in the concept
> Rather than its realization.
> The consonance of the High Renaissance
> Is present, though distorted by the mirror.
> (226–29)

The form (the "concept") is "present" only through the distortion. The punctilious observance of the representational rules—the "laws of perspective" (153)—has produced something unutterably strange looking, thus constituting a kind of deconstruction of the rules themselves.

The "laws of perspective" come into the poem where Ashbery is talking about living in the present, as opposed to dreaming about the future:

> Tomorrow is easy, but today is uncharted,
> Desolate, reluctant as any landscape
> To yield what are laws of perspective
> After all only to the painter's deep
> Mistrust. . . .
>
>   (151–55)

The laws of perspective are inventions of the painter, impositions on the uncharted landscape, which result perhaps from the painter's lack of confidence in his personal perceptions. They are "a weak instrument though / Necessary" (155–56). Not necessary in any absolute mathematical sense—the Cubist laws of perspective are different from the Renaissance laws of perspective. But it is necessary that some laws of perspective be invented for painting to go on. Laws of perspective are culture-bound:

>   it is certain that
> What is beautiful seems so only in relation to
>   a specific
> Life, experienced or not, channeled into some form
> Steeped in the nostalgia of a collective past.
>   (325–28)

The difficulty of living each day, like the difficulty of creating art, is the difficulty of channeling experience into some preselected, culturally validated form. Forms have no "ideal" beauty, then, in the Platonic sense. And yet human beings cannot help thinking of them that way, extrapolating from the distortions of experience to the consonance of form.

All of these reflections should shake the confidence of a critic who wants to make interpretive statements derived from observations of physical form. Freedberg looks at Parmigianino's painting and sees nothing but distortion. From that he infers consonance. This procedure should at least make one suspicious. Suppose I find a poem that is sixteen lines long and has an odd rhyme scheme and few or no lines that scan as iambic pentameter. What would I mean by calling this poem a "sonnet," or saying that it "resembles" a sonnet? For that matter, what did I mean above by suggesting that Frost's poem looks like a sonnet, when it exhibits neither rhyme, nor iambic pentameter, nor the correct number of lines? If I try to wriggle out of the difficulty by saying that the poem will remind somebody or other of a sonnet, the question becomes, Whom will it remind? If physical form is (and it already seems strange to say so) a cultural phenomenon, then is it possible for one culture to learn to appreciate the physical forms of another, and if so, how is it done? The problem of form slides over here into the problem of theme, which I will take up later. But Ashbery's poem says enough, anyway, to show that the concept of "form" is as slippery as the concept of "meaning" itself.

Ashbery comments on poetic diction indirectly. His most obvious tactic is to knit fairly long swatches of critical prose (normally thought to be as far from the poetic as anything linguistic could possibly be) surprisingly seamlessly into the fabric of the poem. Most of the quotations are from Freedberg (e.g., 187, 191, 218–21) or from the translation of Vasari (e.g., 9–15, 211). There are also quotations from music criticism (315) and from Shakespeare (317–18). In the vicinity of some of these quotations, Ashbery himself lapses into critical prose, incorporating paraphrase of his sources:

> Later portraits such as the Uffizi
> "Gentleman," the Borghese "Young Prelate" and
> The Naples "Antea" issue from Mannerist
> Tensions, but here, as Freedberg points out,
> The surprise, the tension are in the concept
> Rather than its realization.
>
> (222–27)

It is an interesting study in itself to see the ease with which Ashbery modulates from passages such as this one to ones that might be called poetic. The obvious point, of course, is that it makes little sense to distinguish between "poetic" language and "ordinary" language. The surprise is not the usual surprise of "found" poetry, namely that ordinary or even ugly pieces of language can be elevated, so to speak, into the poetic by removing them from their mundane contexts. Instead, the surprise is that these bits of language function in the poem by remaining precisely what they are: passages of critical prose.

A similar tension appears in two categories of words that Ashbery calls attention to by means of the normal typographical devices. There are a few foreign words, which are italicized: *speculum* (49), *le temps* (86), *en permanence* (490). In two of these cases, Ashbery translates: "the Latin *speculum*, mirror"; "the weather, which in French is / *Le temps*, the word for time." These are words recognized as strange. There are also words that by placement in quotation marks are exposed as being too familiar, as being clichés from which Ashbery to some degree dissociates himself: "programmed" (171), "poetic" (387), "art" (390), "Play" (423), "it was all a dream" (533). These two categories represent linguistic extremes: the odd, and the used-up. Again, Ashbery does not impose the foreign words as neologisms, nor does he attempt to rehabilitate the clichés. He uses the bits of language as exactly what they are.

Certainly this sounds strange, considering what peculiar things Ashbery does elsewhere with language. Perhaps a passage from "Grand Galop," another poem in the collection, can serve as a gloss here. In that poem Ashbery is working the metaphor of art (here, sculpture) as preservation:

> Better the cleanup committee concern itself with
> Some item that is now little more than a feature
> Of some obsolete style—cornice or spandrel
> Out of the dimly remembered whole
> Which probably lacks true distinction. But if one
>   may pick it up,
> Carry it over there, set it down,
> Then the work is redeemed at the end. . . .
>   (Ashbery, 15)

Words are like pieces of language left lying around for the poet to use. They always depend for the fullness of their meaning on some lost situation, some "obsolete style." But they can to some degree be "redeemed" by being set into a new situation. This theory would explain how the familiar, considered as familiar, can be reassembled to make what is strange. But it is also clear that by this theory it makes no sense to distinguish between "poetic" diction and "ordinary" language. All pieces of language, strange or familiar, are equally lost from their original structures and equally available for new building.

In both the first and last sections of the poem, Ashbery expresses skepticism about the ability of works of art to have themes, to convey messages. Parmigianino's argument about the soul is to be read, if anywhere, from the face of his self-portrait. But it is difficult or impossible to be sure what the face indicates:

>   the face
> On which the effort of this condition reads
> Like a pinpoint of a smile, a spark
> Or star one is not sure of having seen
> As darkness resumes. A perverse light
> Whose imperative of subtlety dooms in advance its
> Conceit to light up: unimportant but meant.
>   (65–71)

The result is that Parmigianino's gesture in the painting becomes a "pure / Affirmation that doesn't affirm anything" (98–99).

The portrait has, in other words, no theme. To have a theme means to belong to a cultural form. But all cultural forms belong to some other culture, even if it is only yesterday's. Human beings are always moving into the present from some past that is beyond their control. They are "thrown," as Heidegger says, on some trajectory. They must both rely on and try to escape from the artifacts of the past, the cultural forms that have produced and bound them. But no past cultural form can be completely adequate to the present, because today is always subtly different from yesterday: "No previous day would have been like this" (382). And so human beings

> have been given no help whatever
> In decoding our own man-size quotient and must rely
> On second-hand knowledge. Yet I know
> That no one else's taste is going to be
> Any help, and might as well be ignored.
> (504–8)

Because cultural forms are historically bound, the themes that depend on them lose status. They cannot aspire to be verities and must settle for being mere conventions, like everything else cultural.

It does not convey much information to say that a poem or painting employs Renaissance conventions to talk about the soul, when the soul itself is only a Renaissance convention. As for conventions,

> we have really
> No time for these, except to use them
> For kindling. The sooner they are burnt up
> The better for the roles we have to play.
> (521–24)

Human beings never escape the conventional. They always play roles. But the impossibility of fully participating in or even of understanding the cultural forms of the past argues also the impossibility of stating themes. The hermeneutic enterprise that aims at finding messages for the present in texts of the past is fundamentally misguided.

Now, what has been going on here? It would not much stretch the customary use of the term to say that I have been "interpreting" Ashbery's poem, and doing so using elements of Jakobson's model of communication. My interpretation has depended, in one sense, on the Cartesian version of Jakobson's model, because that is the structure that (I have been arguing) Ashbery's poem deconstructs.

But it is important to see that the relation between Jakobson's model and Ashbery's poem is not the same here as the relation I explored earlier between the model and Frost's poem. One way of putting it is to say that with Frost, I took the Peircean version of Jakobson's model as an interpretive system that underwrote interpretive statements by providing rules to connect the statements with the text of the poem. For example, the concept of "addresser" ("author") with its corollary notion of "voice" made it necessary to decide the extent to which Frost's poem is "ironic" or "serious." More precisely, I made certain kinds of interpretive statements; and then by comparing the statements with the text of the poem I discovered that an author, who speaks in a more or less ironic voice, had been presupposed in my interpretation. At that point, I uncovered a latent concept of the interpretive system. I understood that in interpreting, in writing statements that were supposed to be signs of the poem, I had been guided by some chain of signification that I had postulated to have occurred in Frost's consciousness. If I had wanted to state the heuristic principle explicitly, I would have said something like, "Decide what the author wants to mean."

Or, I compared Frost's poem with a sonnet. That involved an interpretive decision about which physical features of the text were relevant and which were irrelevant. But I had already made that decision implicitly at the moment it occurred to me to compare Frost's poem with a sonnet. So the concept of "channel" ("form") was another latent concept that underwrote interpretation by providing a rule for connecting Frost's text with my interpretive statements. Stated as a heuristic principle, the rule was something like this: "Identify the relevant physical features of the text." And similarly with the other elements of Jakobson's model, as I applied them to Frost's poem.

The situation is quite different with my interpretation of Ashbery's poem as a metapoem. This is not to say that Ashbery's poem cannot be interpreted from the perspective of Jakobson's model. Only, I have not done so. The elements of Jakobson's model in my interpretation so far have been the subject matter postulated for the poem and not the concepts of the system that underwrites interpretation. I have treated these elements, in other words, as names of entities that Ashbery is talking about and not as ways of connecting his text with my interpretive statements. Jakobson's elements come in simply as the vocabulary of my interpretive statements, not as methodeutic concepts in Peirce's sense.

With Frost, I might say something like this: " 'Truth?' in the last line means that there is no truth. I think so because I think the author is being ironic." With Ashbery, on the other hand, I might say something like this: "'The soul is not a soul' means that you cannot reconstruct an author's intention. I think so because of some (as yet unspecified) interpretive system that underwrites the connecting of the 'soul' with an author's intention." With Ashbery, the author is mentioned in my interpretive statement itself. With Frost, the author is not mentioned until I try to explain why my interpretive statement says what it says.

Is there any special reason for rejecting Jakobson's model as an interpretive system appropriate for Ashbery's poem? Theoretically, I see none. No doubt in some of my interpretive statements above I have even lapsed back into the model of poetry as communication. It is often easier, and sometimes almost unavoidable, to say that "Ashbery means" this or that. Interpreting in accordance with Jakobson's model or some variation of it has seemed natural for a long time. But since it appears to me that Ashbery's poem specifically aims at deconstructing the Cartesian version of that model, I want to play along, as it were, and see what possibilities for an interpretive system might remain once the model has been demolished.

I think Ashbery's poem gives a clue, in the word *metaphor*:

> Since it is a metaphor
> Made to include us, we are a part of it and
> Can live in it as in fact we have done,
> Only leaving our minds bare for questioning
> We now see will not take place at random
> But in an orderly way that means to menace
> Nobody—the normal way things are done,
> Like the concentric growing up of days
> Around a life: Correctly, if you think about it.
> (302–10)

At least to those nostalgic for absolutes, these lines must seem the most optimistic ones in a poem that generally affirms or even celebrates relativism. Of course, what is asserted here is denied elsewhere. But the lines leave room for order, and even for doing things "correctly." Maybe there is hope even for an orderly and nonmenacing "questioning" of poems. The *it* in line 302 is one of Ashbery's ambiguous pronouns. It might refer to Parmigianino's painting, to his "argument" (291), to the "other life" that is "stocked there" (296), or to the "globe" (300), which itself might be the painting, the sun, or the earth. In fact, the blurred *it* seems to include almost anything you please. And that suggests part of the logical nature of a metaphor. A metaphor is one sort of sign, and, given the right situation, anything can become a sign of anything else by virtue of being both similar to that other thing in some respects and different from it in others. Metaphor is not possible without similarity on the one hand, and difference on the other.

I want to argue that it is just the concept of "metaphor" that has underwritten most, if not all, of the interpretive statements about Ashbery's poem that I have made so far. I have been able to see the poem as a deconstruction of Jakobson's model just because I have taken the painting as a metaphor for the poem, or the process of painting as a metaphor for the process of writing, or the processes of painting and writing as metaphors for human consciousness, or the painting and the poem as metaphors for particular states of consciousness, and so on. Parmigianino's self-referential painting becomes a "metaphor / Made to include us" as "we" self-consciously reflect upon it. One possible reaction to Ashbery's poem is to read it feelingly and remain silent. But if there is a question of interpreting it, where *interpreting* means making interpretive statements, then the concept of "metaphor" seems crucial. It seems to remain as necessary even after all the concepts of Jakobson's model have been swept away.

I do not have a general theory of metaphor. But I would like to make a few observations about how metaphors work in literary texts, in order to explain how "metaphor" by itself can be regarded as a sort of minimal interpretive system.

The first point is that I am using the term *metaphor* in its broader sense to include verbal comparisons that have other technical names. So "My luve's like a red, red rose" is a metaphor, as is "darkness visible." I prefer the term *trope*, but that term, too, has taken on a life of its own in critical discourse. And so I shall just continue with the term that Ashbery provides. If I had a better definition of *metaphor* than this handwaving sort of ostensive definition, then I think I would have a general theory of metaphor after all.

The second point has to do with *metaphor* considered as the name of a relation. At first it might seem obvious that *metaphor* is the name of a relation between two words or the referents of those words, where the words or their referents are called the terms of the metaphor. "My luve's like a red, red rose" relates my love to a rose, and so on. But I think it is not quite that easy. "My love is an old woman" and "My love is Jane Doe" also relate subject-term with predicate-term; depending on the situation, these sentences might or might not count as metaphors. (The "love" referred to in the first sentence could be male, for example, and the "love" referred to in the second sentence could have some name other than *Jane Doe*.) Something else is going on in metaphors besides the relating of subject-terms to predicate-terms.

I would put it this way: something can be construed as metaphorical only after an interpretation takes place in which a "literal" meaning is constructed. "My luve's like a red, red rose" appears as a metaphor only when I say, "That means that the woman he loves is young and very beautiful." The concept of metaphor is then uncovered as the rule underwriting the connection of the interpretive statement with Burns's text. I want to say, then, that *metaphor* is the name of a particular kind of relation between a text and an interpretive statement. Instead of saying simply that "rose" is a metaphor for "my love" in Burns's text, I would prefer to say that the text "My luve's like a red, red rose" constructs a metaphorical relation between its terms and the terms of the interpretive statement "My love is young and very beautiful" (or whatever else I say the line means).

Third, the examples "My love is an old woman" and "My love is Jane Doe" demonstrate also that it is not *just* the terms of the comparison that are brought into relation by the metaphorical statement. To interpret "My luve's like a red, red rose," I have to know that the class of women is not included in or coextensive with the class of roses. Considerations such as this make people want to say that metaphors relate not just terms, but "different universes of discourse," or something of the sort. (At this point, one might mention, for example, Paul Ricoeur's theory of metaphor in *The Rule of Metaphor*, in which Ricoeur systematically moves the analysis of metaphor from the level of the individual word and sentence to the level of "discourse" in general. I shall have more to say about Ricoeur in Chapter 4.) In other words, I have to know how the terms of the comparison are used in the language, and that means knowing their relations to other terms in the language that are paradigmatically related with them, as Saussure would say. What seems to happen with a metaphor is that I sort through, as it were, the numberless possible associations of each term of the comparison until I find predicates that match. "Youth," "beauty," "ephemerality," and some other predicates seem to belong to both women and roses, and so I mention these predicates in my interpretive statement. But what is being brought together in the comparison is not just two terms, but two paradigms—two universes of associations. When through triteness of the metaphor most users of the languages hit immediately on the relevant predicate, without being conscious of the separate universes of associations, then the result is a "dead" metaphor, a locution that is no longer considered metaphorical.

Now it might be easier to see how a metaphor can be a kind of limiting case of an interpretive system: a structure (in this case, unitary) of relations that determine their relata also to be relations. The metaphor is the relation between the terms of the text and the terms of the "literal" interpretive statement. On the side of the text: to read metaphorically is to regard a text as constructing a relation of comparison between two terms, where those terms in turn are conceived as loci in their respective networks of differential relations (that is, their paradigms). On the side of the interpretive statement: it constructs a relation between the subject-term of the metaphor (e.g., the beloved woman) and the predicates conceived as common to the subject-term and the vehicle of the comparison (e.g., the predicates "young" and "beautiful," which belong to both the woman and the rose). And the terms of the interpretive statement also belong to a differential structure within the vocabulary of the literal. Somebody might ask, "Why do you say 'woman' instead of 'girl'? Why do you say 'young' instead of 'nubile' or 'mature'?" Getting the interpretive statement "right" means considering the terms of the critical vocabulary also as loci in a differential structure.

The potential of a single metaphor for becoming a whole interpretive system is implied in certain uses of the word. "The metaphor of knowing as seeing dominates Western metaphysics." "The metaphor of Euclidean geometry dominates classical optics." "The metaphor of the solar system underlies the Bohr atom." "The metaphor of pilgrimage explains everything that happens in Chaucer's *Canterbury Tales*." "The metaphor of the way or path is central to Taoism." "The metaphor of consumerism is destroying the modern American university." And so on. In fact these large, compelling metaphors tend to generate subordinate metaphors in a process that seems as natural as the "concentric growing up of days / Around a life" (309–10), but which is conceptually akin to the construction of the most pyrotechnical Metaphysical conceits (from Italian *concetto* = "concept").

Ashbery's poem, given the logical incoherence that is part of its program, is surprisingly coherent in terms of its controlling metaphors. The poem is almost Metaphysical in shape, as though Ashbery is seeing how many conceits he can tease out of one painting. But the effect is anti-Metaphysical. Instead of feeling gratified surprise at how things can be made to fit together, one is "restive" and yet "serene" (96) like Parmigianino in observing how the most artfully elaborated metaphors fail to hold things together.

To demonstrate this quasi-Metaphysical structuring of Ashbery's poem, I want to trace the complex interweavings of two of the most striking patterns of metaphor. First, there is the pattern of metaphors involving Parmigianino's painting itself, which because it is a painting of a reflection in a spherical mirror produces images of surfaces, mirrors, and spheres or circles. Second, there is the pattern of metaphors involving weather, wind, and water, which in the poem often seem to stand for everything that is not the painting or is outside the painting.

To read the poem this way means to impose on it the coherence demanded by a particular interpretive system: in particular, the interpretive system whose central concept is "metaphor." This interpretive system requires that answers be given to questions such as, What is this poem about? How does the poem hang together? That is, when I write interpretive statements answering such questions, it appears that my answers presuppose the concept of "metaphor" considered as interpretive system. The metaphors give the rule. So far, American New Critics would perhaps not be unhappy with this approach to the poem. But that is not the whole story. Later, I will show how the concept of "metaphor" also transcends or deconstructs itself, as do the concepts of the interpretive system I applied to Frost's poem.

Meanwhile, though, I will argue that to interpret the poem from the perspective of metaphor means to read it as a poem about human life in time. Since human consciousness is temporal, it is historically bound, and one great question of the poem is the extent to which the past (for example, artifacts such as the painting) can touch the present. The other great question (foreshadowed in 179–80 and taken up explicitly in 311ff.) is related to the first. It is the question of the meaning of death, which is the cessation of consciousness in time.

Both of these questions have their linguistic counterparts in the phenomenon of metaphor itself. The past is continuous with the present, determines the present, and is inextricably involved with the present. It is, in one sense, the same as the present; yet, in another, it is not. Similarly, for metaphor to exist, the metaphorical statement must be conceived as at once similar to (determining of) and different from the literal statement, and the terms of the metaphor must be conceived as at once similar and different. Also, language can be conceived as radically metaphorical, so that literal language, too, has its historical roots in metaphor. Then every metaphor must always be dying, hardening toward its own absence. To interpret a metaphor is unavoidably to give it a little death: "Something like living occurs, a movement / Out of the dream into its codification" (205–6). Or, as the poem says in another context,

> the moment
> Takes such a big bite out of the haze
> Of pleasant intuition it comes after.
> The locking into place is "death itself". . . .
> (312–15)

The ambiguous relationship of the present with the past is reflected visually in Parmigianino's painting. In the first lines of the poem the hand in the self-portrait is

> thrust at the viewer
> And swerving easily away, as though to protect
> What it advertises.
> (2–4)

The result is a "gesture which is neither embrace nor warning / But which holds something of both" (97–98). The dead painter seems to reach out to the viewer and to turn away, to put himself forward and to withdraw into reticence, to welcome and to repulse. And still at the end of the poem:

> . . . I beseech you, withdraw that hand,
> Offer it no longer as shield or greeting,
> The shield of a greeting, Francesco. . . .
> (525–27)

Between beginning and end there is not the rise and fall of the Aristotelian simple plot, but instead a wavering, a back-and-forth movement between accepting the portrait as a valid comment on its own irrelevance—"pure / Affirmation that doesn't affirm anything" (98–99)—and rejecting the relevance of the portrait on the grounds of having understood its argument—"no one else's taste is going to be / Any help" (507–8). The portrait both is and is not the consciousness of the poet; the depiction of the convex mirror both is and is not the depiction of the postmodern consciousness. The poem is a metaphor of metaphor.

I mark what I call movements of the poem by the explicit references to the movement of attention away from or back to the painting. In the first movement (1–99) Parmigianino's face in the portrait expresses his "soul," which "establishes itself" (24) as the face remains "lively and intact in a recurring wave / Of arrival" (23–24). The face "swims /

Toward and away" (6–7), and so the soul is said to "swim" out and "return" (25–26). Since the pigment on the wooden ball does not move, the watery images seem to express something that happens in the living consciousness of the viewer as he stands in front of the painting. They reflect the temporal dimension of experiencing the portrait in the present.

But the face itself in the painting is a surface, and furthermore, it is the "reflection once removed" (17) of the surface of a convex mirror. Everything visible from any particular point in space can be reflected, though distorted, in the surface of a convex mirror; and as one moves around the mirror to see what is reflected in it, the reflection of one's own face always remains at the center. The mirror with the central face, then, becomes a metaphor for "our moment of attention" (46), what is before the consciousness at any particular time. And at least in that sense, for human consciousness "everything is surface" (80). At any particular moment, nothing can be present to the consciousness that is not present to the consciousness: "The surface is what's there / And nothing can exist except what's there" (80–81).

Parmigianino's self-portrait depicts "life englobed" (55), the life of consciousness inevitably confined to the "globe" that is "its dimension" (57) just as the surface of the globe of the earth is the inescapable dimension of human biological life. Words themselves cannot get outside the "moment of attention" to mirror the consciousness from some other perspective. Instead, they usurp the consciousness and themselves become part of the mirroring surface: "speculation / (From the Latin *speculum*, mirror)" (48–49). Even the painter's hand—the active, tool-using faculty of the human being—that is "big enough / To wreck the sphere" (73) must nevertheless "join the segment of a circle, / Roving back to the body" (63–64).

In this first movement of the poem, Ashbery uses the pun on *le temps* to say that the weather as a metaphor for time is not important, "doesn't matter much" (83), because it

> Follows a course wherein changes are merely
> Features of the whole. The whole is stable within
> Instability, a globe like ours, resting
> On a pedestal of vacuum, a ping-pong ball
> Secure on its jet of water.
> (87–91)

The earth turns and the weather repeats itself with the seasons, just as the ping-pong ball holds steady on its changeable jet. The changes brought about in time are outside the stability that is the whole. In that sense, the painting, too, is timeless and can speak its argument to viewers of any time. The painting is impervious to what is outside it. The face with its message seems "tiny, self-important" (78) with relation to the technological hand, but it floats on top of the unstable ocean, a timeless "ship / On the surface" (78–79). Although the soul longs toward the wind and weather, is "restless, hearing raindrops at the pane, / The sighing of autumn leaves thrashed by the wind" (35–36), it is confined and "must stay / Posing in this place" (36–37). The soul longs to live in time, but its "condition," which feels like an "effort" (66), is to transcend the temporal.

The second movement of the poem (100–206) seems to stress the other thing: the historical boundedness of any human consciousness and the inescapable differences between Parmigianino and the viewer of his painting. The timeless globe of the first movement metamorphoses into a "balloon" that "pops" as "the attention turns dully away" (100–101). The lapse of attention is like a shift of wind or a change in the weather: "Clouds / In the puddle stir up into sawtoothed fragments" (101–2). The self is not the absolutely simple Cartesian soul. It is a composite of the weather outside itself, "Like light behind windblown fog and sand, / Filtered and influenced by it" (111–12). The consciousness itself is now involved in the "turning seasons" (117), controlled by some mysterious "curved hand" (116) and filled with

> thoughts
> That peel off and fly away at breathless speeds
> Like the last stubborn leaves ripped
> From wet branches. . . .
>
> (117–20)

From this perspective the "round mirror which organizes everything" reflects a "chaos" (120–21). The passing of time is like a "carousel" that, "going faster and faster," makes everything outside the present moment blur into one "neutral band" (124–27). What was important yesterday loses its identity today and merges into the indecipherable "silver blur" (141) around the edges of the convex mirror, the blur of experiences outside the central present moment, all compressed and distorted by the passage of time.

The only way to break the circle that now begins to look vicious would be to touch the past again—perhaps, to understand Parmigianino's experience and grasp the significance of one's own experience by contrasting it with the painter's otherness. "I can only know the straight way out, / The distance between us" (135–36). But the painter himself has been caught in the "circle of . . . intentions" (145). Parmigianino set out to paint everything he saw in the mirror, the whole of the world visible from his perspective. And yet the convex shape of the mirror conspired with him to "perpetuate the enchantment of self with self" (146). He was always at the center, wherever he looked. However "extraneous" the individual self might seem, it is impossible to "rule out" (144). The viewer is in the same situation. However much he wants to understand Parmigianino, the viewer is always at the center.

The meditation on how "Tomorrow" is "easy" and "today" is "uncharted" (151ff.) seems to be a meditation on the possible versus the actual. Tomorrow is the country of the dream (180ff.). It is the locus of the "forms" that "retain / A strong measure of ideal beauty" (190–91). Parmigianino's entrapment in the circle of "enchantment of self with self" in fact "doesn't matter" (147) if the important things about the painting are its ideal features, which transcend Parmigianino's historical time and gesture toward the "tomorrow" of the viewer.

But the human sense of the possible or the ideal ultimately depends on the experience of the actual in day-to-day living. The possible is precisely that which is never experienced, just as tomorrow is the day that never arrives. Human beings try some things, and they succeed at them. From that, they infer the existence of other things left untried, the "supposition of promises" (165) from which one can

> ramble
> Back home . . . so that these
> Even stronger possibilities can remain
> Whole without being tested.
> (166–69)

It is as though human beings deliberately refrain from trying some things, so as to leave a space, as it were, for the merely possible. Today as actual is like a "Landscape sweeping out from us" (163), but it too is bounded by a circle, the "horizon" (164) that moves as human beings move through time. There seems to be a deep pessimism about escaping from the circle of the actual and establishing contact with the ideal beauty that is supposedly what makes Parmigianino's painting timeless.

> Actually
> The skin of the bubble-chamber's as tough as
> Reptile eggs. . . .
> (169–71)

All of the possible interactions of the subatomic particles are observed and "programmed" there (171) in the realm of the actual from which there is no escape. Human beings can no longer dream of the forms and their ideal beauty,

> And we realize this only at a point where they lapse
> Like a wave breaking on a rock, giving up
> Its shape in a gesture which expresses that shape.
> (198–200)

The wave here, as elsewhere (e.g., 23, 386), seems to represent the temporal. The timeless is expressed in the failure of time to stand still. The actual gestures toward the possible by failing to achieve it. The portrait now seems to stand for a lapsed dream, the High Renaissance dream of a life lived in time among the eternal forms.

The third movement of the poem (207–310) oscillates the other way. It brings back the painting as an artifact that somehow escapes the conditions of its creation and preservation. If life in time is a wave, Parmigianino's face in the self-portrait is like a ship "Riding at anchor, issued from hazards" (210). If this can happen, then the painting can touch the postmodern viewer after all, or even momentarily supplant the viewer:

> you could be fooled for a moment
> Before you realize the reflection
> Isn't yours.
> (233–35)

But this interchange is a personal matter, something between the individual viewer and the individual painter in the mirror. The new challenge in this section of the poem is the challenge of the urban experience: "The shadow of the city injects its own / Urgency" (251–52).

The postmodern human being lives in the city. It is much easier in the impersonal modern city to appreciate the insignificance of one's own private concerns; it is much easier to see oneself as a not-particularly-important cell of the giant urban organism. It is much harder to believe in the accuracy of the convex mirror, which places a huge, distorted version of oneself at the center and reduces everything else to a silver blur. The economic life of the city has always wanted to reduce art to production and consumption, and thus to cut off the artist from any relations with fellow humans that cannot be mediated by money:

> It wants
> To siphon off the life of the studio, deflate
> Its mapped space to enactments, island it.
> (264–66)

And the economic life of the city is admittedly the matrix of artistic creation, "The backing of the looking glass" (263).

But so far art has not succumbed: "That operation has been temporarily stalled" (267). The real challenge is the "new preciosity" that is "In the wind" (268–69) and that "brings what it knows not, is / Self-propelled, blind" (271–72). The wind is part of the weather that means life in time. If I were forced to supply a name for the unexpressed subject-term of the metaphor here, I would read the wind as the blind movement of history in the postmodern period and the preciosity that it bears as the nostalgic surrendering of the substantial Cartesian soul. The wind "Acknowledged saps all activity, secret or public" (274), for what can a soul that is not a soul do apart from the blind social forces that are the condition for its being? The whisper of the wind is felt as a "chill" that moves outward from the landscape of the private body to the "open sea" that is that body's life in time (276–79). The poem asks whether Parmigianino is "strong enough for it" (270). But it might be, after all, that this is what the painting has been trying to say to the postmodern viewer all along: that Parmigianino's problem already was the same problem, that the High Renaissance already foresaw the postmodern problem. If that is the case, there is "another life stocked there" (296) in the painting, and the painting can become the "globe" (300) that is "a metaphor / Made to include us" (302–3).

The next movement of the poem (311–479) begins a meditation on death as the decisive marker of the difference between the present and the past. As elsewhere (100ff., 482ff.), a change of weather—here, a "breeze"—becomes a metaphor for the shifting of the viewer's attention. Later, the sunlight on the sidewalks paradoxically "reproduces" what is unique to the present moment, "that special, lapidary / Todayness" (379–80). Yet it seems impossible to stop looking for beauty, and that seems to involve crossing the boundary between the present and the past (325–28) and trying to imagine whatever one sees as "outside time—not as a gesture / But as all, in the refined, assimilable state" (340–41). What does it all mean (342–44)? The answer once seemed to be "Love"—love, maybe, as Socrates meant it. But love experienced in time is like vaguely winding rivers that lead to an unknowable ocean (349ff.). The look in the beloved's eye is as ambiguous as the look in Parmigianino's eye in the portrait, and one can never know anyone else's experience even in the present:

> I used to think . . .
> That the present always looked the same to everybody
> But this confusion drains away as one
> Is always cresting into one's present.
>
> (383–86)

Surfing, as it were, on the wave of experience in time. The only constant is the movement into the future, which becomes a falling back into the present as the "waterwheel of days / Pursues its uneventful, even serene course" (393–94). The image of the waterwheel unites the two major patterns of metaphor I am discussing here, like the ping-pong ball on the jet of water in lines 90–91.

If the present does not look the same even to contemporaries, how much more difficult must it be to enter into the experience of the dead? You can visit a museum, but

> You can't live there.
> The gray glaze of the past attacks all know-how:
> Secrets of wash and finish that took a lifetime
> To learn are reduced to the status of
> Black-and-white illustrations in a book where
>   colorplates
> Are rare.
>
> (398–403)

And anyway, what the artist paints is not his own experience. It is something that "necessity" (455) creates according to the "Stringent laws" of the "history of creation" (458–59), something beyond the artist's control, and that is all that guarantees its existing. If the painting is a mirror, the important point about the reflection is its otherness from what is reflected: "This otherness, this / 'Not-being-us' is all there is to look at" (475–76). All the artist does, along with the viewer, is to enter the circle of the whisper game where a "phrase passed around the room / Ends up as something completely different" (445–46). These whispers, like the "whispers out of time" in the last line (where "out of" may be taken in both senses), are the whispers of the wind of the historical present (275). You can understand the painting only by letting it whisper to you what the currents of your time are already whispering. The artist was never in the painting in the first place. Parmigianino's face, as earlier, may be a "ship" that "has entered the harbor," but it is "Flying unknown colors" (478–79).

In the last movement of the poem (480–552) the portrait becomes a "crystal ball" that is clouded by the internal weather of wavering attention and failing imagination: "Its scene drifts away / Like vapor scattered on the wind" (482–83). By the end of the poem the soul that is not a soul has been dragged through and worn by the experiences in time that it once (33–38) longed toward and thought it could not get to:

> The fertile
> Thought-associations that until now came
> So easily, appear no more, or rarely. Their
> Colorings are less intense, washed out
> By autumn rains and winds, spoiled, muddied. . . .
> (483–87)

The painful paradox is that though the self does not exist apart from the social forces that shape it, nevertheless nobody else can help. Everybody gets just one chance: "There is room for one bullet in the chamber" (528). There is room only for Parmigianino in the chamber he paints, and the viewer ultimately cannot enter the painter's sphere:

> you fall back at a speed
> Faster than that of light to flatten ultimately
> Among the features of the room, an invitation
> Never mailed. . . .
> (530–33)

One must look for "clues," if there are any, in the "April sunlight" (546) that is the emblem of todayness.

And one is hampered by the urban experience: "We have seen the city; it is the gibbous / Mirrored eye of an insect" (541–42). This metaphor seems as densely packed intellectually as some of Donne's or Marvell's. The insect's eye replaces Parmigianino's convex mirror. As if reflected in the swelling, multifaceted eye of an insect, one sees oneself repeated over and over in the faces of the millions of others who also make up the organism of the city. Individual differences vanish. Moreover, the eye of the insect is "Mirrored" in one's own pupils. Oneself and one's seeing are constituted by one's relations to the social body. The insect is huge, horrible, and campy, a figure from a cheap science-fiction film. The individual has no more significance than a single member of a hive. And yet one does not even have the comfort of release from the enchantment with self, because the insect's eye retains all the distortions of the convex mirror along with the further distortion of repeating the self endlessly in every other self. The death of the individual would mean nothing and would snuff out the world.

Now, it seems reasonable to ask again at this point, "What has been going on here?" In this reading of Ashbery's poem I have imposed on it what is no doubt a false coherence. The interpretive system based on the concept of "metaphor" requires that imposition. Or, more accurately, once I have constructed this more or less coherent reading, I explain the connections I have made by appealing to the concept of "metaphor." Ashbery might be revolted by this sort of interpretive practice. He might suggest that I need to experience his poem more with my "nervures" and less with my critical intellect. He might even say that his poem deconstructs the concept of "metaphor" at least as efficiently as it deconstructs the Cartesian version of Jakobson's model of communication.

And that brings me to my next point. To understand an interpretive system from the inside, which is the only way to understand it, it is necessary to see what answers the system gives to the questions put to it. But then it is necessary also to see what questions the system poses that cannot be answered within its boundaries. What can be said along these lines about the concept of "metaphor" as applied to Ashbery's poem?

First, as I have argued, the term *metaphor* names a relation between the terms of two statements: a "metaphorical" statement in the poem and a "literal" interpretive statement. Thus, a metaphor comes into existence only by means of an act of interpretation. The concept of "metaphor" itself, then, cannot be what determines the particular predicates I find to be common to the subject-term and the vehicle.

That is just to say that there would be other ways of articulating all of the metaphors I have discussed here; and if there are arguments for articulating them as I have, those arguments are not grounded in the concept of "metaphor" itself. For example, if I am sure that the insect's eye in the last lines of the poem suggests that urban humanity is a hive organism, how do I know that? Not all insects are hive insects. The multiple facets of the insect's eye are not specifically mentioned. Maybe Ashbery is just talking about the material city, the glittering windows of the buildings, which in some lights seem inhuman. Ultimately, my interpretive decision has been made on the basis of other interpretive decisions about other metaphors. I have tried to read the insect's eye to make it coherent with my reading of other passages. And of course, my reading of all the other metaphors is also open to the same kind of questioning, especially since the poem seems to be a critique of the possibility of coherent experience.

The concept of "metaphor" itself, as interpretive system, opens the question of why any particular metaphor is what it is, without providing any way of answering that question. In Peirce's terms, the concept of "metaphor" is a methodeutic concept. It is not productive. It explains *how* I have connected the words of the poem with the words of my interpretive statement (namely, metaphorically) without explaining where the words of my interpretive statement came from. That remains so far mysterious, in a situation exactly parallel with the mysterious finding of interpretive statements for Frost's poem.

The concept of a "correct interpretive statement" means something here. It means an interpretive statement that is consistent with the overall metaphorical pattern. The interpretive system determines what *correct* means. Indeed, there might be other metaphorical patterns produced by different readings, which might also be self-consistent and therefore correct. Or, other interpretive systems might produce readings whose correctness would have to be decided on other grounds. So the notion of "correctness" is not meaningless, but it is not unitary either. There might be many correct interpretations.

I think that a major reason Ashbery's poem seems "postmodern," as opposed to Frost's "modern" poem, is that Ashbery carries the explicit deconstruction of interpretive systems one step further than Frost does. The generalization applies also to the concept of "metaphor," and to show that, I want to look for the third time and even more closely at the first section of Ashbery's poem. The early lines are about representational art, where "representation" is the general category under which metaphor is a particular species:

> ". . . he set himself
> With great art to copy all that he saw in the glass,"
> Chiefly his reflection, of which the portrait
> Is the reflection once removed.
> The glass chose to reflect only what he saw
> Which was enough for his purpose: his image. . . .
>   (14–19)

There are some oddities in Ashbery's expression here. (What is odd about that?) For example, it might seem more accurate to say simply that the portrait reflects (represents) the mirror image. But the portrait is the "reflection once removed," as if there were another, intervening reflection or representation between the mirror and the painting. And in fact, there is. The painting could not exist without previous representations in Parmigianino's eye and brain of the mirror image. The line "The glass chose to reflect only what he saw" oddly endows the mirror with free will, but at the same time makes the representation in the mirror depend on what Parmigianino is in fact capable of seeing. Nothing could be represented to him in the mirror that his eye and brain could not represent. Thus the mirror image represents what is in Parmigianino's eye, and the portrait represents what is in the mirror. But it is equally accurate to say that the eye represents what is in the mirror, and the portrait represents what is in the eye. In this infinite circling of representation the signified drops out, so to speak. All three elements—eye, portrait, mirror—exist only in the mode of representing, with relation to the other elements that are themselves representations.

If this is Ashbery's representation of representation, the lines would apply also to metaphors, which are representations. Metaphors represent only other metaphors, in an infinite circling of which Parmigianino's attempt to represent is a microcosm. But the concept of "metaphor" itself depends on there being a "literal" statement outside the metaphorical, as I have argued. Ultimately, then, in Ashbery's representation of representation the concept of "metaphor" deconstructs itself. As Peirce might put it, the "meaning" of a metaphor is not the discovery of some literal signified, but only the translation from one system of signs into another. "Metaphor," like all concepts of interpretive systems, is a methodeutic concept only, the name of a relation between signs. "Metaphor" is not some abstract category that can be known apart from and previous to actual interpretation of poems. Instead, metaphor appears as a category only in the relations between poems and interpretive statements. To employ the concept of "metaphor" as interpretive system means to consider the relation between that concept and the poem as reciprocal. Neither, that is, can be understood without the other.

The first section of Ashbery's poem deepens the critique of the literal by confusing subject-terms and vehicles of the metaphors. When Burns says, "My luve's like a red, red rose," it seems fairly clear that the literal woman is the subject being discussed, whereas the imaginary rose is "brought in" as vehicle to "carry" the meaning. But in Ashbery's poem, the separation between subject-term and vehicle gets progressively less clear.

The initial "As" (1) hints that Parmigianino's painting is the vehicle for some elliptical metaphor. Maybe the title means that the poem is a "Self-Portrait" as Parmigianino's painting is. The face in the portrait "swims" (6) as the soul is said to "swim out through the eyes" (25), and so the face becomes the vehicle for representing the soul. In this metaphorical structure, however, the hand in the painting is set in opposition to the face. It is not "in repose" (8); it is "Bigger than the head" (2);

it is "on another scale" (76) like a "dozing whale on the sea bottom" (77) with respect to the "tiny, self-important ship" (78) of the face. The face seems to be what the hand swerves to "protect" as it "advertises" (3–4). If the face represents the soul, the hand must represent what is not the soul, what simultaneously presents and conceals the soul by providing another scale in terms of which to measure it. In short, the hand represents the painting itself as a metaphor for the soul, and thus the painting refers to itself and is transformed from vehicle to subject-term.

The hand is not the "right hand" as Ashbery says in the first line. Parmigianino in fact extended his left hand. A convex mirror, like a flat mirror, produces a virtual image. It is possible to imagine that the right hand is extended only if (1) the viewer in imagination assumes the spatial position of the figure depicted "inside" the mirror; or (2) the viewer imagines that the image is real—for example, that a real though distorted other is extending his right hand. Under the assumption that Ashbery was not just confused by mirror games, this switching of left and right is perhaps an overly ingenious way of talking about how the portrait works—namely, by causing an identification with the artist (as in lines 237ff.) while preserving a strong sense of "otherness, this / 'Not-being-us'" (475–76). In any case, clearly the metaphorical structure causes the painting to flicker back and forth between representing something else and self-representing, between vehicle and subject-term.

So this structure of sameness and difference that characterizes the experience of metaphor characterizes also the experience of the portrait. Often it is difficult to tell whether the subject of the metaphor is Parmigianino's experience in painting the self-portrait or the viewer's experience in looking at it. To the extent that the viewer understands or appreciates the painting, the two can stand for each other in a relationship that is perhaps best described as metaphorical. The viewer's experience cannot be identical to Parmigianino's, nor can the postmodern universe of associations be the same as that of the Renaissance. If Parmigianino and the viewer of his painting are to be brought into relation, it will have to be through something like metaphor. But which experience is the subject-term and which is the vehicle?

> [I]t is life englobed.
> One would like to stick one's hand
> Out of the globe, but its dimension,
> What carries it, will not allow it.
> (55–58)

Who is "one" here? It could be Parmigianino. It sounds that way in the lines that follow. His self-portrait could express his argument that the soul "Longing to be free" must nevertheless "stay / Posing in this place" (37–38) because this place is the surface and the surface of the painting is all there is. Then Parmigianino's experience, expressed in the painting, would become the vehicle for a metaphorical statement about what is also the postmodern condition. The "laws of perspective" (153) that constrain Parmigianino's art become emblematic of the postmodern discovery that the soul is confined to "its room, our moment of attention" (46).

Or, "one" could be the viewer, as also, for example, in line 42. Then, the viewer's "speculation" (48), the words that succeed only in demonstrating that "there are no words for the surface" (92), would become the vehicle for a metaphorical statement about what Parmigianino was trying to express in paint. Is Parmigianino's experience a metaphor for mine, or is mine a metaphor for his? Although two universes of discourse are brought into relation, is the concept of "metaphor" even applicable any longer?

To write a metaphorical interpretation, I must have decided what is being talked "about" in the poem—that is, which term is subject-term and which is vehicle. The concept of "metaphor" itself, as Ashbery's poem illustrates, provides no definitive rule for making this decision. If there is nothing but representation of representations, how can I tell which way the vector points? The concept of "metaphor" allows me only to articulate what connections I have in fact made. Like other interpretive systems, the concept points toward questions that cannot be answered within its boundaries.

My purposes in this chapter, as I said at the beginning, have been three: (1) to illustrate the sense in which a theory of interpretive systems is "methodeutic," (2) to illustrate how interpretive systems of textual hermeneutics are "self-transcending," (3) to illustrate how the relationship between interpretive systems and particular texts is "reciprocal," in that neither can be observed except in interaction with the other. Later I shall discuss the implications of what I have said here for study of the humanities. If textual hermeneutics is taken as the paradigm of the study of the humanities, then what I have said in this chapter should have important implications about what kinds of knowledge are possible for the humanities and about what methods are appropriate. But I hope I have shown here at least that interpretive systems are not sets of rules for producing knowledge of texts, as the so-called scientific method, for example, is commonly (and I think wrongly) understood to be a set of rules for producing knowledge of nature. No more are interpretive systems sets of axioms from which to deduce new theorems about texts. If they are anything, interpretive systems are ways of getting at an understanding of interpretation, the fundamental concern of the humanities, from the inside—which is the only way to get at it.

3

The Arts of War

1. The Martial Arts as Languages

A good deal has been written in Western languages about the Oriental martial arts. A recent monograph in the *Journal of Asian Martial Arts*, for example, includes a closely printed thirty-nine-page bibliography of books and articles, most of them in English (Maliszewski, 65–104). But Westerners often find expositions of the Oriental martial arts confusing or mystical. It might be worth speculating on why this is so.

First, verbal descriptions of movement are notoriously hard to write and to read. Anyone knows this who has tried to learn from a book how to dance or how to tie a knot. The complexity of systematic methods for recording movement (e.g., Labanotation) evidences the difficulty of describing even the most ordinary motions. Written descriptions of movement often make sense only after the movement has been demonstrated or learned through imitation. Descriptions of techniques in the martial arts are properly used to remind or to correct. The Oriental martial arts are traditionally taught by example, where the teacher stands to the student in a relationship that a Westerner might describe as that of master to disciple. Discourse forms only a part of the training, and not necessarily the most important part. Traditionally, masters of some martial arts have been reluctant to write down what they know or even to demonstrate their arts in public. Presumably, they fear that misunderstanding of the actual movements or of the philosophical foundations of their arts will result in corruption or misuse of the techniques.

Second, anyone who lacks mastery of Oriental languages lacks at least to some extent the conceptual framework that even the most skillful translation relies on. For example, the notion of "ki" (Japanese, Korean) or "ch'i" (Chinese) is central to many of the martial arts, but *ki* has no exact English equivalent. Its various translations ("breath," "vital spirit," "life force," "mental energy") tend to sound to speakers of English vague and vaguely unlike each other. An instructor of the Japanese martial art aikido, for example—literally, the way (*do*) for harmony (*ai*) of *ki*—might deal with the central notion by using the word *ki* frequently in many situations, as if the students already knew or would soon experience what it means. The process seems very similar to teaching language to a child. At first, talk of "extending *ki*," or "experiencing *ki*," or "respecting the partner's *ki*," might seem quasi-mystical. Gradually, the word begins to make sense, although no one ever gives a satisfactory English translation. To the members of the class, the word becomes useful for describing or modifying behavior; to those not members of this linguistic community, *ki* appears to have no obvious referent.

Another example is the word *do* itself, which appears in Japanese in *aikido*, *judo*, and elsewhere, and in the Korean *taekwondo*. (The corresponding Chinese word is *tao*.) *Do* is usually translated "way" or "method," but it can also be translated "art" or even "way of life" or "way of being in the world." "Martial art" already sounds like an oxymoron to some Westerners; even stranger is the suggestion that taekwondo ("the art of kicking and punching"), for example, could become a way of life. One major task of this essay is to see whether this difficult idea can be articulated by regarding the martial arts as interpretive systems, where interpretive systems are understood from the perspective of textual hermeneutics.

Finally, discourse about the Oriental martial arts confuses Westerners because most Westerners have to make a strenuous effort to keep from thinking of body and mind in terms of Cartesian dualism. Generally, the vocabulary of body-mind dualism gets used even when an attempt is being made to think beyond that opposition. For example, the authors of *Aikido and the Dynamic Sphere* define *ki* this way: "The closer unity of mind and body—the fusion of these two functions (direction and action)—seems to come closest to an acceptable Western explanation of the strange strength which aikidoists call *ki*" (Westbrook, 22). This book, which was called to my attention by Jeff Baygents, a long-time student of the martial arts, is one of the clearest expositions in English that I know of. But obviously, a split between mind and body is being presupposed here in order to talk about their unification. The picture is Cartesian: there are two opposing principles that the martial artist or the concert pianist or the ballet dancer forces together through arduous practice.

There is truth in that picture. I cannot kick at the level of my head unless the muscle of my hamstring is flexible, and so I develop my kick by doing stretching exercises. It does make sense to say that practice in the martial arts aims at disciplining the body to carry out the intentions of the mind. But it is equally clear that to use the vocabulary of "body" and "mind" or of "physical" and "mental" already takes a long step toward instituting the very opposition that the martial artist wants to think beyond. The phrase "unity of mind and body" sounds mystical because of the Cartesian world picture in which the terms *mind* and *body* are embedded. Nor can it help someone learn a martial art to instruct the person, "Unify your mind and your body." Trying to identify something vaporous called "mind" as distinct from some machine called "body" just sharpens the cleavage. Instead, the instructor says, "Move this way," or "Put your hand here and your foot there," or "Watch how I do it."

So I am going to argue that the vocabulary of mind and body is not the right vocabulary to talk about the martial arts and, maybe, about other activities involving what is commonly thought of as bodily learning. Ultimately, even reading and writing are activities that involve bodily learning: movements of the eyes, the vocal apparatus, and the hands.

What vocabulary is right, then? Obviously, I am going to say that it is the vocabulary of textual hermeneutics—in Peirce's terminology, the vocabulary of symbol and replica. But what would justify this vocabulary? Only the results of applying it. The vocabulary would be justified in the same way as any hypothesis is justified. That is, the vocabulary is justified if using it produces interesting results about the martial arts and about textual hermeneutics itself.

Specifically, if a martial art can be conceived of as a kind of language, then I think that reflecting on such a language produces an interesting assessment of Wittgenstein's famous private-language argument. One might be tempted to say (and instructors do say), for example, that to perfect a technique of taekwondo the practitioner must get the internal "feel" of the technique, which even the advanced practitioner cannot quite communicate verbally. Some instructors try imagery; some rely almost exclusively upon demonstrating or placing the student's body in the correct positions. If a martial art can be thought of as language-like, then it might at first seem to be very close to a nonverbal "sensation language," where the referent of each technique for each practitioner is the private "feel" that accompanies its performance. What might Wittgenstein, who wants to deny the possibility of private language, say about this?

Before diving into such deep waters, however, it is necessary to ask how a martial art can be construed as an interpretive system, where the concept of "interpretive system" is defined from the perspective of textual hermeneutics. How can a martial art be construed as semiotic activity?

A disclaimer is in order. It is more or less an accident of my background that I take taekwondo as the exemplary martial art. I happen to have practiced taekwondo for a number of years. Each of the martial arts has its own techniques and what is commonly called its own "philosophy." Taekwondo is not normative in any important sense. I shall mention other arts, at times; much of the time, what I have to say would be applicable to more than one of the martial arts. Where it is important to know that I am speaking particularly of taekwondo, I shall say so.

There are striking similarities between learning a martial art and learning a language. Learning proceeds by imitating in a context someone who has mastered the techniques to be learned. A child learns the word *table* by observing and imitating the way adults use it in particular contexts, and a student of taekwondo learns a particular kick by observing and imitating the movements of the instructor's body in relation to real or imaginary opponents. And as with a formal language class, a class in the martial arts usually involves a series of formal exercises.

Private practice also seems to be essential—as when a child repeats a word over and over in an apparent attempt to fasten the word to an object, or when an adult student of a language repeats a word over and over to get some fluency in articulating the unfamiliar phonetic material. The idea of private practice in a martial art such as aikido at first seems strange, since the point of this art is to perceive and react to an attack. It would seem that a partner is necessary for meaningful practice. But of course the individual student can practice postures, breathing, and sequences of movements; and soon a student can begin to remember and imagine the kinesthetic sensations of interacting with a partner, so that it becomes possible to practice even while sitting still.

Private practice in taekwondo, on the other hand, sometimes seems to be the major part of training. Serious students spend hours perfecting their techniques by kicking, blocking, and striking in the air or at posts or punching bags. Instructors tell stories of learning a kick by doing a thousand repetitions a day. But as with aikido, even this sort of private practice is not strictly speaking private. A student is told even when kicking or punching in the air always to imagine an opponent, and even to imagine which part of the opponent's body the striking surface contacts. An experienced instructor can tell when a student is not imagining an opponent, and the instructor in such cases is likely to call the student's attention to the poor practice by asking the student to explain what the technique "means." So even in private practice the techniques are conceived as having meaning only in relation to a potential opponent, just as practice of a language always implies a linguistic community.

The parts of the traditional taekwondo class correspond neatly with the various levels at which speech may be analyzed. The class normally beings with calisthenics and stretching exercises. This is the phonemic level, as it were, the level where the capacity of the vocal apparatus to produce meaningful movements is developed. Practice of basic techniques follows. The basic techniques are the "words" of the language. Everyone realizes the technique differently, but everyone who is minimally competent performs movements that can be recognized as replicas of the particular technique. The technique is like a word, in Peirce's terms, in that it is a rule prescribing the qualities of its replicas. It is word-like also in that it symbolizes intent or has "meaning"; the technique means to strike the real or imagined opponent in a vital spot, but also it means to strike in accordance with the ethical or philosophical principles that underlie the art.

This needs clarifying. Advanced practitioners might not be aware of any separation of technique and intent, either on the part of opponents or on their own part. They might respond to attacks "instinctively" or "without thinking." But a similar sort of thing happens in speaking, perhaps in spirited dialogues where one has a sense of answering "what is being said" without attending particularly to the words used or to the interlocutor's motives. Nevertheless, just as the conventions of language make possible the give-and-take of dialogue, so the conventional symbolism of a technique in the martial arts makes possible the accurate and efficient reaction to it. Someone who does not know the techniques of taekwondo is likely to be injured by a kick because the person does not understand what the martial artist is doing. The symbolism of the techniques explains also a phenomenon of taekwondo that at first seems odd. The more advanced students are more likely to be injured by less advanced students than by students of their own level; but no one can manage to touch the instructor. This phenomenon makes sense when taekwondo is compared with a language. The more advanced students are in exactly the position of someone who knows a language fairly well, but is not yet fluent enough to deal with deviant or ungrammatical versions of the language.

Traditional taekwondo training involves also forms (*poomse*), or patterned sequences of techniques in which one reacts to attacks from a series of imaginary opponents. These represent the syntax of the language, ways of putting the techniques together in meaningful patterns that can be adapted to many actual situations. Perhaps the forms in taekwondo can be seen as corresponding to the passages that a student of a language memorizes for recitation.

Finally, the traditional taekwondo class involves sparring, either pre-arranged exercises or freestyle, where the students attempt to use the language by constructing sequences of techniques that are meaningful when applied to an actual opponent. Taekwondo sparring might be thought of as friendly dialogue, where the partners control the deadly force of their techniques in order to help each other become more fluent. The actual use of taekwondo in a life-or-death situation might be compared with violent verbal argument, where a serious attempt is made to reduce the opponent to silence. (Aikido, by contrast, is more like gentle persuasion.)

Obviously, learning a martial art is different from learning one's own language, in that the language is already in place and serves as a medium of instruction for the martial art. It is possible to imagine learning a martial art as a nonverbal pattern of behavior, as, for example, one might imagine a feral child's learning foraging behavior from wolves. But even though some martial arts imitate the movements of animals, the kind of "instinctive" response that the martial artist aims at is clearly not a return to the instinctive response of the animal. A martial art is a cultural activity.

It is more accurate to compare learning a martial art to learning a second language. Or, as I would prefer to say, learning a martial art is like learning to read and write. Even if one pursues the implications of making writing conceptually prior to speech, as I sometimes do in this book, nevertheless speech seems chronologically prior to writing. It is possible to imagine instituting a visual (written) language in the absence of a spoken language, but human beings seem not to go about things that way. Certainly individual human beings in a literate culture do not.

Taekwondo is to a large extent a visual language. It is therefore more susceptible than some other martial arts to analysis in graphic terms. Practitioners try to control breathing and minimize the sound of movement in order to give opponents as few auditory clues as possible. Even the loud yell used in taekwondo, which sometimes in practice serves to signal an impending attack or the completion of an exercise, is meant primarily to concentrate one's own force. With judo or aikido, being in contact with the opponent's body is sometimes important in sensing an attack. In taekwondo, on the other hand, the opponent is touched only at the point of impact of a kick, a strike, or a block.

The importance of private practice in taekwondo also connects this art closely with writing. Techniques in taekwondo can have "meaning" even if no actual opponent is present, just as the writing of a meaningful text does not depend upon the presence of an actual audience. In sparring, students try to "read" the opponent's intent from movements, but also to treat each attack as if it were "real"—that is, as if the opponent's intent were to kill. Obviously, students of taekwondo do not usually in fact try to kill each other. Breaking boards and rooftiles, another feature of traditional taekwondo training, is meant to test the force of techniques that must be carefully controlled in practice. In reading the opponent's intent in training, then, one reads an intent that is not really there, just as the reader of a text conceives of an absent author as the source of the text. Because of the lethal force of the techniques, the absence of the signified is necessarily built into the practice of taekwondo.

Taekwondo, like many martial arts, conceives of movements in terms of spatial diagrams in various ways. In aikido, for example, the center of gravity in the lower abdomen is thought of as the center of a circle representing the arc of the technique. In some techniques, the circle is the actual path of the opponent's body as the opponent is thrown or immobilized. Sometimes, martial artists associate the practice of their art with the reading or writing of ideographs. Howard Reid and Michael Croucher quote portions of an interview with a Taiwanese master of *hsing-i*, a Chinese art. *Hsing* refers to the external shape or form, and *i* refers to the idea or intention underlying that form (Reid and Croucher, 97). Master Hung I-hsiang points out that the written Chinese language is the basis of Chinese culture, and specifically connects hsing-i with textual interpretation: "Hsing-i is based on ideograms or picture ideas which assume the image and likeness of an external object. . . . Some people refer to this form of training as *hsin-i* or 'heart and intentions'; in other words, it is an attempt to express the ideas of the mind, literally 'shaping the mind' or 'shaping the intention'" (97). Reading the opponent's intention from the posture is like reading ideographs, and the techniques of the art express ideas that can also be expressed in ideographs. Hsing-i, in particular, is usually taught in conjunction with *pa-kua*, a martial art based on the eight trigrams of the *I-Ching*, the *Book of Changes* (*pa-kua* means "eight diagrams").

The use of some of the forms in taekwondo training has apparently been influenced by other martial arts. For example, some schools of taekwondo use a series of eight *Palgwe* forms. *Palgwe* is sometimes translated "eight trigrams" (i.e., the equivalent of the Chinese *pa-kua*), and the forms are associated with the ideographs of the *Joo-yeok*, the Korean term for the *Book of Changes* (World Taekwondo Federation, 223). The eight *Taegeuk* forms are now official forms of the World Taekwondo Federation. Each of these is associated with one of the ideographs of the *Joo-yeok* (World Taekwondo Federation, 83), and each *Taegeuk* form is to be performed as an expression of the principle suggested by the corresponding ideograph. For instance, the sixth *Taegeuk* form corresponds to the ideograph for "water," and the form is supposed to be performed in a "flowing" manner (World Taekwondo Federation, 113).

In some cases the pattern of a form is actually said to trace out an ideograph on the ground. One of the advanced forms in taekwondo is called *Keumgang*, which suggests "diamond" and appears as part of the name of a famous mountain in Korea. Accordingly, the pattern of the form is said to trace out on the ground the Chinese ideograph for "mountain" (World Taekwondo Federation, 148). The form *Sipjin* ("decimal"), similarly, traces out the Chinese character for "ten" (World Taekwondo Federation, 174).

The modern Korean set of Hankil characters is a phonetic alphabet, but Koreans still use some Chinese ideographs. The Hankil characters themselves are construed as schematic pictures of the physical arrangements of the vocal apparatus. Thus, the connection between reading and writing and the practice of the martial arts would not sound so far-fetched to Korean practitioners as it might sound to Westerners used to the Roman alphabet.

I will briefly anticipate a later argument by calling attention to a passage in Wittgenstein's *Philosophical Investigations*. In 1.156ff., Wittgenstein discusses the word *reading*. He has been arguing that there is no particular mental process that corresponds to the word *understanding*, in the case where someone is given a series of numbers (e.g., 0, 2, 4, 6, 8, and so on) and then, having demonstrated an ability to continue the series, is said to "understand" the rule of the series. By *reading* here Wittgenstein means only "the activity of rendering out loud what is written or printed"; he is "not counting the understanding of what is read" (1.156).

Wittgenstein imagines an educated Englishman, and asks, "what takes place when, say, he reads a newspaper?" (1.156) The Englishman need not be "attending to what he is reading," and so as far as his reading of any particular word is concerned, there is no difference between his consciousness and the consciousness of a pupil who has memorized a passage and who is, someone might want to say, only "pretending" to read. Wittgenstein then imagines several other cases: a human pupil being trained to function as a reading machine (one inevitably thinks of Milton's daughters), whose teacher will say that the pupil is "reading" only after the pupil gets a certain number or certain proportion of words right (1.157); a man who reads a text he has never seen before but who has a drug-induced sensation of reciting a passage learned by heart (1.160); a man who is given a series of characters not of any known alphabet, and who says words while looking at the characters with the drug-induced sensation of reading (1.160).

Then, an example of writing brings this discussion more clearly into line with Wittgenstein's earlier discussion of rule following. Wittgenstein imagines someone who is given a printed text to convert into cursive writing. This person is also given a table that shows how to make the conversion (1.162). But this person could use the table in any number of ways: "suppose . . . he always wrote b for A, c for B, d for C, and so on, and a for Z? —Surely we should call this too a derivation by means of the table" (1.163). Wittgenstein's point is that reading cannot be defined simply as derivation of spoken from printed words. The notion of "derivation" itself disappears, like an artichoke when one divests it of its leaves in search of the real artichoke (1.164).

Wittgenstein wants to say, of course, that "we . . . use the word 'to read' for a family of cases. And in different circumstances we apply different criteria for a person's reading" (1.164). There is no particular mental process that can be identified as "reading," just as there is no particular mental process that corresponds to the word *understanding* in the case of the numerical series.

Presently, I will discuss some of the implications of Wittgenstein's private-language argument, but for the moment my point is only this: *if* one assimilates the martial arts to textual hermeneutics, taking quite seriously the remarks above about the intimate connection between techniques and ideographs, and *if* one entertains Wittgenstein's picture of reading, *then* there would be no particular mental process that corresponds to "understanding how to do a sidekick," for example, or to "reacting to a sidekick." Hypothesizing a profound connection between the martial arts and language, as some arts do, implies that Wittgenstein's arguments about reading, understanding, and rule following are applicable also to the practice of the martial arts.

And in one sense that sounds right. Advanced practitioners of the martial arts talk about acting without thought or without intent, or acting with an "empty mind." This is difficult to understand in the terms of traditional Cartesian dualism. In those terms, it is also necessary to say that the body must be disciplined precisely in order to carry out the intentions of the mind, and an apparent contradiction arises.

But the difficulty disappears in the vocabulary of textual interpretation. In terms of Wittgenstein's argument, there is no particular mental process separable from the word itself that corresponds to reading the word or using the word. In precisely the same sense that the author's intention to mean is absent from the written text, the martial artist's mind is absent from the technique. The vocabulary of body and mind seems unsatisfactory for talking about language, if for no other reason, because in using language human beings are normally most oblivious to any distinction between body and mind. If I think too hard about what my tongue is doing, in fact, I can no longer talk. I have to make a strenuous effort to see the black configuration on the white page as anything other than a word, or to hear the sequence of sounds as anything other than a sentence. Masters of the martial arts are presumably in a similar situation, in that the intention is identified with the technique to such an extent that it seems that there is "no mind" beyond the technique itself. That is to say, like Wittgenstein's Englishman they are fluent in the language; unlike beginners, they can use it "without thinking."

Before going any more deeply into Wittgenstein's puzzles, however, it will be helpful to see how taekwondo, considered from the perspective of textual hermeneutics, fits the definition of "interpretive system" given in the first essay: a structure of relations such that each relation determines its relata also to be relations. This discussion should furnish a clue about how some of Wittgenstein's reflections on private language can be translated, as it were, into Peirce's terms, and thus can reflect some light on the theory of interpretive systems.

If one takes even the first step down the Cartesian path by thinking of the body as an especially complex machine with a ghostly operator inside, one has already precluded the possibility of considering any martial art as an interpretive system. Hands and feet get mentioned in taekwondo training, but never as mere pieces of self-subsistent matter. The training concerns itself instead with *surfaces*: supporting surfaces, striking surfaces, and blocking surfaces. The talk is of stances and techniques, rather than of hands and feet purely and simply.

At first it might seem that *stance* refers merely to a relation among parts of the body: as if to say that a stance is a relation among head, hands, feet, pelvis, torso, and so on. But the notion of "stance" itself implies a balancing in the gravitational field and thus a contact—a surface—between the body and the earth. What a stance brings into relation, strictly speaking, are supporting surfaces. When an instructor says that seventy percent of the weight is on the right foot, not just the right foot is involved. The whole body as informed by the intention is involved. To assume a stance, then, means to make whatever complicated adjustments are necessary so that certain surfaces become supporting surfaces in a certain way.

A surface is just that. It is not the skin on the sole of the foot. Rather, one has to place his foot in such-and-such a way to constitute a supporting surface. *Supporting surface* is the name of a relation between the person (body and mind) and the earth. One could not assume a taekwondo stance, for example, in a weightless environment, even though one's hands and feet could have the same spatial relation to each other as they might have in a gravitational field. Also, someone might speak of the "supporting surfaces" of a dead body lying on the ground, but these would obviously not be the kind of "supporting surfaces" that the interpretive system of taekwondo is concerned with. One would not be likely to refer to the dead body's "stance."

Similar arguments apply to blocking and striking techniques. To call the first two knuckles of the fist a "striking surface" is not to make a statement about the skin of the knuckles. To think of a "striking surface" is precisely to think of the relation between oneself and one's opponent (real or imagined). Similarly, to think of some part of an opponent's body as a "target" is to think of the opponent in relation to the attack, and to think of the spot on the opponent's body in relation to the opponent's total behavior.

Of course, it is natural to speak of the skin as the surface of the body. I am speaking in this somewhat odd way to make two points: first, that the stances and techniques of taekwondo are not susceptible to exhaustive analysis in terms of the movements of a physical body conceived in isolation, and, second, that the stances and techniques have the characteristic essential to the parts of an interpretive system. The stances and techniques, as relations, themselves determine their relata to be relations. Their relata are not just body parts, but are instead surfaces—relations between a person and the person's environment. Surfaces in taekwondo should be conceived not as "surfaces of," but instead as "surfaces between."

English translations of the Korean terminology of taekwondo perhaps obscure an important point. English words such as *stance, kick, block,* and *punch,* for example, when applied to taekwondo techniques all sound like nouns, even though the last three words can also be verbs. That is, each term is thought of precisely as the name of a "technique," where *technique* is unequivocally a noun. The impression is strengthened when a block is identified as a "high" block or a "low" block, or a kick is described as a "front" kick or a "side" kick. The phrases sound as though they are constructed on the adjective-noun pattern, even though the modifiers can also have adverbial uses.

Here are some Korean terms, by contrast: *soki* (stance), *jiluki* (punch with the fist), *chiluki* (thrust), *chaki* (kick), *makki* (block). All of these words are formed from the relevant verb stem by addition of the nominalizing suffix *-ki*. Better translations would be "standing," "punching," "thrusting," "kicking," "blocking." A front kick, for example, is *ap chaki*—literally, "kicking to the front," where *ap* is clearly adverbial in force. The verb-like and therefore relational character of the techniques is more obvious in Korean. There is no self-subsistent entity called a "kick." Instead, a relation of "kicking" obtains between a practitioner and a target.

I argued above that taekwondo techniques (the same arguments would apply to stances) are in important respects like words. In Saussure's analysis, the words of a language are constituted by the differential relations that set any particular word apart from the others. In Peirce's analysis, words are relations when considered from either side: they are rules prescribing the qualities of their replicas; and they are places in the infinite chain of signification. Can similar things be said about the techniques of taekwondo?

I said something above about how the techniques of taekwondo are word-like in prescribing the qualities of their replicas—that is, in determining the characteristics of the actual movements of those who perform the techniques. Are they also word-like in being constituted as part of a system of differences, as in Saussure's analysis of language? If the techniques of a martial art are its lexicon, then taekwondo has a limited vocabulary in comparison with some other arts. Some arts distinguish many hundreds or even thousands of separate techniques. In taekwondo, on the other hand, there are numberless variations on the low block, for example, but the technique is still thought of as a low block.

Nevertheless, I think it makes sense to look at the techniques of taekwondo as constituting a differential system in Saussure's sense. Instruction in taekwondo often proceeds by building on previously learned techniques, pointing out similarities and differences between the old and the new techniques. "The back kick is just like the side kick, except you turn the other way." "With the round kick, you pick up your knee to the outside, not straight ahead as with the side kick." "This block is just like the knife-hand block, except that you make a fist." I return also to the curious phenomenon that advanced students sometimes seem more likely to be injured when sparring with beginners than when sparring with students of their own rank. Part of the problem is that the beginner's kick is often more an uncontrolled flinging-out of the foot than a properly executed technique. The advanced student might not defend properly, being unable to tell "what kind of kick it is supposed to be." Being able to "control" a technique means, among other things, being able clearly to differentiate that technique from similar techniques.

Finally, is there a way that the "words" of taekwondo, the techniques, can be said to take their place as symbols in a chain of signification? One way to get at this question is to look at what martial artists say about the practice of forms. From their interviews with Master Hung I-hsiang, Reid and Croucher comment as follows on the practice of *pa-kua*, which is based on a circular arrangement of eight trigrams:

> At the root of this lies the Taoist belief in the eternally changing nature of the universe. Existence is in a constant state of flux and this art teaches the student to become one with the process of change and to go with the flow of things. Initially, the student is taught postures that correspond with the trigrams. When performing pa-kua forms he or she will turn at the correct point in the circle, abandoning one posture and taking on a new one corresponding to the point of reentry into the circle. (101–2)

Thus the student acts out, as it were, a particular (Taoist) way of being in the world.

In *Tae Kwon Do: The Korean Martial Art*, Richard Chun describes the *Palgwe* forms as referring to

> a philosophy of universal being, which comprehends Truth as a constant within the phenomenon of an ever-changing cosmos. Inherent in the concept of "form," in this context, is the awareness that the universe is infinite and unknowable, having no apparent ties binding it together—and yet some integrating force of cosmic cohesion keeps order. . . . The principle of Pal-Gwe is that one who knows himself and his environment . . . will find the path of harmony between the changeable forces of the world in which he lives and the constant values of human ethics. Such a man will act effectively in the world, without falling into moral error. (370–71)

Chun in fact translates *Palgwe* as "law" or "command" (371). Whether the philosophy expressed here is the same as the Taoist philosophy of *pa-kua* is a deep question which I have no means to answer.

But one similarity between the quoted passages is obvious: namely, the practice of the forms is said in both to express a particular relationship between the person and the environment—to use the phrase once again, a way of being in the world.

Each of the *Taegeuk* forms used by beginners in modern taekwondo training is, as I have mentioned, associated with a Chinese ideograph that stands for the principle that is expressed also by the form. The second *Taegeuk* form, for example, is associated with the Chinese character meaning "joyfulness" (World Taekwondo Federation, 88). The eighth *Taegeuk* form, which is thought of as containing the elements of all the previous forms, is associated with the Chinese ideograph for "earth." The form is said to express the relation that human beings have to the earth as the source of all energy (World Taekwondo Federation, 129). *Taegeuk* itself refers to the Yin-Yang symbol on the Korean flag. The word is written with the Chinese characters meaning "bigness" and "eternity": "it is something that contains the essence of everything" (World Taekwondo Federation, 82–83). Advanced forms used in modern taekwondo training have such names as *Keumgang*, which I have already mentioned, suggesting "diamond" or perfection, and *Ilyo*, or "oneness."

The point is that the techniques of the martial arts take on their full meaning only by entering into a syntax, only by symbolizing a particular kind of relation between the person and the environment. The particular way of being in the world is more all-encompassing, apparently, than eating and sleeping properly so as to be able to strike harder. It is even more than considering the ethical question of when it is proper to use the techniques of the art. Different arts might have different philosophies, but the art becomes a fully developed interpretive system only when the complex structure of relations between the martial artist and the environment determines the performance of the techniques to be significant—that is, determines the techniques as themselves relations (words) that can be taken up into the chain of signification. Sometimes there is so much concentration on mastering techniques that it might appear that the techniques are ends in themselves. But the techniques ultimately symbolize.

This is another way of stating the obvious point that the martial arts are ascetic disciplines. The usual way to talk about ascetic disciplines, however, is in the Cartesian vocabulary of body and mind or body and soul. The soul "subdues" the desires of the body, the body is "disciplined" by the mind, and so on. I am arguing here that the vocabulary of hermeneutics provides a better way of talking about ascetic disciplines.

2. Wittgenstein and "Private Language"

Now I want to take up Wittgenstein's discussion of "private language." It would be silly of me to suppose that I understand Wittgenstein on this subject very well, given that professional philosophers still debate these matters vigorously. I am especially indebted to Saul Kripke's *Wittgenstein on Rules and Private Language: An Elementary Exposition*. All I would like to do here is note some interesting parallels between Wittgenstein's remarks on private language and Peirce's remarks on semiosis, and to apply some of their conclusions to the martial arts considered as interpretive systems.

Here, roughly, is Wittgenstein's argument about private language. Some philosophers (including Wittgenstein himself, in *Tractatus Logico-Philosophicus*) have held that the language of logic can provide a picture of reality because the elements of the proposition can correspond to the objects of the world. Here is a short anthology of propositions from the *Tractatus*.

> The world is all that is the case. (1)
> What is the case—a fact—is the existence of states of affairs. (2)
> A state of affairs (a state of things) is a combination of objects (things). (2.01)
> We picture facts to ourselves. (2.1)
> A picture is a model of reality. (2.12)
> In a picture the elements of the picture are the representatives of objects. (2.131)
> What a picture represents is its sense. (2.221)
> A logical picture of facts is a thought. (3)
> In a proposition a thought finds an expression that can be perceived by the senses. (3.1)
> A thought is a proposition with a sense. (4)

In the *Philosophical Investigations* Wittgenstein rejects this view of language.

The *Philosophical Investigations* begins (1.1) with St. Augustine's account (*Confessions*, 1.8) of learning language. Augustine essentially talks about learning nouns by observing people's behavior in relation to physical objects. The noun "means" the thing. As Wittgenstein says, "That philosophical concept of meaning has its place in a primitive idea of the way language functions. But one can also say that it is the idea of a language more primitive than ours" (1.2). How does one learn numbers, for example, on Augustine's model? Or prepositions or conjunctions? It is not easy to say. Through the first part of the *Philosophical Investigations*, Wittgenstein constructs or alludes to various simple and complex "language games" to show that there is no single "*essence* of language, of propositions, of thought" (1.92), although there may appear to be: "now it may come to look as if there were something like a final analysis of our forms of language" (1.91). But logic, if that is what this "final analysis" aims at, is not "something sublime" in this sense.

Wittgenstein's concept of "game" is crucial. There are many different kinds of games. They are so many and so different, in fact, that it is impossible to identify a single essence, something that all games have "in common" (1.66). At best, what games share is what Wittgenstein calls "family resemblances" (1.67), "a complicated network of similarities overlapping and criss-crossing" (1.66). If the various uses of language are like different games, "language games," then there would be no particular thing for logic to aim at, no single essence of language that could be used as a rule for analyzing propositions and for solving philosophical problems by speaking more exactly. "It is not our aim to refine or complete the system of rules for the use of our words in unheard-of ways" (1.133).

On the contrary, philosophical problems arise in the first place because people get confused about which language game they are playing. For example, they try to use the word *pain* the same way they use the word *table*—as the name of a thing—and so philosophical problems arise. You can experience my table, but you cannot experience my pain. So what does it mean to "know" that someone else "has" a pain? It cannot mean the same kind of thing it means to "know" that someone else "has" a table. The problem, in a deep way, is in the language. All the philosopher can do is "To shew the fly the way out of the flybottle" (1.309). "The real discovery is the one that makes me capable of stopping doing philosophy when I want to" (1.133).

This line of thought brings Wittgenstein to his discussion of "rules." A possible objection to his notion of "game" is that all games at least have rules that govern play. Can logic, then, be regarded as a refinement or clarification of the rules of the language game that aims at making a picture of reality? As Wittgenstein imagines his interlocutor saying, "But still, it isn't a game, if there is some vagueness *in the rules*"

(1.100). But of course, all rules of games are more or less vague in one sense. The rules of chess do not specify whether I have to move the pieces with the right hand or the left, or how many fingers I have to use. But there is a deeper objection to the notion of "rule," which Wittgenstein gets at by considering various kinds of rule following.

I mentioned earlier the rule following involved in the continuing of a numerical series (*PI*, 1.143ff.). Suppose I give you the series 0, 2, 4, 6, . . . , and ask you to continue it. Suppose you write an 8. I say, "Yes, that's right. The rule of the series is to write the next even number." But suppose you write a 14. Then I say, "No, that's wrong. Why did you think you should write a 14?"

You answer, "Well, obviously you got a 2 by doubling the zero and adding 2; then you got the 4 by doubling your 2; then you got the 6 by doubling your 4 and subtracting 2. So the next thing I should do is to double the 6 and add 2. That makes 14. The next number in the series would be 28, and the next would be 54."

Or suppose you do write an 8, and I then ask you to explain why. You say, "Well, I took the number representing the place in the series, doubled it, and subtracted 2. The first place in the series corresponds to a 1, 1 doubled is 2, and 2 minus 2 is zero. Then, you take the 2 representing the second place, double it, and get 4; 4 minus 2 is 2. So 2 goes in the second place. Now, whatever comes after the 6 will be in the fifth place of the series; 5 doubled is 10, and 10 minus 2 is 8."

At that point, I might be tempted to say, "Yes, I see that your rule will produce the same series that my rule will produce, but it seems to me the wrong rule. At least, it wasn't the rule I meant. Isn't it easier just to think of adding 2 each time?"

In fact, there are any number of functions (rules) that will produce the series I began with. Some of them will produce 8 as the next number, and some of them will not. Wittgenstein's point is not just that I can find rules that will produce different series. His point is to question the conversation about the rules that you and I have just had. What sense does that conversation make, if any? What justification can I possibly have for saying *that you are wrong, whatever* you produce? Whatever you do produce, some function can be found that will produce that value at that spot.

It is when I want to say that you are wrong (or to justify my own rule) that I want to point to something that goes on in my head, something called "understanding" of a rule, that I have and that you (apparently) do not. But what, exactly, is this "mental process" of "understanding"? Wittgenstein argues that various different kinds of things might happen before a person says, "Now I can go on" to continue the series: the person might be trying out various algebraic formulae to find one that works, or the person might just notice that each term in the series is 2 larger than the preceding term, or the person might at some point simply recognize the series as something familiar, and so on (1.151). But there seems to be no particular "mental process" that is common to all cases, no "essence" of "understanding." As Wittgenstein says, "Try not to think of understanding as a 'mental process' at all. — For *that* is the expression which confuses you" (1.154).

At this point in the *Philosophical Investigations* Wittgenstein interpolates his discussion of "reading" (summarized earlier), in order to make clearer what he means about "understanding." As with "understanding," there seems to be no single essence, no particular mental process, common to all the cases that people might want to call "reading."

The upshot of Wittgenstein's discussion seems to be that I cannot point to any internal, mental process (anything that exists only "in my head" or "in your head") to justify my statements about whether you have followed a rule (or whether I have, for that matter). The justification for judgments about rule following is social. Consequently, rule following cannot be a private matter.

> Is what we call "obeying a rule" something that it would be possible for only *one* man to do, and to do only *once* in his life? —This is of course a note on the grammar of the expression "to obey a rule".
>
> It is not possible that there should have been only one occasion on which someone obeyed a rule. It is not possible that there should have been only one occasion on which a report was made, an order given or understood, and so on. —To obey a rule, to make a report, to give an order, to play a game of chess, are *customs* (uses, institutions). (1.199)
>
> ... [I]t is not possible to obey a rule 'privately.' ... (1.202)

Wittgenstein's reflections represent not a solution so much as a dissolution of the philosophical problem of rule following: "This was our paradox: no course of action could be determined by a rule, because every course of action can be made out to accord with the rule. The answer was: if everything can be made out to accord with the rule, then it can be made out to conflict with it. And so there would be neither concord nor conflict here" (1.201). Wittgenstein seems to mean here that the issue is what behavior is "made out" to be (in the social context). The issue is not one of accord or conflict with some mental entity called a "rule." It is always true that at some point or other, "I obey the rule *blindly*" (1.219). The accord or conflict in question is the accord or conflict of behavior with what is called "obeying a rule" in a particular language game.

The philosophical problem arises in the first place because people try to use the word *rule* the same way they use the word *path*. The problem is not, however, that rules are not like paths. The problem is that the phrase *following a rule* is a move in a different language game from the language game in which the phrase *following a path* is a move.

But this same line of argument applies also to the use of concepts. A concept is a kind of rule. Presumably, the concept of "table" is the rule that enables me to decide which particular objects in the world I *should* call "tables." The *should* here implies, again, the question of justification. It is not just a question of what any individual in fact has called or will call "tables." It is a question, instead, of whether my uses of the word *table* constitute appropriate moves in the relevant language games. Wittgenstein's argument here apparently leads to the strange notion that concepts are not "in my head," that there are no particular mental entities or processes that I can point to as constitutive of my understanding of a concept. The criterion for my understanding of a concept is, in general, my appropriate use of a word.

As Wittgenstein says, "For a *large* class of cases—though not for all—in which we employ the word 'meaning' it can be defined thus: the meaning of a word is its use in the language" (1.43). That is, the meaning is not some idea in my head or in yours. It is part of the language, which Wittgenstein likes to speak of as a "form of life" (1.19, 23): "It is what human beings *say* that is true and false; and they agree in the *language* they use. That is not agreement in opinion but in form of life" (1.241).

Even if people do tend to think of concepts as residing in their heads, still they do not think of them as private property (unless, of course, they are worried about patents or copyrights). The Pythagorean theorem is understood by me, but it is not my own. The case is harder with sensations. What about the sensation of red? Or the sensation of pain, which seems even more "private" than red, in that pain is not externally instantiated? These seem to be obvious objections to Wittgenstein's arguments, if he means the arguments to apply to sensations as well. And clearly he does. In dealing with such objections, Wittgenstein explicitly discusses for the first time the notion of a "private language" (1.243ff.).

It is at this point, too, that Wittgenstein's arguments might seem most counterintuitive from the perspective of the martial arts. When someone does a side kick, for example, there must be some sort of kinesthetic sensation accompanying the kick. The martial artist must get the "feel" of the kick, as some people say. And so it seems to make sense to say that knowing how to do a side kick is constituted by having a particular kinesthetic sensation "in mind." But this kinesthetic sensation, it turns out, can never be communicated in words to anybody else. The instructor can say only, "Do this," and demonstrate; or, the instructor can say, "Lift your knee higher," or "Think about your balance." Such instructions at best refer only to part of the organic whole that is the kinesthetic sensation the instructor "means." More accurately, both instructor and student recognize that the student's kinesthetic sensation is not going to be the same as the instructor's, since the student is differently constituted. The instructor has only various strategies to help the student develop his or her "own" kinesthetic sensation.

And if this is the true picture, it seems that the student could give the kinesthetic sensation, once developed, a "private" name. And similarly with front kicks, high blocks, and so on, so that these names would fit Wittgenstein's definition of a sensation language: "The individual words of this language are to refer to what can only be known to the person speaking; to his immediate private sensations. So another person cannot understand the language" (1.243). This would be, then, a "private language." Is this not an accurate picture of what goes on in learning a martial art?

The situation I have just proposed is like what Wittgenstein describes in 1.258: ". . . I want to keep a diary about the recurrence of a certain sensation. To this end I associate it with the sign 'S' and write this sign in a calendar for every day on which I have the sensation. . . . I speak, or write the sign down, and at the same time I concentrate my attention on the sensation—and so, as it were, point to it inwardly." It is as though the student of taekwondo were to lie in bed after the day's practice and think, "Here is S, which is the kinesthetic sensation I had today when I practiced the side kick; and here is B, which is the kinesthetic sensation I had when I practiced the back kick," and so on. And in fact this sounds like an accurate description of certain trains of thought, especially when one is learning forms by making the sequence of movements automatic, patterning them in the muscles, as it were.

But as with rule following, Wittgenstein might suggest, the difficulty would come in *justifying* the application of S or B to particular kinesthetic sensations: "in the present case I have no criterion of correctness. One would like to say: whatever is going to seem right to me is right. And that only means that we can't talk about 'right'" (1.258). In other words, how do I know that it is always the same sensation that I have called by the same name?

If I answer that the justification is that whenever I experience the sensation in practice, I always produce a proper side kick, then Wittgenstein will point out that the criterion of correctness is now public. It is the side kick itself, the word in the common language of taekwondo, and so there is still nothing purely private that allows me to be sure that I have applied S to the same sensation each time. And if I cannot be sure of that, what use is there in inventing the name S or in applying it at all?

> Let us now imagine a use for the entry of the sign "S" in my diary. I discover that whenever I have a particular sensation a manometer shows that my blood-pressure rises. So I shall be able to say that my blood-pressure is rising without using any apparatus. This is a useful result. And now it seems quite indifferent whether I have recognized the sensation *right* or not. Let us suppose I regularly identify it wrong; it does not matter in the least. And that alone shews that the hypothesis that I make a mistake is mere show. (We as it were turned a knob which looked as if it could be used to turn on some part of the machine; but it was a mere ornament, not connected with the mechanism at all.) (1.270)

The engineer's simile of the unconnected knob has real force, here. The question now becomes not whether I can identify something in my head correctly as "the same sensation," but whether I can tell that my blood-pressure is rising. The question is not whether I can have the proper kinesthetic sensation every time, but whether I can actually do a side kick. If I can do a side kick, it makes no difference what particular kinesthetic sensation I am having or think I am having, or whether I am conscious of any kinesthetic sensation at all. As with rules, there is no particular mental entity or process I can point to that justifies my belief that I understand the side kick. I can only point to a side kick—my own, or someone else's.

As strange as this line of argument sounds, I think that on closer inspection the experience of practicing the martial arts tends in large measure to confirm it. In fact, in learning how to do a side kick one is never thinking consciously of all the movements involved in the whole technique from beginning to end. Much is already automatic, for example. The large muscles that keep the body erect and preserve equilibrium are always making adjustments without conscious awareness, though one can learn to be aware of these muscles. And as one develops the technique, various movements are "put on automatic" so that other movements can be concentrated on. Or, inefficient habitual movements have to be brought temporarily to consciousness so that they can be corrected. Sometimes I am thinking about my foot and not paying attention to my knee or my hip; sometimes I am thinking about the leg that is under me and not the leg that is kicking; sometimes I am thinking only about the position of my head or hands; and so on. An instructor soon discovers that different verbal instructions have to be given to different students to produce the same results. Some students have to be told, "Lift your foot"; others have to be told, "Fold your knee more"; others have to be told, "Point your knee toward the target"; others have to be told, "Bring the leg up from the hip."

Presumably, too, an advanced martial artist in combat or even in sparring practice is able to perform a side kick with no conscious thought of kinesthetic sensation at all. That is precisely the condition the martial artist aspires to, the condition where the technique no longer seems an expression of some "inner" reality that is separate from it. The technique expresses, instead, by becoming an inseparable part of a way of being in the world. The technique is then fluent, as speaking is fluent when the speaker is not conscious of having to struggle to "find words to express a meaning," but where the meaning is there in the words that come.

How is it that people can become confused about sensations and mental processes in this way? Wittgenstein does not want to deny that sensations and mental processes exist (1.304–8). His point is only that it does not make sense to say that I can correctly judge whether something is correctly called "pain," or "red," or "remembering" by comparing that something with some particular private mental entity or process of my own. Whether something is correctly named depends on how the language is used, and language neither is nor can be my private property. People get into philosophical difficulties when they get confused about what language game they are playing, when they "construe the grammar of the expression of sensation on the model of 'object and designation'" (1.293): "The paradox disappears only if we make a radical break with the idea that language always functions in one way, always serves the same purpose: to convey thoughts—which may be about houses, pains, good and evil, or anything else you please" (1.304). Just because there is a noun *pain* that can appear in syntactic slots where nouns such as *table* can also appear, no one has a warrant for supposing that one can always play the same language games with pains that one can play with tables.

There is a children's story by Barbara Williams, called *Albert's Toothache*. It is about a young turtle who takes to his bed and refuses to eat his gray spider-legs, because, he says, he has a toothache. It does no good for his parents to point out that turtles have no teeth. Notice that at this point, it is legitimate for the turtle parents to make a very odd move in the language game of pain reports: namely, to tell someone else that he *does not* feel pain. The impasse continues until the wise grandmother turtle thinks to ask the sufferer *where* he has a toothache. The young turtle indicates an injured toe. The pain is real, as anybody would say after the confusion is cleared up; but the young turtle's understanding of the language game of pain reports is incomplete. He could not have experienced a toothache, but he has understood the language game just well enough to disrupt the domestic arrangements. The young turtle is a philosopher, in Wittgenstein's sense, and he needs to be shown the way out of the fly-bottle.

It makes sense, then, to say that a martial artist can practice without moving, if by that is meant that one can imagine or remember the kinesthetic sensations that in fact accompany the performance of a technique. It does not make sense if one means that the martial artist is constructing a mental picture of the technique to consult as a rule for performing the technique the next time. The martial artist might think of things to *try*, and might even express sensations verbally—"Turn more quickly; lift the foot sooner"—but these things must *be* tried and, as it were, inscribed in the technique before they can be said to count. Although the context of Wittgenstein's remark is different, I think he is getting at a similar point when he says that the sensation by itself "is not a *something*, but not a *nothing* either! The conclusion was only that a nothing would serve just as well as a something about which nothing could be said" (1.304). Or, to translate into the terms of the martial arts as interpretive systems, a nothing would serve just as well as a kinesthetic sensation isolated from its technique.

3. *Ascetic Disciplines and Language Games*

Should one regard the martial arts as so many "language games"? Here I want to distinguish between the martial arts considered as sports and the traditional practice. Sport taekwondo as exhibited in the Olympic Games, for example, requires strenuous training similar to that of traditional taekwondo. But the orientation of traditional taekwondo is quite different. Traditional taekwondo is a style of unarmed self-defense in which the aim is to develop techniques of such devastating force that a single technique properly executed will incapacitate and perhaps kill an opponent. Such techniques are appropriate only when carefully controlled during practice, or in actual life-and-death situations.

In this essay I am considering taekwondo as an example of a traditional martial art that most people would not call a "game." Is that a serious objection to considering taekwondo as a "language game" in Wittgenstein's sense? Certainly the fact that traditional taekwondo is "serious" does not constitute an objection. Some people take sports or chess or other nonverbal games with life-or-death seriousness, and some language games are deadly serious. But I want to argue that nevertheless one misses something by assimilating the martial arts to the notion of the language game. As I have already suggested, I would prefer to call them "ascetic disciplines."

What is the difference between ascetic disciplines and language games? I hope to throw light on this question by exploring how some crucial points in the private-language argument can be articulated in terms of Peirce's semiotic. But before doing that, I will indicate very roughly why to me Wittgenstein's arguments seem less than completely satisfactory for analyzing ascetic disciplines.

Normally, an ascetic discipline is thought of as a lonely business. Monastic communities may be ordered around communal activities, but private prayer or meditation is at the heart of the monastic experience. Similarly, serious practitioners of taekwondo, for example, often spend more time in solitary practice, "forging" their techniques, than they do in practice with others. Wittgenstein's private-language argument, on the other hand, occurs entirely within the context of a discussion about justification—how particular linguistic behaviors are to be justified for a community. The context of justification is what the Western tradition is accustomed to think of as the philosophical context. A philosopher is someone who has, or who wants, reasons for beliefs and actions. Once Wittgenstein has demolished the long-standing notion that justification can be given in terms of some "inner" standard, some mental process, the notion of the language game arises as an alternative kind of justification. I start thinking in terms of language games just when I ask myself, How can I justify this application of a rule or a concept, or this kind of talk about sensation? I want to call something a language game because, with the other possibilities demolished, the language game provides me with criteria for justification. The way out of the fly bottle is the way into the communal language game.

But the way of the ascetic seems to lie in a different direction. It seems to me at least strained to say that the ascetic has concern for or interest in justifying personal behavior in terms of communal practice.

The question of justification just does not come up when the martial arts or other ascetic disciplines are practiced as disciplines. Looking at ascetic disciplines as language games is useful insofar as it demonstrates how ascetic practices have meaning in communal terms, but it is misleading insofar as it makes one suppose that justification before a community is the central question.

Of course, a martial artist is interested in whether a particular technique "works." The point of trying out the technique, however, is not to justify one's practice before a community, but instead to improve it. Except in life-or-death situations, trying out the technique means only further practice. Even the notion of justifying oneself to oneself, of being "consistent," seems to make little sense in talking about ascetic disciplines. The martial artist does not want to write the technique in stone. The ascetic discipline seems rather to involve the experience of ridding oneself of the need for justification, of stripping away, as it were, veil after veil of self-justification. One might consider what it means to "improve" a martial-arts technique by solitary practice. It is a commonplace in the martial arts that no one has ever performed a "perfect" technique. Practice, then, becomes almost the opposite of self-justification. It is the discarding of each successive performance as inadequate to the technique.

A second problem, as it seems to me, with regarding ascetic disciplines as language games is that ascetic disciplines often or always seem to be seeking some "rock-bottom" level of reality. This rock-bottom reality might turn out not to be different from "everyday" reality, but is what is thought to contain or explain it. The martial artist seeks the perfect technique, which would imply the perfection of a whole way of being in the world; the mystic seeks God; Thoreau sought the "facts" of "Life." Even the Eastern ascetic who perceives that all is illusion believes that this perception constitutes an enlightenment. If there is a rock-bottom reality, it must be outside any current language game, since any current language appears to be only a "form of life" of a particular community at a particular time.

Of course, all ascetics might be deluded. They might be laboring under some philosophical illusion engendered by a bad move in some language game. But there is testimony against this conclusion. Moreover, if ascetics are deluded, they are at least not confused by being unwittingly entangled in the language game of philosophical justification. People who suffer from that confusion—philosophers—have the problem because they are unaware that they can get out of the fly bottle. But no matter how strict a rule the ascetic discipline imposes, and no matter how unforeseen the consequences of following the discipline may be, one is always aware of deliberately choosing the discipline, and of being able deliberately to turn aside from it. This does not sound like philosophical confusion, which is the kind of confusion that Wittgenstein's concept of the "language game" is designed to explain.

It seems best to me, then, to leave open the possibility that there is something outside language games, which ascetics aim at whether they truly get there or not. Wittgenstein's arguments seem to show only that if there is such a thing, it cannot be philosophized about. It is, perhaps, in the language of the *Tractatus*, that about which one must "remain silent." Ascetics might reply here that if what they are doing cannot make sense in the language game of philosophical justification, so much the worse for that language game.

Now, how can Peirce's reflections help in talking about ascetic disciplines? It is true that sometimes Peirce sounds as though he is making exactly the philosophical move Wittgenstein criticizes. For example, in one place Peirce, commenting on the proposition "Ezekiel loveth Huldah," says, "Now the effect of the word 'loveth' is that the pair of objects denoted by the pair of indices Ezekiel and Huldah is represented by the icon, or the image we have in our minds of a lover and his beloved" (*CP*, 2.295). It sounds as though Peirce is referring to exactly the kind of justification by mental image that Wittgenstein demolishes. But I think that in this particular passage Peirce had other things on his mind than Wittgenstein's problem. Where Peirce addresses that problem or similar problems more directly, his thought is closer to Wittgenstein's than it might seem at first.

I turn again to Peirce's two remarkable essays against Cartesianism, "Questions Concerning Certain Faculties Claimed for Man" and "Some Consequences of Four Incapacities." The essays appeared in the *Journal of Speculative Philosophy* for 1868. Both are reprinted in Wiener's anthology *Charles S. Peirce: Selected Writings (Values in a Universe of Chance)*. The discussion of Peirce's realism that follows will draw mainly from these early essays. Peirce's realism of course developed as he matured. Discussions of the development are available, among other places, in Christopher Hookway's *Peirce*, in Max Fisch's essay "Peirce's Progress from Nominalism toward Realism" (Fisch, 184–200), and in the essays in section 5 of *Studies in the Philosophy of Charles Sanders Peirce*, second series, edited by Edward C. Moore and Richard S. Robin (*Studies*, 345–474).

The mystical-sounding notion of "ultimate reality" can be given a definite sense in Peirce's philosophy. Peirce distinguishes between the "real" and the "unreal" as follows:

> ... cognitions ... are of two kinds, the true and the untrue, or cognitions whose objects are *real* and those whose objects are *unreal*. And what do we mean by the real? It is a conception which we must first have had when we discovered that there was an unreal, an illusion; that is, when we first corrected ourselves. Now the distinction for which alone this fact logically called was between an *ens* relative to private inward determinations, to the negations belonging to idiosyncracy, and an *ens* such as would stand in the long run. The real, then, is that which, sooner or later, information and reasoning would finally result in, and which is therefore independent of the vagaries of me and you. ("Consequences," *W*, 69)

Peirce had earlier pointed out that human beings first become aware of ignorance and error, and thus hypothesize a private self in which that ignorance and error can inhere, when they become aware of the reliability of *testimony*. The little boy believes that the stove is not hot, because he does not feel the heat when he is not touching it. The adult tells him that the stove is hot, and the little boy by touching finds that the testimony of the adult is more reliable than his own impressions. As Peirce puts it, "testimony gives the first dawning of self-consciousness" ("Questions," *W*, 28).

Wittgenstein might say here that the child comes to know sensations *as* sensations when the child learns the language game of reporting sensations. Private language is impossible because before communal language (testimony) there is nothing private to talk about; there is no category of the private.

Wittgenstein's reflections lead him to the conclusion that justification of rule applying, concept applying, and sensation reporting must always be social. Similarly, Peirce's notion of the "real" depends crucially on a corollary notion of a community. But the community Peirce means is different from Wittgenstein's language community:

> the very origin of the conception of reality shows that this conception essentially involves the notion of a COMMUNITY, without definite limits, and capable of a definite increase of knowledge. And so these two series of cognitions—the real and the unreal—consist of those which, at a time sufficiently future, the community will always continue to reaffirm; and of those which, under the same conditions, will ever after be denied. ("Consequences," *W*, 69)

Peirce's "community" represents, as he would say, a "would-be." It is likely that it will never be completed. The life of the solar system is presumably finite. Entropy increases everywhere, and in the longest run, everybody is dead. Never mind. The notion of a community "sufficiently future" and "without definite limits" still exerts its force on present cognitions. Human beings seem to experience a certain constraint when they believe that such-and-such is the case regardless of whether they individually perceive it that way or like it that way. This constraint is not necessarily put on them by the object itself. Nor is it necessarily put on them by a concept that exists "in their heads." It is a constraint exerted by the community without definite limits.

The crucial similarity between Peirce and Wittgenstein here is the conclusion of both that the idea of the "real" depends on a community. The crucial difference is that Peirce's community is different from Wittgenstein's. Wittgenstein's community is the actual, existing language community that shares the form of life in which the language game is played. Peirce's community is the virtual, future community that will gradually arrive at a confirmation of what is real by seeing what cognitions in the long run survive the various language games played in particular actual communities, and by seeing in what form those cognitions do survive.

In Peirce's analysis, then, it makes *sense* to say that the ascetic aims at a cognition of what is real by separating himself or herself, if necessary, from the particular linguistic community. In Wittgenstein's analysis, that way of putting it does not make sense—it is "nonsensical." In Peirce's analysis, it is even possible to hit on the real; though, in accordance with Peirce's doctrine of "fallibilism," it is not possible for human beings to be sure that they have done so in any particular case: "There is nothing, then, to prevent our knowing outward things as they really are, and it is most likely that we do thus know them in numberless cases, although we can never be absolutely certain of doing so in any special case" ("Consequences," *W*, 69). Peirce's qualification that confines knowledge to "outward" things is not so narrow a qualification here as it might seem. As part of Peirce's refutation of Cartesianism, his essay takes as one of its central hypotheses that "[w]e have no power of Introspection, but all knowledge of the internal world is derived by hypothetical reasoning from our knowledge of external facts" (*W*, 41). Wittgenstein might agree with this hypothesis, on one level, when he argues that we know what pain is by learning the language game of pain reports, and that we learn the language game by observing pain behavior.

Certainly, Peirce could be wrong. He acknowledges that his reflections imply an unfashionable scholastic realism. If we can think "the real, as it really is," and since "no cognition of ours is absolutely determinate," then "generals must have a real existence." Peirce goes on, "Now this scholastic realism is usually set down as a belief in metaphysical fictions" ("Consequences," *W*, 69). And even if Peirce is right, one might think that the ascetic is foolish to sacrifice any normal satisfactions of human life in pursuit of a reality that, if it is grasped, cannot be known to have been grasped. But all of that is beside the point I am trying to make. My point is only that Peirce's notion of the relation between the real and the community leaves room to make certain statements about ascetic disciplines without talking nonsense, in a way that Wittgenstein's notion does not.

A deeper articulation in Peirce's terms of the private-language argument is possible when one considers that for Peirce all thoughts are signs. Human beings, in fact, are signs. The point of going into this is, first, to use Peirce's semiotic to reinforce the connection between textual hermeneutics and ascetic disciplines that are apparently nonverbal (such as the martial arts). I want to show how those ascetic disciplines might appear from the perspective of textual hermeneutics. A second and more important point, however, is to show how reflecting on ascetic disciplines from this perspective might help to understand textual hermeneutics itself better.

In "Consequences," Peirce attempts to confirm certain anti-Cartesian hypotheses put forth in "Questions," by tracing out the consequences of those hypotheses. The crucial moment in that argument is to demonstrate that all cognition conforms to the formula of valid inference. That means that Peirce has to show that, contrary to what most people would be inclined to say, such things as sensations, emotions, the focusing of attention, and imagination, among others, are all results of some process of inference. Peirce's discussion of sensation, emotion, and attention particularly interests me here, because in this discussion Peirce seems very close to some of the things Wittgenstein says in the private-language argument.

Peirce argues his theses about sensation, emotion, and attention by appealing to his constant theme that all thought is in signs. "When we think . . . we ourselves, as we are at that moment, appear as a sign" ("Consequences," *W*, 51). The problem seems to be that sensation, emotion, and attention feel different, somehow, from reasoning in syllogisms. And they also feel different from each other. How can the different feelings be accounted for, if all thought is essentially the same—that is, thought in signs?

Peirce's solution is as follows. Every sign, he says, has three elements: (1) a representative function, by which the sign stands for something to someone. This is the sign considered purely as the triadic relation of sign ground, object, and interpretant ("Consequences," *W*, 51–53). But in addition, any actual sign has what Peirce calls (2) "*material qualities*": "Since a sign is not identical with the thing signified, but differs from the latter in some respects, it must plainly have some characters which belong to it in itself, and have nothing to do with its representative function" (53). These are the irrelevant qualities of what serves as the sign, a Firstness of the sign that is not taken up into the chain of signification. For example, whether a weathercock is painted red or blue normally has nothing to do with its capacity to function as a sign of the wind. Finally, something actually carries out the task of connecting the sign with its object—what Peirce calls "a real effective force behind consciousness" (55). This effective force results in (3) the "pure demonstrative application" of the sign (54). It is a Secondness of the sign that consists in a physical connection of the sign with its object. In the case of a picture, for example, the pure demonstrative application results from "the power of association which connects the picture with the brain-sign which labels it" (53–54). Here Peirce seems to be talking about what today might be called the physical correlate of a thought, the electrochemical activity of the central nervous system that accompanies thought.

Now Peirce can explain why sensation, emotion, and focusing of attention feel different from reasoning and from each other. Sensation and emotion do conform to the formula of valid inference because they are *hypotheses*. That is, they are simple predicates taken in the place of complex predicates about the external world and bodily states. I hypothesize that the table is red, because a complex set of events is occurring in my central nervous system, because in similar situations I have heard other people use the word *red*, and so on. The difference between a sensation and an emotion is only that an emotion arises later than a sensation in the development of the chain of signification, and "produces large movements in the body . . . blushing, blenching, staring, smiling, scowling, pouting, laughing, weeping, sobbing, wriggling, flinching, trembling, being petrified, sighing, sniffling, shrugging, groaning, heartsinking, trepidation, swelling of the heart, etc., etc." (60). Peirce seems very close to Wittgenstein, here. Wittgenstein's point is that I know when I am justified in calling my "inner" experience by a certain name ("pain," "fear," "anger"), because I have observed how the terms are used in connection with certain behaviors (pain behavior, fear behavior, anger behavior). Peirce is saying that my emotion itself is a hypothesis, a simple predicate substituted for the complex predicates that include my own emotion behavior. Peirce concludes, "That which distinguishes sensation and emotion from the feeling of a thought is that in the case of the two former the material quality is made prominent . . ." (60). The material quality of the sign, insofar as it is separate from the representative function, is just a feeling that is determined by the particular constitution of the individual. It is an idiosyncrasy, something that cannot stand in the long run, and as such is "unreal" in Peirce's sense.

This, I believe, is how Peirce would explain Wittgenstein's aphorism that a sensation is not a something, but is not a nothing, either (*PI*, 1.304). Wittgenstein imagines a society in which everybody has a box containing something called a "beetle" (*PI*, 1.293). Nobody can look in anybody else's box, and so everybody knows what a beetle is only by looking in his or her own box. Wittgenstein points out that the word *beetle*, if it is used in the language of these people, "would not be used as the name of a thing. The thing in the box has no place in the language-game at all; not even as a *something:* for the box might even be empty. —No, one can 'divide through' by the thing in the box; it cancels out, whatever it is." One might compare the following passage from Peirce, where he is trying to show that sensations are not immediate intuitions, but are instead cognitions determined by previous cognitions: "If it be objected that the peculiar character of *red* is not determined by any previous cognition, I reply that that character is not a character of red as a cognition; for if there be a man to whom red things look as blue ones do to me and vice versa, that man's eyes teach him the same facts that they would if he were like me" ("Questions," *W*, 36). Only the character of red *as a cognition*, in Peirce's vocabulary, has a chance of being real. One can "divide through" by the private character of red, whatever it might be.

Sensation and emotion differ from rational thought, then, only in the relative prominence of the material quality of the sign. When one sign is connected with another by rational relations (I think one might just as well say *real* relations, here), the material quality of the sign is not so prominent as the representative quality. If, on the other hand, the connection of one sign to another depends on the peculiar, idiosyncratic constitution of the individual, then the material quality becomes prominent just because the rational connection is missing.

Focusing of attention for Peirce means putting emphasis upon some element of consciousness, and that means making that element more capable of "producing an effect upon memory, or otherwise influencing subsequent thought" ("Consequences," *W*, 61). It turns out, then, that "attention is the power by which thought at one time is connected with and made to relate to thought at another time; or, to apply the conception of thought as a sign, that it is the *pure demonstrative application* of a thought-sign" (62). Attention is an *induction*, a kind of inference, because attention is aroused when human beings notice the same phenomenon repeated in different cases, and look for the further repetition of that phenomenon in similar cases. Thus, the analysis of consciousness as semiosis gives Peirce an explanation of why attention feels different from rational thought, even though attention conforms to the formula of inference.

These arguments lead Peirce into some interesting observations on the nature of consciousness: "We have seen that the content of consciousness, the entire phenomenal manifestation of mind, is a sign resulting from inference" ("Consequences," *W*, 70). If the human being is identified with human thought, then the human being is the sign. Other notions of consciousness confuse the representative function of the sign with its material quality or its pure demonstrative application. If by *consciousness* is meant "that emotion which accompanies the reflection that we have animal life," Peirce contends, then that sort of "consciousness" is "the more lively the better *animal* a man is, but which is not so, the better *man* he is." Such a "consciousness" is a "mere sensation," and therefore is "only a part of the *material quality* of the man-sign" (70–71). If by *consciousness* is meant the unity or consistency in thought (71), that is only the bringing into connection of subsequent thoughts with previous thoughts. Therefore, though Peirce does not say so explicitly, the implication seems to be that this Cartesian unity corresponds merely with the pure demonstrative application of the thought sign.

In short, the reality of the human being is the sign. The reality of the sign is that which can be taken up in the chain of signification and handed on to the future community without definite limits. What is real in me is what I have a chance of handing on through signification. What is real in me is, namely, the representative function of the thought sign. The rest is unreal:

> . . . reality depends on the ultimate decision of the community; so thought is what it is only by virtue of its addressing a future thought which is in its value as thought identical with it, though more developed. In this way, the existence of thought now depends on what is to be hereafter; so that it has only a potential existence, dependent on the future thought of the community.
>
> The individual man, since his separate existence is manifested only by ignorance and error, so far as he is anything apart from

his fellows, and from what he and they are to be, is only a negation. ("Consequences," *W*, 72)

Again, this line of thought seems very similar to Wittgenstein's private-language argument. And again, the difference between the two arguments seems to be the use that is made of the notion of "community." Peirce's community is an indefinitely future, virtual community. Wittgenstein's community is a particular actual community that plays a particular language game as part of its form of life.

But it is important not to get confused about this difference. As Kripke stresses (111–12 and elsewhere), Wittgenstein does not mean that a particular community's saying something is so makes it so. Wittgenstein is saying only that confusion about the language games of a particular community produces nonsense. It just so happens that in the Western tradition confusion about the language games involving "rules," "concepts," "inner" and "outer" experiences, "sensations," "emotions," and so on, have produced philosophical questions and answers that are nonsense. Wittgenstein's arguments in fact seem extremely helpful in dispelling some illusions about what actually goes on in martial-arts training. But unfortunately for my purposes here, the private-language argument finally seems unsatisfactory for getting at the question of ascetic disciplines. It seems to me that Wittgenstein leaves me with the choice of talking nonsense on this subject, or remaining silent.

Wittgenstein might be right. But it seems that Peirce's way is worth exploring before giving up, especially since Peirce's semiotic also suggests deep affinities between the practice of ascetic disciplines and textual hermeneutics. I ask now, with Peirce's reflections as a guide, what does the practice of ascetic disciplines look like from the perspective of textual hermeneutics?

For Peirce the reality of thought is the representative function of the sign. The reality of the human being in the moment of thought is the reality of the sign. And Peirce identifies himself as a realist, or "one who knows no more recondite reality than that which is represented in a true representation" ("Consequences," *W*, 69). (To avoid a possible confusion, I should mention a point that I shall take up more fully in Chapter 5. The point is that Peirce's notion of "representation" here and elsewhere is not simply the notion of undistorted reflection as in the surface of a well-polished mirror. Peirce's pragmatism requires a more developed notion of representation. I represent something not just by reflecting it in my mind as it is in itself, but instead by conceiving its potential effects—to speak loosely, its uses.)

I want to argue, then, that from a Peircean perspective it would make sense to say that an ascetic discipline aims at total absorption in the real. All that has a chance of being real about human beings is the representative function of the sign in human consciousness. So an ascetic discipline aims at total absorption in the representative function of the sign. That would mean, in turn, an attempt to purge from consciousness, so far as possible, awareness of the material qualities of signs (the idiosyncratic "feel" of the signs) and of their pure demonstrative applications (the "I think" of attention).

This resolves the ascetic paradox of knowing the self by denying the self. It also provides a way of talking about ascetic experience that might seem less esoteric than some of the traditional ways. That is, ascetic experience is like being totally absorbed in a conversation, to the point that words come without seeking, and one is not aware of any separation between the words and the meaning. Or it is like fluent reading, where there is no sense of having to decode the marks on the page and no sense of having to extrapolate from what is written to some absent authorial intention. One reads, and the meaning comes. It is not separate, but is given in the experience of reading. Almost everyone has had such experiences with language. Presumably, that is also the kind of total absorption in techniques experienced by the accomplished martial artist.

Trying to talk about the martial arts in terms of the traditional vocabulary of mind and body, physical and spiritual, inner and outer, produces descriptions that sound mystical to Westerners. At least sometimes, however, these descriptions can be translated into the vocabulary of semiotics, and thus can be brought into relation with the familiar experiences of reading, writing, and speaking.

Here is an example from one of the classic texts of karate: *Karate-do Nyumon*, by Gichin Funakoshi, who brought Okinawan karate to Tokyo in 1922 and founded what his students call the *Shotokan* style of karate. Funakoshi points out that the *kara* of *karate* was once written with the character meaning "China"—thus, "China hand." But *kara* can also be written with the character meaning "empty," and this is the usage that Funakoshi himself advocated:

> Just as an empty valley can carry a resounding voice, so must the person who follows the Way of Karate make himself void or empty by ridding himself of all self-centeredness and greed. Make yourself empty within, but upright without. This is the real meaning of the "empty" in karate. . . . Once one has perceived the infinity of forms and elements in the universe, one

> returns to emptiness, to the void. In other words, emptiness is none other than the true form of the universe. . . . Form equals emptiness; emptiness equals form. (24–25)

This passage is obviously rooted in Oriental philosophy, and it makes explicit the ethical dimension of the martial arts. I am more interested, however, in Funakoshi's metaphor of the voice that resounds in the empty valley, and in his remarks about emptiness in general. The metaphor of the voice seems very close to implying a semiotic understanding of the martial arts. The techniques of karate are like the resounding voice—the linguistic sign—which is realized (made real) precisely to the extent that private (unreal) idiosyncrasies are kept from interfering with it.

In Peirce's terms: the emptiness of the self means total absorption in the representative function of the sign, since "the individual man . . . so far as he is anything apart from his fellows, and from what he and they are to be, is only a negation" ("Consequences," *W*, 72). Also, it seems possible to translate Funakoshi's aphorism about form and emptiness into Peirce's terms. Peirce says, "thought is what it is only by virtue of its addressing a future thought. . . . In this way, the existence of thought now depends on what is to be hereafter; so that it has only a potential existence" ("Consequences," *W*, 72). The emptiness of the universe for human thought consists precisely in the form of thought— namely, the form of the sign, whose reality is always virtual.

Now, I would guess that all of this is very far from the line of argument that Funakoshi is pursuing, which is informed by a long tradition of non-Western philosophy. Peirce's philosophy is thoroughly Western, and that is its virtue for my purposes. My point is only that there sometimes exists a translation of descriptions of ascetic experience into the terms of semiotics.

In a very interesting passage, Shigeru Egami, a student of Funakoshi's and his successor as head of the Shotokan school, describes the effects on students of practicing *kata* (forms) to exhaustion:

> Continuing to practice, they will become . . . exhausted, to the point of not being able to stand up, their breath will come in gasps, and their vision will blur. Out of sheer exhaustion, they may wish for unconsciousness. But they should not stop. Continuing in this state, they will become like automatons and will be unable to concentrate any power in their movements. To put it simply, they will not know what they are doing.
>
> At this stage, they will realize that their movements have be-

come soft and natural. The mind is useless, but the movements will have been acquired by the body.

If practice continues, they may come to the stage where the mind is very clear and the movements of the body understood. Or they may simply forget everything and crawl on the floor. They may repeatedly lose themselves and find themselves until they discover that they feel greatly exhilarated. It is then that they will understand that they have fallen down, or fainted, from exhaustion. But even then, if a command is heard, they will react in some way, though not necessarily physically. At the same time, they will come to comprehend the relation between themselves and the person giving the orders, the relation between the performers and the relation between mind and body.

The body movements and the flow of feeling will at first be very confusing, then they will become very quiet, and finally one will enter a state of tranquility and concentration, and the breath will become regular despite the strenuousness of the movements. (Egami, 106–7)

The vocabulary of mind and body gets seriously in the way here, since in the process described by Egami the relation of mind and body seems to be constantly changing in confusing and unpredictable ways. But what Egami seems to be describing is one strategy for experiencing complete absorption in the techniques of the kata. The point is to make oneself "too tired to think," while yet continuing to perform the techniques. The process might be compared to learning and overlearning a poem or a prayer until through fatigue the text comes into the mind unbidden and crowds out of consciousness everything except itself. In Egami's description the students, wavering on the verge of unconsciousness, nevertheless come to "comprehend the relation" between themselves and others and between mind and body. That is, in semiotic terms, they come to comprehend the meaning of the techniques in the community in which they are performed.

I will summarize, then, this long reflection on the martial arts. It seems useful to consider the martial arts as interpretive systems, where *interpretive system* itself is defined from the perspective of textual hermeneutics. The martial arts are language-like, and in deep ways learning them is like learning a second language, or learning to read and write. If one takes this view of the martial arts seriously, then the experience of training seems to confirm several crucial theses of Wittgenstein's private-language argument. But Wittgenstein's ideas seem not fully satisfactory for talking about ascetic disciplines as they are usually conceived. Many of the statements that one wants to make about ascetic disciplines must appear, from Wittgenstein's perspective, to be nonsense. Peirce's ideas seem more useful, and there seems to exist at least a partial translation of Wittgenstein's private-language argument into Peirce's terms. If this is so, then Peirce's thought provides a way of talking about ascetic disciplines as interpretive systems, without on the one hand sacrificing all of Wittgenstein's insights into how language works, or on the other hand talking nonsense.

4. Textual Hermeneutics as Ascetic Discipline

Finally, I want to turn this whole discussion on its head for a moment. My aim so far has been to look at ascetic disciplines from the perspective of textual hermeneutics. But now I want to suggest that *textual hermeneutics can be looked at as an ascetic discipline*. Of course, one need not look at textual hermeneutics that way. But one way of describing what goes on in interpreting a text is to say that the interpreter tries, so far as possible, to become totally absorbed in the signs of the text, such that the interpreter purges from consciousness purely private feelings and awareness of the separate "I" of the "I think." That is, the interpreter aims at a pure consciousness of the representative function of the signs woven together to make the text.

It is important to understand that I do not necessarily identify this pure consciousness with undistorted mirroring of a preexisting object. Peirce's notion of representation is not that simple. Nor do I necessarily identify this pure consciousness with consciousness of an author's intention, or of something that the text imitates, or of a structure determined by norms of a particular linguistic community, or of a Platonic form, or of a particularly complex emotion, or of any of the other things that texts have been said to represent. The consciousness I am talking about might be a consciousness of any or of none of those things. The interpreter who practices interpretation as an ascetic discipline is oriented toward the representative function of the text for the virtual, indefinitely future community that gives signs their reality. To be totally absorbed in the text means to have nothing in one's own reading that is not potentially real.

Practicing textual hermeneutics as an ascetic discipline is not equivalent to writing interpretations that "mean the same thing" as the texts in question, or trying to double the author's meaning in contemporary language, or anything of that sort. Translating the text into another sign system might be one exercise, perhaps a necessary exercise, for the practice of the ascetic discipline or for helping others to practice it. But it is only an exercise. The ascetic discipline aims at absorption in the text such that translation of it seems no longer necessary, and perfect translation of it seems impossible. That is why what is experienced as a profound insight into a text sometimes comes out sounding like either a platitude or a mysterious oracle when one tries to translate it into the vocabulary of critical discourse.

Many people say that they read texts for pleasure, whereas they associate ascetic disciplines with pain or at least effort. I am not saying that people do not or should not have pleasure when they read. It is even possible that what some people count as "pleasure"—that slippery word—is "real" in Peirce's sense. It is only that I do not identify textual hermeneutics with the pursuit of pleasure. One can read purely for pleasure without doing textual hermeneutics at all.

Regarding textual hermeneutics as an ascetic discipline would have profound implications for the teaching of the humanities. These implications are the subject of the last chapter of this book. In some cases, the behavior of teachers of texts might remain much the same, but their understanding of what they are doing would be radically changed. Textual hermeneutics would not appear as the handing down of a definitive inspiration that occurred at some point in a critic's head. One might present interpretations as if they happened that way, but only as a strategy to help students see what it means to aim at the pure representative function of the sign. Nor would textual hermeneutics consist of the codification of definitive rules of interpretation, determined by the essential nature of texts, and supposed always to work in the same way with every text. There might be rules, but these would also appear as strategies: a set of empirically developed methods that might work in different ways for different people and different texts, methods that sometimes do and sometimes do not lead interpreters to an ascetic experience of interpretation.

Nor would textual hermeneutics conceived as ascetic discipline consist in extending the free play of the signifiers by foregrounding the private association—though this, too, might be a strategy. And I will add one more negative: textual hermeneutics as an ascetic discipline would not be the attempt to construct an actual "interpretive community" of those who have agreed to use the text for particular purposes. Observing that interpretive communities exist and noting how they behave, or even trying explicitly to construct an interpretive community, might, again, be strategies among other strategies of the ascetic discipline, exercises among other exercises. Instead of all these things, textual hermeneutics as ascetic discipline would be very close to—might even be the Peircean translation of—Heidegger's "listening" to the speaking of Language in the masterful poem.

Clearly, textual hermeneutics has been and is being regarded as all of these things: special inspiration, rules, play, politics. And others. Why one might want to regard textual hermeneutics as an ascetic discipline for the purposes of humanities education nowadays is a big question that I must postpone until the final chapter. Here I want only to establish the possibility of regarding textual hermeneutics that way, and to suggest some of the implications. In one sense, looking at the martial arts as interpretive systems is a strategy for understanding more concretely what it means to regard textual hermeneutics as an ascetic discipline.

4

Terminus at the Real

1. Privileging Texts

In the third chapter I said that it is possible to think of textual hermeneutics as an ascetic discipline, and the applying of any particular interpretive system as one among many possible exercises of the discipline. In this chapter I want to explain more fully what all of that means. My method here is indirect. I want to look at a particular hermeneutic problem as it appears in the work of Paul Ricoeur, and to show how that particular problem is one manifestation of a general problem that the theory of interpretive systems can illuminate. I will ultimately argue that the problem cannot be solved if it is conceived as Ricoeur conceives it, but that the problem disappears if textual hermeneutics is regarded as an ascetic discipline.

If the point of the ascetic discipline is to get to rock bottom, to know oneself as sign by being conscious of nothing but the representative function of the signs of a text, then it is clear that one neither has nor wants this kind of relationship with every text. Certain texts are treated as "privileged." They are set apart and accorded higher value than other texts. Other texts, such as dictionaries, biographies, criticism, commentary, newspapers, and bad poems, may be read, but their value for interpretation is only instrumental. They are read in order to help the interpreter stand in the proper relation with the privileged texts. The Anglo-American New Critics, for example, implied that texts written in "literary" language are somehow different from and in some ways better than texts written in "ordinary" or "scientific" language. There have been arguments about what makes "poetry" different from rhythmical "prose." My particular concern with Ricoeur is the kind of privileging that occurs when a text is read as "scripture." The readiest alternative nowadays to reading, say, the Bible as "scripture" seems to be to read it as "literature," and so the terms *scripture* and *literature* come to stand to each other in a kind of dialectical relationship where scripture occupies the privileged pole. Perhaps the easiest, and certainly the most fashionable, way to state the general problem is to talk about the difference between "canonical" and "noncanonical" texts. What makes the difference in interpretation?

Obviously, the causes for my actually taking any particular text as canonical are complex and have to do with various physical, psychological, historical, political, economic, and sociological factors. I have to admit that the fact that I today think that *Paradise Lost* is a great poem is not completely unrelated to the fact that Milton was a white male of the leisure class of his own time. To trace such causes is of course an extremely important moment in the understanding of interpretive systems in general. But it is not these causes that I am interested in here. When I ask how privileged texts are different from nonprivileged texts, I am not asking how anybody's canon got to be what it is. Instead, given that everybody has a canon, I am asking how the interpretation of canonical texts differs from the interpretation of noncanonical texts.

Let me put this specifically in terms of "scripture" and "literature," since I want to take that opposition as exemplary of the phenomenon of privileging. It would be confusing to ask simply, How is scripture different from literature? People would rightly object that these terms lack clear reference. The only way to meet the spirit of such objections would be to construct a general theory of language that would establish *scripture* and *literature* as the names of separate, well-defined categories of texts. Lacking such a theory, I lack a general answer to the question of how scripture is different from literature. But by the same token, I lack a good reason for discarding either term or reducing the opposition.

By way of getting around this difficulty, one might ask instead, How is "taking" a text as scripture (whatever scripture might turn out to be) different from "taking" a text as literature (whatever literature might turn out to be)? But this version of the question makes the difference seem to depend upon the reader's experience, however vague or confused. Somebody might want to say, "I know when I am reading scripture, because of a certain indefinable warm feeling I get inside with these texts and with no others." The warm feeling might seem definitive to that particular reader. But as Wittgenstein would point out, the warm feeling is not very useful in talking about interpretation or anything else. One does not normally question the quality or validity of someone else's private experiences.

One questions explicit interpretive statements. And so a further refinement of my question might be, How is the interpretation of scripture different from the interpretation of literature? Or, in other words, can I articulate something distinctive in the structure of explicit scriptural interpretation that, while it might not enable me to define scripture, will at least let me make sense when I say that a text has been taken as scripture instead of as literature?

I want to pursue this problem and connected problems in the work of Ricoeur. As I have said, I think that Ricoeur does not answer the question. But I hope to suggest the significance of this question for at least one strand of contemporary hermeneutics. For some people, the question might be important in itself; but Ricoeur's failure to deal with it is also a symptom of a deeper problematic. Later in the chapter, I shall propose one answer to the question and discuss some implications of that answer, including its compatibility with the project of Ricoeur's hermeneutics.

2. *Ricoeur in the 1970s*

I shall confine my discussion of Ricoeur's work mostly to a particular stage in the development of his thought—roughly, the decade of the 1970s—since the problem I want to address is clearest there. Ricoeur foreshadowed his engagement with this problem in an address before the Divinity School at the University of Chicago in 1971. This address was translated by David Pellauer, published in *Criterion* 10 (Spring 1971), and finally reprinted as an appendix to *The Rule of Metaphor* (315–22). Ricoeur said, "What we need now is a new framework which would allow us to connect Biblical hermeneutics to general hermeneutics conceived as the question of what is understanding in relation to text-explanation" (321). Ricoeur's works of the following decade often seem to be trying to construct such a framework. He offers a succinct and more or less systematic treatment of his theory at this stage in *Interpretation Theory: Discourse and the Surplus of Meaning*. For the most part, my other citations will be to two collections: *Essays on Biblical Interpretation* and *Hermeneutics and the Human Sciences*.

The fundamental theses of Ricoeur's hermeneutics (at least, those that will be important in what follows) can conveniently be discussed under three headings: (1) the autonomy of the text; (2) the world of the text; and (3) the appropriation of the text.

The autonomy of the text. For Ricoeur, writing frees discourse from what he calls the "dialogical situation": that is, the situation of speech events between particular interlocutors, where each interlocutor tries to reconstruct the intention of the other and where either interlocutor can "point out" the element in the context to which reference is made, if there is any doubt. As he puts it: "Inscription becomes synonymous with the semantic autonomy of the text, which results from the disconnection of the mental intention of the author from the verbal meaning of the text. . . . What the text means now matters more than what the author meant when he wrote it" (*IT*, 29–30, 87, 92). Thus, Ricoeur accepts the "main presupposition" of the "anti-historicism" in the human studies that followed from Frege's concept of "sense" (*Sinn*) and Husserl's concept of meaning as an "ideal object." It is the presupposition, namely, of the "objectivity of meaning in general" (*IT*, 91). Though a philosopher such as Gadamer might think of this "distanciation" (*Verfremdung*) between author and reader as a kind of "ontological fall from grace" ("Hermeneutics and the Critique of Ideology," *HHS*, 91), Ricoeur conceives of it as "constitutive of the phenomenon of the text as writing" and as the condition of interpretation and understanding ("The Hermeneutical Function of Distanciation," *HHS*, 139–40).

A "working definition" of hermeneutics, then, is "the theory of the operations of understanding in their relation to the interpretation of texts" ("The Task of Hermeneutics," *HHS*, 43). Note that this definition does not mention the author.

So far, Ricoeur's hermeneutic theory seems compatible with the insights of structuralism and poststructuralism that I have mentioned before. Also, the "working definition" of hermeneutics could easily be read from the perspective of Peirce, as indicating that the task of hermeneutics is methodeutic: a study of how intelligences in fact connect the signs in texts with the signs in explicit interpretations.

The world of the text. Ricoeur criticizes "Romantic" hermeneutics for trying to use texts to get back to the intention of the author or the mental life in which the author was submerged. What the interpreter should try to get at is

> Not the intention of the author . . . ; not the historical situation common to the author and his original readers; not the expectations or feelings of these original readers; not even their understanding of themselves as historical and cultural phenomena.

> What has to be appropriated is the meaning of the text itself, conceived in a dynamic way as the direction of thought opened up by the text. . . . If we may be said to coincide with anything, it is not the inner life of another ego, but the disclosure of a possible way of looking at things, which is the genuine referential power of the text. (*IT*, 92)

In the text fixed in writing, and thus liberated from the dialogical situation, the reference is no longer directly to the world as the "totality of manipulable objects" that can be pointed to in the immediate context of any speech event ("Phenomenology and Hermeneutics," *HHS*, 112). Instead, especially with the poetic text, there is another kind of reference, which Ricoeur calls "non-situational," "second order," or "non-ostensive." The text refers, in other words, not to things in the world, but to a way of looking at the world.

Literary texts, in particular, deliberately break down the "first order" of reference, to call attention to the second order:

> poetic texts speak about the world. But not in a descriptive way. . . . the reference here is not abolished, but divided or split. The effacement of the ostensive and descriptive reference liberates a power of reference to aspects of our being in the world that cannot be said in a direct descriptive way, but only alluded to, thanks to the referential values of metaphoric and, in general, symbolic expression. (*IT*, 37)

Ricoeur recalls Heidegger's remarks about understanding (*Verstehen*) to support his contention that what a reader understands in a text is in fact "the outline of a new way of being in the world" (*IT*, 37). Ricoeur also connects the non-ostensive reference of the literary work with the Aristotelian concept of *mimesis*, "the Greek term for the disclosure of a world" ("Metaphor and the Central Problem of Hermeneutics," *HHS*, 180).

Even historical texts, insofar as they are narratives, share something with fictional narratives. What has happened in the past represents a possibility for the present: "to recognize the values of the past in the *difference* with respect to our values is already to open up the real towards the possible. The 'true' histories of the past uncover the buried potentialities of the present," and thus history, in a sense, like fiction "explores the field of 'imaginative' variations which surround the present and the real that we take for granted in everyday life" ("The Narrative Function," *HHS*, 295). Ricoeur's formula is as follows: "by opening us to what is different, history opens us to the possible, whereas fiction, by opening us to the unreal, leads us to what is essential in reality" (296).

Thus, Ricoeur arrives at another definition of hermeneutics from a different viewpoint: "Hermeneutics can be defined . . . as the explication of the being-in-the-world displayed by the text. What is to be interpreted in the text is a proposed world which I could inhabit and in which I could project my ownmost possibilities" ("Phenomenology and Hermeneutics," *HHS*, 112).

From a poststructuralist perspective, Ricoeur might seem for a moment simply to have replaced the Cartesian ego of the author with the Cartesian ego of the reader. But construing Ricoeur's ideas in terms of Peirce's semiotic might shed a different, more sympathetic light. When Ricoeur says that a reader can "inhabit" the world proposed in the text, perhaps Ricoeur means that the reader can allow the sign chain that is the interpretant thought to be taken up by the sign chain of the text. The reality of the sign chain is virtual, pending the decision of the future community of rational minds. Then, there would be no need for talk about substantial Cartesian egos. There is, instead, the absorption of one sign chain in another. For human beings, to live in a world means to be a chain of signs that postulates an object at its limit. Postulating a self as substance, as Cartesian ego, is not necessary then in order to talk about inhabiting the world proposed in a text. Ricoeur's formula can avoid the Cartesian trap if it can be translated into Peirce's formula that "man is a sign."

The appropriation of the text. Ricoeur in fact does not want to say that interpretation is purely a "subjective" matter, purely relative to what the interpreter finds in the text (or puts there) because of idiosyncratic concerns. With his concept of "appropriation"—comparable to Gadamer's concept of "fusing of horizons" (*IT*, 94)—Ricoeur tries to meet the possible objection that his theory leads to a vicious relativism. Appropriation is the dialectical counterpart of distanciation. It is the interpretation of a text that "culminates in the self-interpretation of the subject" ("What Is a Text?" *HHS*, 153), or the "application (*Anwendung*) to the present situation of the reader" ("The Hermeneutical Function of Distanciation," *HHS*, 143). But the reader who stands before the world of the text is not just the same old Cartesian ego who inhabits the familiar, everyday world. The new world of possibilities imaginatively projected in the text creates a new subjectivity to inhabit it. "World" and "self" are not separable entities, but instead are correlatives.

Thus to understand the world of the text is to understand or temporarily become a new self that stands in a reciprocal relation with that world. And this self, as much as the projected world, is a creation of the text, not of the reader: "If the reference of the text is the project of a world, then it is not the reader who primarily projects himself. The reader is rather enlarged in his capacity of self-projection by receiving a new mode of being from the text itself" (*IT*, 94). Ricoeur insists that "we understand ourselves only by the long detour of the signs of humanity deposited in cultural works" ("The Hermeneutical Function of Distanciation," *HHS*, 143), and he is fond of saying that in interpretation one understands, not the author's intention behind the text, but "oneself *in front of the text*" ("Phenomenology and Hermeneutics," *HHS*, 113; *IT*, 87).

In literary works especially, the "imaginative variations" of the real find a counterpart in the "imaginative variations" of the ego: "The *ego* must assume for itself the 'imaginative variations' by which it could *respond* to the 'imaginative variations' on reality that literature and poetry, more than any other form of discourse, engender" ("Phenomenology and Hermeneutics," *HHS*, 113–14). In reading, the ego is dispossessed; a "self," rather, arises from the understanding of the text the ego claims to precede. Ricoeur's aphorism is that "it is the text . . . which gives a self to the ego" (*IT*, 95). The presumed relation of the reader to the text changes: "I exchange the *me, master* of itself, for the *self, disciple* of the text" ("Phenomenology and Hermeneutics," *HHS*, 113). Here Ricoeur himself employs the vocabulary of asceticism to talk about the relation between reader and text.

The appropriation of the text proceeds by means of a dialectical process, the poles of which Ricoeur calls "explanation" (*explication*, the *Erklärung* of Romanticist hermeneutics) and "understanding" (*compréhension*, Romanticist *Verständnis*). Ricoeur traces this dialectic in chapter 4 of *Interpretation Theory*, in which he rejects the Romanticist use of the concepts. (What follows here is my quick summary of *IT*, 71–88.) Dilthey, for example, had set up an opposition between the "explanation" carried out by the natural sciences, and "understanding," which he said was the fundamental mode of cognition for the human studies. In this view, interpretation is only a particular moment in understanding, a making explicit of what is already grasped in the initial act of understanding.

For Ricoeur, however, *interpretation* is the name of a "complex and highly mediated dialectic," the "whole process that encompasses explanation and understanding" (*IT*, 74). The first movement in the dialectic is a movement from understanding to explanation. The reader grasps the meaning of the text as a whole by means of a "guess" (understanding) that will enable the reader to see how the parts fit together. But this guess can be validated (explanation). Following the reasoning of E. D. Hirsch, Jr., Ricoeur contends that although certainty is not attainable, such guesses can be shown to be more or less probable on the basis of historical evidence.

The second movement in the dialectic is from explanation to understanding or comprehension. The reader can explain the text as a structuralist reading would—that is, not on the model of causal explanation as carried out by the natural sciences, but on a linguistic model. Thus Ricoeur attempts to incorporate the insights of structuralism (or, as he sometimes calls it, semiotics) into his theory. But the full comprehension of the text does not stop with structural analysis. Because structuralism really presupposes the existential situation it means to abstract from, the reader can use structural explanation to point the way toward an understanding of the possible world that the text discloses.

Thus, in Ricoeur's view, understanding in Romanticist hermeneutics tends to be a nonsystematic or irrational activity. Appropriation, however, does not. Appropriation is not another name for subjectivity, since the "subjectivity of the reader is no less held in suspense, no less potentialised, than the very world which the text unfolds" ("Hermeneutics and the Critique of Ideology," *HHS*, 94). And "if fiction is a fundamental dimension of the reference of the text, it is no less a fundamental dimension of the subjectivity of the reader. As reader, I find myself only by losing myself" ("The Hermeneutical Function of Distanciation," *HHS*, 144). Again, this is the vocabulary of ascetic experience.

None of this is to say, however, that Ricoeur accepts Hirsch's definition of meaning as the willed type, or Hirsch's principle that meaning is unitary, that there is one correct (i.e., most probable) meaning. To escape from subjectivism does not require that one sacrifice multiplicity of meaning. As Ricoeur puts it, the "opportunity for multiple readings is the dialectical counterpart of the semantic autonomy of the text," and the "right of the reader and the right of the text converge in an important struggle that generates the whole dynamic of interpretation" (*IT*, 32). In other words, once the text is cut loose by writing from the dialogical situation, its fate is to mean not what its author meant, but what its readers work out its meaning to be. Somewhat like Peirce, Ricoeur seems to gesture toward a future community. For Ricoeur, though, each present reader's "working out" is crucial, for only in the movement between explanation and understanding does interpretation escape subjectivity and become rational. But there is never absolute certainty about the meaning of the text (compare Peirce's doctrine of fallibilism). As Ricoeur puts it, "It is because absolute knowledge is impossible that the conflict of interpretations is insurmountable and inescapable. Between absolute knowledge and hermeneutics, it is necessary to choose" ("Appropriation," *HHS*, 193).

And so I find a third "definition" of hermeneutics, from a third point of view: "To 'make one's own' what was previously 'foreign' remains the ultimate aim of all hermeneutics. Interpretation in its last stage wants to equalize, to render contemporaneous, to assimilate. . . . This goal is achieved insofar as interpretation actualizes the meaning of the text for the present reader" (*IT*, 31–32).

The first of Ricoeur's definitions of hermeneutics quoted above looks to the past: the business of hermeneutics is to explain how the human understanding has in fact operated in the interpretation of texts. The second definition looks to the future: the business of hermeneutics is to project a world that the reader may potentially inhabit. The third definition looks to the present moment, the contemporaneous: the business of hermeneutics is to assimilate the text to the present, and one knows that that has happened when interpretations can be rationally justified. None of this is surprising, considering how Ricoeur is steeped in Heideggerian thinking about the temporality of human being. But it does raise an interesting question. If I say (and Ricoeur sometimes talks this way) that textual hermeneutics is an ascetic discipline, what does that mean I am trying to do with an interpretive theory? Am I trying to explain how I myself and others have practiced the ascetic discipline in the past (Ricoeur's first definition)? Am I trying to explain an exercise that might help with the practice of the ascetic discipline in the future (Ricoeur's second definition)? Or am I actually practicing the ascetic discipline (Ricoeur's third definition)? Two of these things? All three? What, exactly, is the relation between interpretation itself, writing interpretive statements, and interpretive theory? One desideratum of a theory of interpretive systems is that it should suggest answers to these questions.

3. Scripture and Literature in Ricoeur

It is unclear to me whether Ricoeur in the 1970s thought that distinguishing between scripture and literature was a difficulty for his interpretive theory, or whether it was for him only a marginal problem that his reflections had not yet led him to work out. Ricoeur remarks on the generally nonsystematic character of his own works in his response to John Thompson's introduction to *Hermeneutics and the Human Sciences* (32ff.) and in his reply to Lewis S. Mudge (*EBI*, 41ff.).

There is no doubt, however, that Ricoeur had confronted questions raised by this distinction. As early as *The Symbolism of Evil*, Ricoeur asks himself why anyone should adopt a particular symbol system as one's own, from all the various symbol systems that are "iconoclastic" with respect to each other. That is, Ricoeur asks himself the "question of truth": "do *I* believe that? What do *I* make of these symbolic meanings, these hierophanies?" (*Symbolism of Evil*, 354). Philosophy presupposes that the symbol is "a manifestation of the bond between man and the sacred," and it takes as its task to

> make its presuppositions explicit, state them as beliefs, wager on the beliefs, and try to make the wager pay off in understanding. . . . [B]eginning from the contingency and restrictedness of a culture that has hit upon these symbols rather than others, philosophy endeavors, through reflection and speculation, to disclose the rationality of its foundation. (*Symbolism of Evil*, 356–57)

I shall comment later about the "wager" of philosophy and the connection between philosophy and hermeneutics. But for now I want to emphasize only that Ricoeur implies an important difference between a symbolism that one has "appropriated"—that is, for which one has answered the question of truth affirmatively—and a symbolism that one has not appropriated. Ricoeur recognizes the phenomenon of the privileged text. He does not say explicitly what, if anything, grounds the privileging, beyond the happenstance that the particular text has the sanction of one's particular culture. The metaphor of the "wager," in fact, seems to hint at a certain arbitrariness in choosing a particular symbolism for privileging. Nor does Ricoeur say exactly what difference it makes in interpretation when one symbolism is appropriated over another one. The "wager" seems to be something superadded, as it were, to the interpretation.

The closest Ricoeur comes to describing the interpretation of a symbol system that one has appropriated is to say that one must "enter into a passionate, though critical, relation with the truth-value of each symbol" (*Symbolism of Evil*, 354). The phrase "passionate, though critical" seems paradoxical, perhaps deliberately so. Ricoeur seems to want simultaneously to surrender himself to the symbolic text (as one might do with scripture) and to retain his critical faculty as a philosopher (as one might do with literature). So it is clear that there is an opposition in Ricoeur's hermeneutics, even in his earlier work. But this opposition remains below the surface, not fully articulated or clearly delineated there.

In some of Ricoeur's later essays, this opposition is more explicitly brought out. In "Toward a Hermeneutic of the Idea of Revelation" (*EBI*, 73–118), Ricoeur attempts to confront the claim of revelation with the critical consciousness of reflective philosophy. He wants to show that "the apparently unreasonable claim of revelation might be better understood as a nonviolent appeal" (95). His argument connects biblical revelation with poetic discourse, insisting that "the literary genres of the Bible do not constitute a rhetorical façade which it would be possible to pull down in order to reveal some thought content that is indifferent to its literary vehicle"; instead, "the confession of faith expressed in the biblical documents is directly modulated by the forms of discourse wherein it is expressed" (91). Ricoeur's move allows him to plead that the claim made by the revelatory biblical text, an autonomous text that projects a way of being in the world and that is susceptible to appropriation, is like the claim made by the poetic text, and therefore "nonviolent": "the imagination is that part of ourselves that responds to the text as a Poem, and that alone can encounter revelation no longer as an unacceptable pretension, but a nonviolent appeal" (117).

At first glance, one might suppose that the structure of Ricoeur's argument would require him to dispense with, or even argue against, the opposition between scripture and literature. But that is not what happens. Ricoeur continues to maintain that there is a distinction between reading the Bible and reading a poem, without, however, explaining specifically what that distinction means for interpretation:

> Just as the world of poetic texts opens its way across the ruins of the intraworldly objects of everyday existence and of science, so too the new being projected by the biblical text opens its way across the world of ordinary experience. . . .
>
> Yet . . . this areligious sense of revelation . . . does not for all that include the religious meaning of revelation. There is a homology between them, but nothing allows us to derive the specific feature of religious language—i.e., that its referent moves among prophecy, narration, prescription, wisdom, and psalms, coordinating these diverse and partial forms of discourse by giving them a vanishing point and an index of incompleteness—nothing, I say, allows us to derive this from the general characteristics of the poetic function. The biblical hermeneutic is in

turn one regional hermeneutic within a general hermeneutic and a unique hermeneutic that is joined to the philosophical hermeneutic as its *organon*. It is one particular case insofar as the Bible is one of the great poems of existence. It is a unique case because all its partial forms of discourse are referred to that Name which is the point of intersection and the vanishing point of all our discourse about God, the name of the unnameable. This is the paradoxical homology that the category of the world of the text establishes between revelation in the broad sense of poetic discourse and in the specifically biblical sense. (*EBI*, 104)

The Bible, then, is both like and unlike other poems. It is about God; but then, there are other poems about God. Ricoeur declines to say, finally, just how the interpretation of scripture is different from the interpretation of literature. But he apparently wants to imply that it is, nevertheless, different.

He falls back on the phrase "paradoxical homology," which is itself something of a paradox, and in its simultaneous giving and taking is reminiscent of the earlier phrase in *The Symbolism of Evil*: "passionate, though critical." To take a biblical revelation as being "about God"—and truly about God, not just about someone's concept of or name for God—seems to be a move equivalent to the appropriation of a particular symbolism as a true manifestation of the sacred. Like the "wager" on the symbol system, the "religious meaning" of revelation seems here to be something superadded to interpretation. The dialectic between explanation and understanding, it seems, could proceed in the same way if one were dealing only in "areligious" meaning.

The passage just quoted is the best illustration I have found of this spot of vagueness in Ricoeur's interpretive theory. Here I finally get to the nub: why is there this spot of vagueness? Can it be cleared up, or is it an inherent feature of Ricoeur's theory? And if it is cleared up, what will be the consequences for Ricoeur's hermeneutics in general and for the question of canonical texts? In order to get at these last questions, it is helpful to show how the particular problem I am considering is related to other problems in Ricoeur's interpretive theory.

True and false testimony. In discussing biblical interpretation, Ricoeur often uses the concept of "testimony" (a concept borrowed from the philosopher Jean Nabert) to articulate the nature of revelation. Mudge explains the concept this way:

> . . . discourse that claims to be "testimony" claims to be discourse in which, in a moment of total unity between event and

> meaning, an individual or community has found its "effort to exist and desire to be" [Nabert's phrase] interpreted to the point of total dispossession or divestment of the claims of the self. Every attempt of the self to be a source of meaning in its own right has yielded before the question "Who is God?" and the event or combination of events in which this has happened has been interpreted as a "trace" of the Absolute at this historical moment. The event of testimony is set down in discourse which claims, by its own self-reference, to be of this character. (*EBI*, 18)

I note in passing that Mudge uses the vocabulary of asceticism: "total dispossession or divestment of the claims of the self." Testimony attests to an event that is not, like most events, interpreted and given meaning by people. Instead, the event itself gives the people their meaning. And in accordance with Ricoeur's interpretive theory, such an event by being fixed in written discourse can become part of the world of the text.

The problem for Ricoeur's hermeneutics, however, is that claims can be true or false. Thus testimony, with its built-in reference to an original event before and outside the text, can be true or false. Mudge points out that Ricoeur's interpretive theory might not provide a "direct answer" to the question of what distinguishes true and false testimony (*EBI*, 22), and Ricoeur in his response to Mudge agrees:

> That's true. I agree that adding a theory of *structural reading* to the method of historical criticism . . . provides only an incomplete answer. If the stories of the Old Testament are *historylike*, . . . the question of the referential claims of these stories remains unavoidable. . . . The question remains open whether and to what extent the category of testimony may preserve the dialectic of sense and reference—i.e., of immanent meaning and of aboutness. (*EBI*, 44–45)

Ricoeur hints that some sort of answer, though an "incomplete" one, lies in the direction of the more "scientific" or "explanatory" structural reading. The hint seems to me a symptom of the source of the problem in Ricoeur's interpretive theory—namely, his insistence upon thinking of the "true" as the object of philosophy, where "philosophy" means rational justification ex post facto.

The problem of true and false testimony is not logically identical to the problem of scripture and literature, but it is closely related. If I am to read a text as scripture, that might be thought to involve an intellectual commitment to accepting its testimony as truth at some level. Conversely, if I believe the testimony of a text to be historically false, even though I value the text as highly as possible, it might be hard to say how my interpreting of it would be different from my interpreting of any other "great literature." The question might be put another way: as with the decision to "take" a text as scripture, is the decision to accept testimony as true a subjective or irrational matter, something superadded to the rational process of interpretation that moves within the dialectic between explanation and understanding? This is another vague spot, a "vexing problem" (*EBI*, 45) that Ricoeur explicitly recognizes in his interpretive theory.

Metaphor and symbol. Another problem, one that Ricoeur seems not explicitly to recognize, has to do with his concepts of "metaphor" and "symbol." I have mentioned the importance of the symbol for Ricoeur as a "manifestation of the bond between man and the sacred" (*Symbolism of Evil*, 356). In *The Rule of Metaphor* Ricoeur presents a theory of metaphor; but there the term *symbol* does not bear the same weight as an opposite pole to *metaphor*, and Ricoeur does not explicitly address the question of scripture and literature—except in the appendix that I have mentioned. *The Rule of Metaphor* is concerned rather with explaining how metaphorical discourse creates the "second-order" reference to the world of the text (Study 7, "Metaphor and Reference," 216–56), and with elucidating the relationship between metaphorical discourse and "speculative discourse" or philosophy (Study 8, "Metaphor and Philosophical Discourse," 257–313). The understanding of metaphor has at times seemed important to Ricoeur as a model for understanding larger texts ("Metaphor and the Central Problem of Hermeneutics," *HHS*, 165–81). (By the time of *IT*, however, Ricoeur no longer regarded metaphoric and symbolic language as "paradigmatic for a general theory of hermeneutics" [78].) As for symbols in the strong sense, when they appear in language, they appear as metaphor: "Metaphor is just the linguistic procedure . . . within which the symbolic power is deposited" (*IT*, 69). The metaphor, however, is a "purely semantic structure," whereas the symbol, to function as such, must contain "something non-semantic," so that it can bring together "two dimensions, we might even say, two universes, of discourse, one linguistic and the other of a non-linguistic order" (*IT*, 45–46, 53–54).

Symbols of the sacred thus point to something actual, as it were, whereas poetic metaphors construct a hypothetical world. The sky, trees, human breath, the wind, the sun, or other elements of the created world might appear in metaphors in religious discourse; but if these elements are genuine symbols, they have a power to signify in other ways apart from the discourse. So symbols have a "bound character" that "makes all the difference between a symbol and a metaphor. The latter is a free invention of discourse, the former is bound to the cosmos. Here we touch an irreducible element, an element more irreducible than the one that poetic experience uncovers" (*IT*, 61–62). The obvious problem here is to tell whether one is dealing with a metaphor or a symbol in any particular discourse. Symbols come to language in metaphor; in fact, Ricoeur suggests that metaphors can, by being involved in a "whole array of intersignifications," become "root metaphors" and approximate the condition of symbols (*IT*, 64). The problem is analogous with the problem of true and false testimony. That is, when I am confronted with a metaphorical locution in a text, how do I decide whether it is a genuine symbol? Is this decision a result of the interpretation itself, the dialectic of explanation and understanding, or is it something superadded to the interpretation according to subjective and perhaps irrational motives? How do I decide, in short, whether the metaphor is "true," whether it is a manifestation of the sacred? All metaphors must ultimately be constructed from a language rooted in the elements of the created world. Presumably, a felt difference between a believer's and a nonbeliever's reading of the Bible would be that the believer would find symbols there, in Ricoeur's sense, whereas the nonbeliever would find only metaphors. How, then, have the interpretations differed, if they have? What sort of claim can the "objectivity" of interpretation (the dialectic of explanation and understanding) make on either?

Truth and method. A final issue in Ricoeur's interpretive theory that seems related to the question of scripture and literature has to do with Ricoeur's reading of Hans-Georg Gadamer. In several places Ricoeur questions what he feels to be implied in the title of Gadamer's *Truth and Method*; namely, the supposition that "truth" is somehow separate from the "method" of hermeneutics (*HHS*, 61–62, 90, 131). This supposition, in Ricoeur's view, is the major problem in Gadamer's work. Ricoeur seems happy enough with some of Gadamer's crucial concepts (or adapted versions of them)—"belonging," "fusing of horizons," "matter of the text"—but Ricoeur consistently resists the notion that one must choose between participating in ("belonging to") the historical reality (that is, having it present to one as "truth") and knowing historical reality as an object of the human sciences ("method"). Ricoeur finds this "antinomy" to be the "mainspring of Gadamer's work" and an "untenable alternative":

> . . . on the one hand, alienating distanciation is the attitude that renders possible the objectification which reigns in the human sciences; but on the other hand, this distanciation, which is the condition of the scientific status of the sciences, is at the same

time the fall that destroys the fundamental and primordial relation whereby we belong to and participate in the historical reality which we claim to construct as an object. Whence the alternative underlying the very title of Gadamer's work *Truth and Method*: either we adopt the methodological attitude and lose the ontological density of the reality we study, or we adopt the attitude of truth and must then renounce the objectivity of the human sciences.

My own reflection stems from a rejection of this alternative, in an attempt to overcome it. ("The Hermeneutical Function of Distanciation," *HHS*, 131)

That is, truth, Ricoeur would prefer to say, is precisely the object of method considered as philosophical justification.

But the dilemma implied in Gadamer's alternative seems also implicit in Ricoeur's three "definitions" of hermeneutics, quoted earlier. Is it possible to aim *at the same time* at understanding a practice (that is, having a theory of interpretation) and at performing the practice (that is, carrying out the activity of interpreting)? Are the alternatives not exclusive? If they are exclusive, which is the proper goal of the human studies? I shall argue later that the question loses its point when textual hermeneutics is considered as a particular kind of practice—namely, as an ascetic discipline.

Meanwhile, the question is whether the alternative Ricoeur rejects can be overcome within the framework of Ricoeur's own interpretive theory. I stress that I am trying not to adjudicate between Gadamer and Ricoeur but only to delineate a problem for Ricoeur's hermeneutics that appears when he confronts his theory with Gadamer's. Ricoeur attempts to overcome Gadamer's "untenable alternative" essentially by attempting to make the notion of distanciation "productive." He argues that distanciation is the condition of understanding a text. Without its distancing from its author through writing, the text could not become autonomous or project its world; without the distancing of reader from ego that occurs in reading, the new self correlative with the world of the text could not emerge.

But Ricoeur's solution leaves a residue. There is still the possibility that any given reading, even one informed by this "productive distanciation," is wrong. This possibility is inherent in the concept of the "human sciences," because no science is possible where no error is possible. I might have erred in my reading, misunderstood, either because of the ideologies of my own time, or because of the idiosyncratic point of view rooted in my own psychology. Ricoeur, in fact, insists on leaving room for a "critique of the illusions of the subject, in a Marxist or Freudian manner" ("The Hermeneutical Function of Distanciation," *HHS*, 144).

It is hard to see, however, what sort of force this critique might have for interpretation—that is, the dialectic between explanation and understanding. Although Ricoeur wants to place this critique "at the very heart of self-understanding," it seems once again that there is something superadded to the interpretation itself. For how would I simultaneously open myself to the world of the text, allow my ego to be dispossessed, as Ricoeur would have it, and also open myself to the world according to Marx or Freud? Someone—even I myself—might later claim on the basis of a critique of the illusions of the subject that my reading is wrong. But this claim would not touch the structure of my interpretation—again, the dialectic between explanation and understanding. If I insist that someone's reading of a text is wrong, arguing on the basis of ideology or psychoanalysis, but not on the basis of the structure of interpretation itself, then I might have a science called sociology or a science called psychology, but not a science called hermeneutics.

My point is not that Ricoeur is wrong and Gadamer is right. My point is rather that Ricoeur's solution leaves unanswered the question of precisely how "truth" is united with "method"—how, that is, one can know from examining the structure of interpretation itself that it does or does not produce "truth." The problem is of course parallel to the other problems I have mentioned. There seems to be nothing in interpretation itself that distinguishes a metaphor from a symbol, or true testimony from false testimony, or, finally, scripture from literature. If these distinctions are made, they are made on the basis of something that supervenes on the process of interpretation itself: a sense of the sacred in the nonlinguistic elements of creation, a "critique," a "wager."

I am now perhaps in a better position to say how these spots of vagueness in Ricoeur's interpretive theory might be symptoms of a central problematic. To put it crudely, Ricoeur's project is to unite hermeneutics with philosophy. At one point he identifies the "central problem" of hermeneutics, the problem of interpretation, as the problem of reducing the contrast between the scientific objectivity of explanation and the apparent subjectivity of the "hermeneutic circle" in understanding ("Metaphor and the Central Problem of Hermeneutics," *HHS*, 166).

The project begins as an attempt to get beyond the subjectivity of "Romanticist" hermeneutics, which tends to see understanding as the basically irrational (or better, prerational) empathy of one subject for another, and interpretation as merely an articulation of what is understood ("The Task of Hermeneutics," *HHS*, 43–62). Ricoeur's strenuous efforts to incorporate the insights of French structuralism into his theory show, I think, his concern for constructing a hermeneutics that can claim to produce understanding through explanation on the linguistic model. The point is especially obvious in his essay "What Is a Text?" (*HHS*, 153–57, 161). To unite hermeneutics with philosophy means to show that interpretation is rational at its core, that within the dialectic of explanation and understanding there are ways of making truth claims and justifying those claims. More, it means to show that what goes on in interpretation itself is rationally explicable and justifiable.

The spots of vagueness in Ricoeur's theory appear precisely where there is a question of how some sort of truth claim is to be justified. And everywhere, the truth claim seems to be justified on the basis of something external to interpretation itself. The central problematic, then, is the extent to which interpretation, conceived as Ricoeur conceives it, is a rational activity in his sense of "rational." Ricoeur seems to think of rational justification on something like the Euclidean model—that is, deduction from a set of axioms. That is not how Peirce thinks of the rational—namely, as the real, the representative function of the sign that will persist in the long run. I suspect that Ricoeur's implicit notion of philosophy and of the rational is partly what puts him on the hook, and that Peirce's notion could help to get hermeneutics off that particular hook.

Let me put the problematic specifically in terms of the question of scripture and literature. In the interpretation of a text as scripture (or as true testimony, or as symbol), a phenomenon occurs that I have called "privileging." This privileging is not something added to a text after interpretation. Rather, the text is read as privileged. The questions for Ricoeur's hermeneutics would be, first, can this phenomenon be rationally defined? And second, can the privileging be rationally justified? If philosophy has nothing to say about the phenomenon of privileging, then there is at least one aspect of interpretation that is irrational, and there is at least one instance where hermeneutics and philosophy cannot be united.

It might even be that Ricoeur's theory prevents him from making a definite statement about the difference between scripture and literature. Suppose that Ricoeur were to say that the interpretation of scripture is in fact different from the interpretation of literature, in that scripture is "true." Then, since in his theory he is not prepared to adjudicate referential truth claims on the basis of the interpretive dialectic itself (see his response to Mudge), he would have to say that there is something irreducibly subjective and irrational in the process of interpretation itself—

namely, the privileging of certain texts. But that admission would run counter to his desire to show that interpretation is rational. Suppose, on the other hand, that Ricoeur were to say that the interpretation of scripture is in fact the same as the interpretation of literature. Then there would be nothing to prevent the critique of the illusions of the subject from asserting that any privileging of a text is always subjective. The rationality of interpretation itself would be preserved, but at the cost of what means most to a believer in reading scripture. Faith in the truth of the text becomes a nothing, an illusion, as far as the human sciences are concerned. This dilemma sounds suspiciously like the dilemma Ricoeur finds in Gadamer's work. One might even argue that Ricoeur has repressed this fundamental problem of hermeneutics in one place, only to have it surface in several others.

4. *Digression:* Time and Narrative

It might be worth digressing here to consider the more recent reflections in Ricoeur's three-volume work *Time and Narrative*. To avoid confusion, however, a couple of points need to be made right away.

First, in *Time and Narrative* Ricoeur does not explicitly discuss the distinction between scripture and literature. The opposition that drives his thought through these three volumes is rather that between history and fiction, as the "two narrative modes" (1.3). The precritical distinction (which Ricoeur deconstructs) between history and fiction is that history is "true" and fiction is not. So it might at first seem that Ricoeur's reflections on history and fiction would directly parallel his reflections on scripture and literature—since the distinction between scripture and literature is that the former is true and the latter is not. But the temptation to draw this parallel should be resisted. On the one hand, as Ricoeur himself points out, the Bible contains nonnarrative modes as well as narrative (3.272). Nonnarrative portions of scripture cannot be assimilated to "history," and yet these portions also presumably make on the believer whatever claim constitutes the privileging of scripture. And on the other hand, many believers who would say that scripture is "true" would at the same time deny that the kind of truth they are talking about is what is normally called historical truth. So the distinction between the truth of scripture and the fictionality of literature is not the same as the distinction between the truth of history and the fictionality of fiction.

The second point that needs to be made is that Ricoeur does not explicitly discuss in *Time and Narrative* the more general problem of privileging or "canonization." He does acknowledge the phenomenon of canonizing texts (3.179, 246-48), but does not reflect on it as a problem for his hermeneutic theory. Nor can any direct inferences about his interpretation of the phenomenon be made from his treatment of history and fiction. Neither of these modes is privileged with respect to the other. In the earlier parts of *Time and Narrative*, Ricoeur holds history and fiction apart to clarify their differences; ultimately, however, he brings them back together and talks about their "interweaving" (3.180-92). The "basic hypothesis" of *Time and Narrative* is that "*time becomes human to the extent that it is articulated through a narrative mode, and narrative attains its full meaning when it becomes a condition of temporal existence*" (1.52). There is no distinction in this "basic hypothesis" between the narrative called "history" and the narrative called "fiction."

Having cleared the ground some, I would nevertheless like to suggest now that the fundamental problem I have been discussing surfaces again in *Time and Narrative*. I have explained why solving the problem of the "reality" of history would not immediately constitute a solution to the problem of privileging. But for Ricoeur to show what it means to interpret a text as reconstructing something "real" would at least demonstrate how his hermeneutic theory might philosophize about truth claims of texts. That would be, one might say, some progress.

Ricoeur seems to promise that he will deal with the matter. A mannerism of his writing is the rhetorical *occupatio*, a postponement with a promise: for example, from volume 1, "this opposition between a 'true' narrative and a 'half true, half false' one rests on a naive notion of truth that will have to be thoroughly re-examined in volume 2" (1.226); and from volume 2, "We may now place the accent on the dissymmetries [of historical and fictional narrative] that will only attain a complete elucidation in my next volume, when I remove the parentheses I have imposed on the question of truth" (2.158; similar examples occur at 2.160 and at 3.100). But then, in the ultimate volume, "The relation between fiction and history is assuredly more complex than we will ever be able to put into words" (3.154). One who is searching Ricoeur's work for his solution to the problem of "truth," encountering such a sentence halfway through the third volume, has an uncomfortable sense of arriving after a long journey at a place like Gertrude Stein's Oakland: "There is no *there* there."

Obviously, I am being grossly unfair to Ricoeur, who in fact puts into words many wise and interesting observations about the relation between fiction and history. But the last sentence of his that I quoted, so unkindly ripped from its context, does to my mind signal a kind of shying away from the philosophical problem of truth claims in texts. And as in the other works I have cited, the term *paradox* is prominent at crucial points in *Time and Narrative* where Ricoeur is talking about the relation of either history or fiction to the "real" (1.180; 3.100).

Another symptom in *Time and Narrative* of the problem I have been discussing has to do with Ricoeur's use of two pairs of terms. These terms are, on the one hand, *history* (sometimes *historical narrative* or *historical explanation*) and *historiography* (sometimes *epistemology of history*), and on the other hand, *fictional narrative* (sometimes just *fiction* or *literature*) and *narratology* (sometimes *semiotics*). *History* most often seems to mean just narrative "history writing," and is therefore paralleled with *fictional narrative*: ". . . we have rediscovered in fictional narrative the same configuring operation that historical explanation was confronted with, since . . . narrativist theories . . . authorized the transference of literary categories of emplotment into the field of historical narrative. In this sense, we have simply returned to literature what history had borrowed from it" (2.157; see also, for example, 2.156, and 3.142). *Historiography* and *narratology*, on the other hand, considered as theorizing *about* history and fictional narrative, respectively, are paralleled: "We may, in fact, place on the same level of rationality both nomological explanation, which some theorists of history have claimed to substitute for the naive art of narrating, and the apprehension of the deep structure of a narrative in narrative semiotics" (2.4). One thing that justifies this comparison is that both historiography and narratology try "to approach as nearly as possible a purely deductive procedure, on the basis of a model constructed in an axiomatic manner" (2.29; see also, for example, 2.38, 2.158, and 3.3). I have argued already that this sort of model appears to be what Ricoeur has in mind in his earlier works where he is talking about philosophical justification.

So far, everything seems clear. Historiography and narratology correspond to the moment of the interpretive dialectic that Ricoeur elsewhere calls "explanation." But nomological explanation cannot be "autonomous," as Ricoeur notes in commenting on the narratology of A.-J. Greimas; the ability to carry out this explanation, in fact, depends in part on "our narrative competence" (2.56). So history and fiction, as narrative, are associated with the other moment in the interpretive dialectic: "understanding." Ricoeur can then say in *Time and Narrative*, as elsewhere, "to explain more is to understand better" (2.5).

But a problem arises when Ricoeur does not consistently use his terms as one might expect. Although not precisely confusing them, he does sometimes seem to draw with broad strokes when he is delineating the twin oppositions implied in these two pairs of terms. For example, *historiography* is sometimes set not against *narratology,* but against *literature* or *fiction:* "the two narrative modes in their most elaborated forms, historiography and literature"; "new narrative practices that have appeared as much in the field of historiography as in that of narrative fiction" (2.157). Or, "we must enlarge the space of reading to include everything written, historiography as well as literature" (3.101). Or, "A new sense of the word 'history' will appear . . . , one that exceeds the distinction between historiography and fiction" (3.102).

Perhaps one of the most telling passages is one in which Ricoeur expresses his intention to "do justice to the birth of a new form of rationality within the field of historical explanation, while at the same time preserving . . . the subordination of historical rationality to narrative understanding" (2.157). Ricoeur seems to be alluding to the attempt of some contemporary historians to substitute historiography ("historical rationality") for historical narrative, an attempt which he thinks should be carried only so far. But how does the term *historical explanation* function in this passage? I have been trying to distribute Ricoeur's terms along the dialectical axis of "explanation" and "understanding." To which moment of the dialectic does *historical explanation* belong? It appears to me that the term is ambiguous, and could equally well be assimilated to *historical narrative* (which means to explain historical events) or to *historiography* (which means to explain historical narrative). The tendency of this passage and the others I have quoted is to collapse what elsewhere seems to be a clear distinction between *historical narrative* and *historiography,* perhaps under a more general heading of *historical explanation.* It is as if to say that finally history and historiography are the same thing—as some contemporary historians might in fact say. Now, if the distinction between *historical narrative* and *historiography* collapses, and these terms are in fact respectively parallel with *fiction* and *narratology,* should the distinction between *fiction* and *narratology* collapse, too? Logically, perhaps it should. But nobody wants to say that the narratological texts of French structuralism are an appropriate replacement for the fictional narratives they analyze.

Why does the distinction try to collapse in one case and not in the other? One might answer here that historical texts are different from fictional texts because historical texts are "true" and refer to something "real." So, obviously, the aim of both history and historiography is ultimately to explain something outside the text—namely, the historical "event." But narratology has a fundamentally different aim from fiction—namely, to explain the fictional text itself considered as a structure isolated from its historical contexts. This is a naive answer, as Ricoeur's own work makes abundantly clear. But even the naive answer sets my point in relief. My point is that this sliding of Ricoeur's terms in *Time and Narrative* might well be another symptom of the problem in his work that I have been discussing all along. The sliding suggests the possibility that there is a kind of blur in Ricoeur's hermeneutic theory, that in some as-yet-unspecified way the dialectic between understanding and explanation is different for texts that make truth claims than for texts that do not. At first I can assimilate *historiography* and *narratology* to *explanation*, and *historical narrative* and *fictional narrative* to *understanding*, but then the dialectic between historiography and historical narrative collapses. There still seems to be something in Ricoeur's hermeneutic that needs to be cleared up, and it is something that seems to affect the fundamental dialectic between explanation and understanding, when the truth claims of a text are in question.

The ambiguity of Ricoeur's term *historical explanation* seems to carry over as well into an analogy that he proposes at several places in *Time and Narrative*. He compares the historian's task to that of the judge in a court of law, who must consider several competing narratives and decide which of them constitutes the best explanation of the evidence. This analogy is developed in the following passage:

> For historians, the explanatory form is made autonomous; it becomes the distinct object of a process of authentication and justification. In this respect, historians are in the situation of a judge: placed in the real or potential situation of a dispute, they attempt to prove that one given explanation is better than another. They therefore seek "warrants," the most important of which is documentary proof. Now it is one thing to explain by recounting. It is quite another to set up the explanation itself as a problem in order to submit it to the discussion and to the judgment of an audience, which, if not universal, is at least reputed to be competent, and is composed first of all of the historian's peers.
>
> Making historical explanation autonomous this way in relation to the explanatory sketches immanent in the narrative has several corollaries. . . . (1.175)

Here *historical explanation* seems to correspond in turn to what is elsewhere called *historiography* and what is elsewhere called *historical narrative*. Ricoeur has introduced his analogy at 1.125, where he opposed "judgment" to "deduction": "This way of judging about particular cases does not consist in placing a case under a law. . . . Here historians follow the logic of practical choices instead of that of scientific deduction." The analogy, or the idea of a document as a warrant, appears again, among other places, at 1.156, 3.117, 3.143, and 3.150.

It seems clear how this analogy functions in the economy of Ricoeur's argument. Since *historiography* and *historical narrative* tend to fall together, and since *historiography* is associated with nomological explanation, Ricoeur needs some device for ensuring that narrative remains at the heart of history. If history writing turns out to be deduction from laws, then one of Ricoeur's two narrative modes disappears as narrative. But if history writing *and* historiography essentially involve judging among competing narrative explanations, then narrative is restored as the essential mode of history.

But it is not clear to me how to interpret Ricoeur's use of the analogy of the court of law in the light of his hermeneutic theory in general. An unsympathetic interpretation might ask why, if "scientific" deduction or nomological explanation can occupy the pole of "explanation" in the interpretive dialectic for fiction, it will not work for history. If the answer is that there is no documentary evidence to reckon with in the case of the autonomous literary text, the answer again seems to mean that there is something fundamentally different about the interpretation of texts that are tied to the "real" world by truth claims, something that makes a difference in the fundamental dialectic of explanation and understanding. According to the analogy of the court, the discipline of history possesses only "a critique and a topic," but "has no method"—a point made by Paul Veyne and apparently endorsed by Ricoeur (1.176). But if this is so, how can Ricoeur's general hermeneutic theory aspire in the case of historical narrative to unite "truth" and "method"?

But there might be a more sympathetic interpretation of the analogy, at least from the point of view of my own project. One might argue that the analogy represents an opening of new possibilities for Ricoeur, a new way of looking at philosophical justification. Ricoeur himself does not treat the analogy as anything more than analogy, and he does not apply it outside the discussion of historical texts. But within that discussion, at least, he says some things that have an almost Peircean ring.

Consider, for example, the anti-Cartesian sentiments of the following passage: ". . . a critique of the totalizing intentions of history, joined to an exorcism of the substantial past and, even more, the abandonment of the idea of representation, in the sense of a mental reduplication of presence, do constitute cleansing operations that must be taken up again and again" (3.151). It might be easy to assimilate this passage to a Peircean critique of the Cartesian notion of "representation," or to see here a parallel with the handing on of the Peircean sign to the rational minds of an indefinite future for their reinterpretation. Or, in the sentence just before the one I characterized above as shying away from his philosophical project, Ricoeur mentions the "constraint that the past event exercises on historical discourse by way of the known documents, by requiring of this discourse an endless rectification" (3.154). This sounds very Peircean. The documents, as signs of an event at the limit of the sign chain, are themselves endlessly taken up into new sign chains, with the final judgment left to the virtual future community.

This is not at all the same idea of justification that the axiological method aims at. If I think I have a sound deductive justification, then I think that it does not matter what the community thinks. If they disagree with me, they are wrong. This notion of future judgment by a community, either the historian's "peers" or the virtual future community of rational minds, seems to me a breath, however faint, of a different air in Ricoeur's hermeneutic theory. And this air would be far more bracing for the theory of interpretive systems.

In fact, Ricoeur occasionally says things that come close to what I shall say later when I try to address the problem of privileging from the perspective of a theory of interpretive systems. These statements come precisely where Ricoeur is stressing the relationship between canonical works and the community for whom the works are canonical. Without ever explaining what difference privileging makes in interpretation itself, or exactly how privileging occurs, Ricoeur nevertheless accurately describes the interaction between the community and their privileged texts: "The act of reading is . . . included within a reading community, which, under certain favorable conditions, develops the sort of normativity and canonical status that we acknowledge in great works, those that never cease decontextualizing and recontextualizing themselves in the most diverse cultural circumstances" (3.179). Note the Peircean sound of this "decontextualizing and recontextualizing." And in one of the few places in *Time and Narrative* where Ricoeur does explicitly mention scripture, he stresses how privileged narratives can actually work to constitute the identity of the individual or community: "Individual and community are constituted in their identity by taking up narratives that become for them their actual history" (3.247). Thus, the example of "biblical Israel" is "especially applicable because no other people has been so overwhelmingly impassioned by narratives it has told about itself. . . . The relation is circular—the historical community called the Jewish people has drawn its identity from the reception of those texts that it had produced" (3.247–48). This last sentence, too, is susceptible to a Peircean translation: the signs that were the human beings of the Jewish community were constituted by the signs that were the texts they wrote and read.

So it might be possible to argue that in his more recent work Ricoeur hints that he is moving closer to the Peircean position I am outlining here.

5. The Theory of Interpretive Systems and Privileging

It is time to talk about how a theory of interpretive systems can help with this general problem of privileging texts. Three questions that no doubt need exploring are (1) whether certain culturally sanctioned interpretive systems tend to privilege certain kinds of texts, (2) if so, why, and (3) whether that is a good thing or a bad thing. Those are complicated historical questions that I am not concerned with here, however. My question is whether a theory of interpretive systems can provide a way to articulate what is distinctive in the interpretation of a privileged text—whether, that is, there is anything more in privileging than just cultural selection superadded to the interpretive process. Can I preserve the distinction between canonical and noncanonical texts in terms of the interpretive process itself?

In distinguishing scripture from literature, Ricoeur proposes a supervening category such as "faith" or the "wager." But to distinguish scripture from literature by saying that scripture is that in which one "has faith," or that which one believes to be "about God," does not explain how the interpretation of scripture as text is different from the interpretation of any other poetic (or for that matter, historical) text. To say that scripture is that on which one "wagers" also fails to say anything about the interpretive process. I "wager" when I put a nickel in the slot and pull the handle; if I win, more nickels come out. Ricoeur's concept of the "wager" might indicate what winnings I might expect and how I might count them, but it does not tell me what in the interpretive process corresponds to putting the nickel in. How, in interpretation, do I "wager" on a text? What does it mean to interpret a text as scripture?

Any interpretive system is correlated with the content it interprets. I have expressed this before by saying that the relation between the interpretive system and what is interpreted is reciprocal. The hypothesis that underlies this book is that the world can be construed as text. By that hypothesis, any academic discipline would be an instance of a complex and highly developed interpretive system. I cannot work out this consequence of the hypothesis in any detail, being incompetent in most academic disciplines. But suppose that academic disciplines can in fact be shown to be interpretive systems. Then, I might say, for example, that I apply the interpretive system called "biology" to a living organism when I articulate a meaning for the organism—showing, perhaps, how the organism is exemplary for illustrating a particular biological process, or how it is related with other organisms past and present. I apply the interpretive system "history" to a past event when I articulate the meaning of the event as cause or effect in some historical process. I apply some particular interpretive system of "hermeneutics" to a poem when I articulate, perhaps, an inference about the author's mental life, or a description of the various structures underlying the text, or a description of the "world" of the text. Depending on one's orientation within the field of literary criticism, any one of these things, among others, can be identified with the "meaning of the text."

There is no sharp border around the content correlated with any particular interpretive system. Academic disciplines generally tend to try to mark off particular content areas, but there is no logical necessity and sometimes no possibility of doing so. For example, there are certainly historical interpretations of poems, and there might well turn out to be biochemical or quantum-mechanical ones. Maybe I can explain the phenomenon of poetry in terms of molecular events in glands, or in terms of subatomic events. The example of structuralism shows how one discipline (linguistics) can aspire to swallow them all.

This reflection shows, again, that the relation between the interpretive system and its content is reciprocal. When one explicates the interpretive system that underwrites some particular interpretive statement, one finds out something not only about the interpreted content, but about the interpretive system itself. The concepts of the interpretive system are always more explicitly interpreted, filled out, in use. To extend the methods of structural linguistics, for example, first to the study of myth, then to the study of narrative, then to the study of literature in general, and finally to the study of any system of signs at all, might ultimately teach one more about the interpretive system than about the various contents studied.

Nowhere is the reciprocal relationship clearer than in the study of literary texts. Many of the important concepts of literary criticism might be called "axiomatic" or "empty" terms. These are terms whose understanding depends crucially on knowing at least some situations in which the terms are applied. The term *literature* itself is an example. No one can define it, but people study it. Everyone can give an instance, and no one feels completely helpless when asked to explain what features of a particular text are "literary." The term *metaphor*, as I mentioned in an earlier chapter, is another example, as is, perhaps, the venerable term *plot*. Even the apparently innocuous term *narrator* has revealed depths of complexity. But all of these terms are easy enough to explain once a meaning has been articulated. Once I have said that Wordsworth's "still, sad music of humanity" means "human history," I can explain metaphor by saying that the metaphor consists in using music to talk about history. The notion of "metaphor" enables me to give a name to what I have done in interpreting Wordsworth's poem, but Wordsworth's poem also helps me to understand more explicitly what I mean by *metaphor*.

By Peirce's theory of semiosis, interpreting means connecting one sign (or chain of signs) with another, according to some principle or set of principles. That is, I produce an interpretive statement about a text according to some interpretive system. But by the infinitely replicative nature of semiosis, my interpretive statement is now susceptible to being taken up in another interpretive statement, and so on. In fact, according to Peirce, my interpretive statement is only virtually a sign of the text. It can become a sign only insofar as it has the potential to be taken up in an infinitely self-replicating chain of signs that directs itself toward the perfected knowledge of an indefinitely future community. Having asked and answered the question What is the meaning of the text? then, it makes sense to ask the further question What is the meaning of this interpretive statement?

And here is the crucial point: there seem to be two different ways of answering this latter question. To illustrate, I want to suppose for a moment that the concepts of the Anglo-American New Criticism and of Marxist criticism can be shown to constitute two distinct interpretive systems. Actually confirming that hypothesis might turn out to be difficult, since there are many different manifestations of the intellectual movements that go by those names, since some who say they are practicing one or the other no doubt do not understand what they are practicing, and since some others no doubt interpret according to one or the other of these systems without being aware that they are doing so.

Nevertheless, I am going to suppose that these are two interpretive systems. Then someone might argue, for example, that the interpretive theory of the Anglo-American New Criticism was essentially a device to maintain the coherence of bourgeois values while religion was decaying, by making literature a kind of quasi-religion. (This is a bit of a caricature of Terry Eagleton's argument in the first chapter of *Literary Theory: An Introduction*.)

For instance, the speaker in Marvell's "Garden" talks about "Annihilating all that's made / To a green thought in a green shade." A New

Critic interprets "green" as paradoxical, suggesting a complex and ambivalent attitude that balances on the one hand the valid attractions of repose and contemplation, and on the other hand the repulsion of a vegetative existence that abdicates the responsibility of human action.

A Marxist critic, asked what the meaning of this interpretive statement is, replies that the New Critic implicitly enjoins political quietism by suggesting that the most advanced human types—such as the English gentleman-narrator who is even a sort of proto-Agrarian—ultimately find all experience ambiguous and therefore think it unseemly to be wholehearted enough about anything to rush to the barricades. Thus, a Marxist interpretive system would have been applied to a particular interpretive statement considered as content. The New Critic answers the question of the meaning of a poem in a particular way (or, preferably, explains "how" the poem means); then, the Marxist explains in terms of class struggle the meaning of the New Critic's interpretive statement.

Similarly, my psychoanalyst might explain in terms of Freudian categories why I insist on interpreting Wordsworth's poetry according to the canons of the New Criticism. Then, as part of my resistance to the analysis, I might criticize my analyst from a Jungian perspective for failing to get beyond the limitations of his Freudian categories. Thus, one interpretive system can be bracketed by another, and that by another, and so on.

A corollary of this phenomenon of bracketing is that a text can appear either as content for interpretation or as the articulation of an interpretive system. For example, I might initially interpret Kant's *Critique of Pure Reason* as content, in terms of the categories of Aristotelian logic. Later, I might interpret cosmological or theological concepts in terms of Kant's system. An interpretive system can itself be interpreted.

The structure of interpretation I have been describing is the structure I associate with the interpretation of nonprivileged (noncanonical) texts. This structure of interpretation makes several assumptions. First, it assumes that the interpretive statement is a more or less adequate sign of the interpretant itself (i.e., the sign chain of the interpreter's consciousness). Then, it assumes that there is always something more in the interpretant than the representative function of the sign. There is always some residue of the idiosyncrasies of the interpreter (what Peirce would call the material quality or the pure demonstrative application of the sign), or some artifact of the interpretive system itself. Those impurities, superadded to or even distortive of the meaning of the text, are what one is trying to get at when one asks, What is the meaning of this interpretive statement? The question means to ask, To what extent does the interpretive statement succeed in becoming an adequate substitute for the text? Even the interpreter, by putting the interpretation forward as an adequate articulation of the text, projects this process of further interpretation. That is, the interpreter projects the interpretive statement as a substitute for the text for subsequent interpretants.

But this question about the meaning of the interpretive statement can itself be answered only in terms of some particular interpretive system, and so the whole process seems to imply an endless bracketing of one interpretive system by another. If everyone were agreed on which interpretive system to use, the question What does this interpretive statement mean? would make no sense except as a request for clarification, an attempt to clear the noise out of the system. But people do not agree, and so the bracketing happens. There might sometimes be circlings back to earlier interpretive systems, as when one looks up a word in the dictionary, and then looks up the words in that definition, and so on, until one returns to a word one has already looked up. But in this structure of interpretation there is always the assumption, even on the part of the interpreter, that the text is taken up, "mastered," by the interpretation. There is always something in the structure of the interpretation itself besides the representative function of the sign. There is the text, and there is that which masters it. The interpretation masters the text, and then another interpretation masters the interpretive statement, and so on.

But what about the texts that master the interpreter? Peirce's hypothesis is that human beings can sometimes know the real as it really is, although human beings cannot be certain in any particular case that this is happening. But suppose that it does happen in the case of interpreting a particular text. That would mean that the representative function of the signs—the only thing that can stand in the long run, that can be real, given the nature of human consciousness as semiosis—would be all that there is in the interpretant thought of the interpreter. The sign that is the interpreter would be completely absorbed, as it were, in the sign that is the text. The reality of the sign that is the text is the representative function of the text as it is destined to appear to the indefinitely future community of rational minds. The interpreter would know the reality of the self as sign by knowing the reality of the text as sign. In short, the interpreter would know the text as the object of ascetic experience.

Now, suppose further that this interpreter, for some purpose or other, writes an interpretive statement. This interpretive statement must be underwritten by some interpretive system: New Criticism, Marxist or Freudian criticism, or whatever. But since the interpretive statement is not the same as the text, it cannot be adequate to the text; there is no question of its substituting for the text. At most, its writing is a kind of gesture toward the ascetic experience of the text, an exercise designed to help create or reproduce that experience.

Now I ask, What is the meaning of the interpretive statement? I cannot go about answering that question the way I did before. By hypothesis the interpretive statement is thought not to be adequate to the interpretant thought, and there is nothing in the interpretant thought except what is real, namely the representative function of the complex sign that is the text. All that I can do to answer the question is to translate the interpretive statement into another system of signs. And when I do that, my answer will sound just like—indeed, will be—another interpretive statement about the text.

Before, when the Marxist was asked about the meaning of the New Critic's interpretive statement, the Marxist answered by accounting for the statement in terms of the New Critic's political opinions. The goal of the Marxist, in other words, was to explain why the New Critic produced a certain kind of interpretive statement. Suppose, though, that the Marxist now wants something different. The Marxist wants to understand the ascetic experience of the New Critic. Then, the Marxist might find it helpful to translate the New Critical statement about the text into a Marxist vocabulary. In other words, the Marxist would answer the question about the meaning of the New Critic's statement by explaining the connection between the categories of the New Criticism and the categories of Marxism. The way to do that is to compare the results of applying the two sets of categories to the particular text. The Marxist understands the interpretive statement of the New Critic by translating it into Marxist categories, and in order to do that, the Marxist must refer to his or her own experience of the text.

Marvell says, "Annihilating all that's made / To a green thought in a green shade," and the New Critic points to the paradox in the word *green*. The Marxist might translate this interpretive statement by saying that green becomes a symbol of the paradox of aristocracy, the economically powerful who become spiritually impotent because they consume without producing. (There are Marxists and New Critics, too, who would have subtler interpretations than any I have offered. I am being heavy-handed to make a point.) The Marxist here adapts the New Critical category of "paradox" by explicating it in terms of a Marxist vocabulary. That is how the Marxist explains what the New Critical interpretation means. But the resulting statement is indistinguishable from an interpretive statement about Marvell's poem. The Marxist is saying, as it were, "I understand what the New Critic is talking about, here. I put it a different way. But if you want to see the connection between my interpretive statement and that of the New Critic, you need to understand the text of the poem as both I and the New Critic understand it." Whatever "green" is in the poem (it is called by different names in different interpretive systems) is what underwrites the translation of the New Critical statement into the Marxist statement. In short, the text of the poem itself becomes the interpretive system in terms of which interpretive statements about the poem are interpreted. There is no endless bracketing of one interpretive system by another, but a constant return to the text considered as interpretive system, as a set of rules for translating its various interpretations into each other.

Nor does there even need to be a Marxist in the picture. The New Critic in interpreting the text as privileged already projects an infinite series of interpretive statements, all more or less inadequate to the text, and all connected with each other by the text considered as interpretive system. The text itself becomes a structure of relations that determines all of its possible interpretive statements to exist as translations of each other.

I want to argue that this is the structure of interpretation characteristic of interpreting privileged texts. To call a text "privileged" means that the text itself has been projected as the interpretive system that underwrites the connecting of all the various interpretive statements made about the text from the perspective of other interpretive systems. This is different from nonprivileged texts, which are always taken only as material for interpretation and never as themselves interpretive systems governing their own interpretations. With privileged texts, in inquiring into the meaning of interpretive statements about them, one arrives again and again at new interpretive statements about the texts themselves. In this sense, the privileged text is a kind of terminus of interpretation. It is precisely the limit where interpretation doubles back and interprets itself.

But of course my hypothetical Marxist could treat my hypothetical New Critic's interpretive statement in a more cavalier fashion. The Marxist need not accept the validity of, or even believe in, the New Critic's ascetic experience. The New Critic's interpretive statement has nothing particular in it to distinguish it from an interpretive statement not based on ascetic experience. Does privileging a text after all boil down to some inner feeling of the interpreter, inscrutable to others, that the interpreter has got it right? And if it all depends on some inner feeling of this sort, what about Wittgenstein's private-language argument?

My answer is that there are of course many kinds of behavior, verbal and otherwise, that can be adduced in trying to determine whether someone is privileging a text. Sometimes, in fact, analysis of my own behavior can inform me that I am privileging a text that I was unaware of privileging, or not privileging a text I thought had enormous authority. If I do not understand a line in Nahum Tate, I blame the problem on Tate and criticize him for unclarity. If I do not understand a line in Pope, I worry about it and work hard on it before I give up; and even after I give up, I am likely to attribute the lack of understanding to some deficiency on my own part. A conservative Christian might be able to give no reason for forbidding the ordination of women to the ministry, except to say that St. Paul seems to forbid it. The intensity of the Christian's struggle with the problem is then a sign of the privileging of the Pauline texts. Some biblical inerrantists, if I understand them, imply that it would be a devastating criticism of the Bible to show that some biblical texts are not scientifically and historically accurate—hence the concern of these inerrantists to maintain the scientific and historic accuracy of the holograph manuscripts. Such inerrantists by that implication demonstrate that the Bible is not being interpreted by them as a privileged text. For if the interpretive systems of modern natural science or historical scholarship are needed to produce or verify biblical interpretations, then there is never any moment when the interpretant thought is completely absorbed only in the biblical text. The privileged texts for such an inerrantist are, if anything, the scientific or historical texts, actual or virtual, that the inerrantist takes as normative. And so on. I shall have more to say later about verifying interpretations of privileged texts. But it seems clear that whether I am interpreting a text as privileged can usually be determined on more public grounds than my inner feelings.

Again, I am not considering here the question of why texts are privileged or the question of which texts should be privileged. Nor do I want to suggest that such questions are unimportant. I am trying only to articulate in terms of a theory of interpretive systems what is distinctive about the interpretation of privileged texts. By Peirce's doctrine of fallibilism, not even the interpreter can be certain that any particular interpretant thought is an ascetic experience of the reality of the text—that is, that any particular interpretant is what will stand in the long run. Nevertheless, to project the text itself as interpretive system is to create a distinctive structure of interpretation that is characteristic of the phenomenon of privileging.

The privileged or canonical texts of a culture are the ones that interpret themselves by governing the relations among the interpretive statements that grow up around them. They seem important enough to generate a multitude of interpretations in various modes, and thus seem universal enough to provide the right categories for interpreting the distinctive experiences of the culture. That is why it can seem plausible to say, for example, that the story of Western literature in the last two thousand years is the story of the Bible. A great deal of the history of Western civilization in the same period, similarly, can be construed as a struggle between the Bible and other texts.

I want to return now to the question with which I began, the question of scripture as the exemplary instance of the privileged text. How does the structure of interpretation that I have described work with scripture? The interpretation of a text as scripture is reflexive. Scripture interprets the interpretive statements about it by becoming the interpretive system through which different interpretive statements may be translated into each other. Scripture is therefore the interpretive system through which the interpreter in the moment of the interpretant thought may be understood as the interpreter really is—namely, as a sign. Scripture as interpretive system is also in a sense final, a terminus. Scripture itself underwrites all subsequent explanations of any interpretive statements.

I get into the hermeneutic circle in the first place by writing, say, some interpretive statement. That statement, by the exigencies of interpretive discourse, must be underwritten by some interpretive system—e.g., the historical-critical methodology, "form" or "source" criticism, "existential" categories, or even the concepts of literary criticism. This interpretive system, standing in a reciprocal relationship with the biblical passage considered as its content, allows me to articulate a meaning for the passage. But at the same time, if I am treating the passage as a privileged text (as scripture), I want to project the text itself as the interpretive system that explains the meaning of my own interpretive act by governing the relation between my interpretive statement and all subsequent interpretive statements that translate it accurately.

How does this work? How can scripture interpret interpretation? If I go elsewhere in scripture, for example, to find passages that seem to talk about interpretation, I shall have to interpret those passages before I can apply them to my situation, and I shall have to interpret them in terms of some sort of interpretive system that is not scripture itself. So the whole structure of thought would remain dependent on the interpretive system I happen to choose, and the final interpretive system, scripture itself, would ceaselessly elude me. I would know scripture always only as content. I would have power over it, as it were, the power of the interpretive system I unconsciously employ or consciously elect as a heuristic.

But this regress is avoided in the ascetic experience of a text. That is, a biblical text is interpreted as scripture when the meaning of the interpretant thought is taken to be identical to the meaning of the text. If I interpret the Song of Songs allegorically, for example, and say that it means the love of Christ for the Church, then I have articulated the meaning of a biblical passage, considered as content, in terms of some interpretive system (say, the interpretive system outlined by Augustine in *De doctrina christiana*). But to interpret the Song of Songs as scripture also involves the assertion that the meaning of my self in the moment of my interpretant thought is Christ's love for the Church. The interpretant thought is not taken to be something that can be articulated in terms of my personal psychology, or in terms of some current theory of interpretation. Instead, the interpretant thought is taken to mean precisely what the scriptural passage itself is taken to mean. My self in the moment of my interpretant thought makes sense only as a projection of Christ's love for the Church.

These words, "Christ's love for the Church," are no doubt poor, pale, and inadequate for expressing what I am trying to talk about. The words of the Song of Songs are normative. The words "Christ's love for the Church" are artifacts of my vocabulary and St. Augustine's interpretive system. But if I am going to write an interpretive statement at all, I have to use words different from the normative words of the biblical text. I might even find better words than Augustine's, someday, to serve as signs of the biblical text and of my interpretant thought. The important point is only that I take the meaning of the scriptural passage and the meaning of my interpretant thought to be the same, and the locus of that meaning to be in the scriptural text and not in myself.

Scripture thus becomes at once content and interpretive system. It is as if I assert, in interpreting a text as scripture, that the meaning of my existence in the moment of interpreting is exhausted in the meaning of the text. All that I usually think of as private concerns vanish, and I exist, as it were, only insofar as the meaning of the text comes to light in my interpretant thought. Thus the text has power over me. This surrender to the text in self-interpretation is different from the surrender and self-interpretation that Ricoeur describes as consisting in "imaginative variations" of the ego. The structure of my interpretation here implies that I have finally gotten to rock bottom, to the one real meaning of the interpretant thought that will stand in the long run because it is conscious of nothing but the representative function of the sign that constitutes it.

This characteristic structure of scriptural interpretation means that I can never fully articulate scripture as interpretive system. Any articulation is only as good as the subordinate interpretive system that lets me articulate the meaning of the text considered as content. If somebody asks me what a scriptural passage means, I have to answer in some vocabulary different from the vocabulary of the scriptural passage. This observation suggests how the opposition between "truth" and "method" need not have the force of a dilemma or even of a problem. If textual hermeneutics can, with privileged texts, be construed as an ascetic discipline, then "truth" refers to the ascetic experience of the text, whereas "method" refers to the mode of articulating that experience in interpretive statements. "Truth" is a concern at the level of the interpretant thought and awaits the judgment of the future community of rational minds. It is not that which can be shown to be so by "method." "Method" operates at the level of the interpretive statement and corresponds to Peirce's "methodeutic." What can be articulated is the relation between scripture and the various interpretive systems applied to it. It is pointless to ask whether the human studies aim at the practice of interpretation or at the understanding of that practice. It would be like asking whether the mystic aims at encountering God through the practice of prayer and fasting, or whether the mystic aims at the understanding of prayer and fasting through encountering God. If hermeneutics is taken as an ascetic discipline, the fundamental activity of the human studies—namely, making interpretive statements—presupposes both practice and understanding. "Truth" cannot be separated from practice, nor "method" from understanding.

The structure of interpretation that I have been describing is obviously not always found in the interpretation of literature. When I say that Wordsworth's hearing the "still, sad music of humanity" means that he contemplates human history, I am not necessarily prepared to assert that the meaning of my existence at the moment of my interpretant thought is also that Wordsworth contemplated human history. I would be more likely to say that the meaning of my interpretant thought is that I am committed to the study of poetry, or that I enjoy reading Wordsworth and have a certain affinity for him that enables me to understand him better than other critics do, or that I want to write an article or get a job. Whatever dispossession of the self occurs in my coming to understand a poem, I might still reserve a sense that the poem means "for me," and not that I mean for it. Within the opposition of scripture and literature, Ricoeur's term *appropriation* seems more accurate for literature than for scripture. I appropriate a poem, but scripture appropriates me.

But of course, it could work just the other way. Privileged literary works—even Wordsworth's poetry—or scientific or philosophical works achieve the status of scripture for some, by being interpreted as I have described. Sometimes literature is even put forward as scripture. Wallace Stevens's poetic project, for example, was to construct a "supreme fiction" that would satisfy modern man's religious impulse apart from the claims of religion. There is no logical necessity that prevents anyone from taking any text as scripture, just as there is no logical necessity that prevents anyone from taking the Bible as "mere" literature. But if the opposition between scripture and literature disappears, the opposition between privileged and nonprivileged texts is likely to reappear in other forms, as I have suggested: literary versus scientific, poetic versus prosaic, canonical versus noncanonical, and so on.

The structuralist and poststructuralist idea is that the relativity of canon demonstrates that privileging is *only* a historical, sociological, economic, etc., phenomenon. This idea arises from a disbelief in any absolute standards in terms of which to justify interpretive statements. No universally valid reasons can be given for the value judgments I make when I interpret texts, the argument goes; therefore, privileging is *only* something that a particular culture superadds to certain of the texts they interpret. Peirce's appeal to the judgment of the indefinitely future community, however, allows for the possibility of ascetic experience of the real, even if no certainty is possible and no justification of the experience is currently available. Peirce's semiotic provides a way of talking about the structure of interpretation such that any particular text can be identified as canonical for any particular interpreter, without getting into the question of whether any particular act of interpreting or canonizing is justified. The question of canon, in other words, need not turn on the question of justification. The problem is not to determine some objective difference between canonical and noncanonical texts, or to show, alternatively, that no such determination is possible. The problem is rather to articulate the structure of interpretation distinctive for a text taken as canonical.

Finally, I would like to sketch briefly the consequences for Ricoeur's hermeneutics of the theory of interpretive systems outlined here. First, it might be possible to assimilate Ricoeur's concept of "testimony" to the theory by saying that the reading of scripture is a kind of repetition of an event like the originary one that is "testified" to by the text. That is, just as that event is not given meaning but gives it, so scripture continues to give meaning to the event of interpretation itself. But the problem of true and false testimony remains. That is, the theory of interpretive systems does not tell all Christians what they really want to know about scripture. What some Christians want to know is how scripture should be interpreted and how they can tell which interpretations are correct. These questions would be the business of a "philosophical hermeneutic" such as Ricoeur envisions, where "philosophy" consists in the activity of providing rational justifications. But interpretation can be misguided or wrong. Everything depends upon the interpretive system used to articulate the meaning of the text, which is taken as the meaning of the interpretant thought. The only justifications currently available for any interpretive statement rest on that subordinate interpretive system. There is no certainty about or full knowledge of scripture as interpretive system.

There is another way to verify any particular interpretive statement—namely, by judging the correctness of what the interpretive statement says about one's own personal existence. The theory insists that a statement about the reality of a moment of one's consciousness (the interpretant thought) is implied whenever scripture is explicitly interpreted. But one can never judge the truth about one's consciousness at the moment. I know myself only through representations of what I have been in the past. So I can verify a scriptural interpretation, in a certain sense, by seeing how it works out in my life. I look back from a later vantage point, from which I think the patterns in my life have become more apparent to me, and I can sometimes judge how authentic an expression of my consciousness a particular act of interpretation was at a particular time. This is the beginning of an appeal to the indefinitely future community. The method of verification might be utterly compelling for me. It might even prompt me to make whatever personal claims on someone else I can make as a witness. But it still does not allow me to make rational claims, at least in the more limited sense of "rational" that guided Ricoeur's thought in the 1970s. All scripture thus has something of the quality of prophecy, which always remains more or less inscrutable until its fulfillment.

In short, the loci of possible arguments about scriptural interpretation are the particular interpretive systems that are brought to bear on scripture considered as content. The question is, then, Which interpretive systems? Neither the theory of interpretive systems nor Ricoeur's theory offers any clear way of adjudicating among self-consistent interpretive systems. The role of philosophy—in Ricoeur's sense—in such a situation is purely critical as opposed to productive. The most philosophy can do is to point out inconsistencies in any given interpretive system, lay bare the presuppositions of a given system, or confront the systems with one another to show how they are conceptually similar or different. A new interpretive system constructed by philosophy is just that, a new system, one among many, and without absolute claims.

It seems, then, that the theory of interpretive systems implies a notion different from Ricoeur's of the relationship between philosophy and hermeneutics. Specifically, one would have to give up the nostalgia for a philosophy that produces meaning from a text. Ricoeur himself perhaps moves in this direction in *Time and Narrative*. Peirce's notion of the rational as the real, taken together with his doctrine of fallibilism, implies an idea of philosophy that is radically different from the theory Ricoeur expounded in the 1970s. Philosophy is not in the business of justifying past statements or behaviors, but is instead in what might be called the empirical position—the position of remaining open to what the real will in fact turn out to be.

One would have to read as misguided Ricoeur's attempts to incorporate the insights of French structuralism. As Ricoeur himself seems to recognize at points, precisely to the extent that structuralism, a science of texts, can be incorporated into his theory, it ceases to be structuralism at all. Peirce would agree that the reality of the text is not necessarily the structures that generate it. Instead, the reality of the text is what the text will turn out to be in the interpretant thought of the indefinitely future community. Ricoeur himself comes close to saying this of historical texts, at least, in scattered passages of *Time and Narrative*. I think Ricoeur has accurately identified the central problematic of "Romanticist" hermeneutics. But the considerations taken up here suggest that Ricoeur's own hermeneutics will not be able to solve the problem fully.

These reflections suggest that it is possible to distinguish the interpretation of scripture from the interpretation of literature, without multiplying entities by adding categories such as the "wager." Similar arguments apply, mutatis mutandis, in distinguishing any kind of privileged text from nonprivileged texts. But making such distinctions has meant giving up Ricoeur's central program of the 1970s. It has meant accepting scripture (or any privileged text) as mysterious, as the text in which the interpreter is most aware of being interpreted and in which the interpreter's pretensions to know through interpreting come to least. Whether Ricoeur himself really wants to banish the mysterious from the realm of interpretation is another, and perhaps larger, question. But the internal paradoxes in Ricoeur's theory already suggest that the distinction between privileged and nonprivileged texts loses its theoretical force precisely to the extent that philosophy as justification is placed at the heart of hermeneutics.

5

The Corpse in the Iron Lung

1. The Pragmatics of Literary Education

I have argued that it makes sense to think of textual hermeneutics as an ascetic discipline. Then, the various "approaches" to texts, the applications of various interpretive systems, appear as so many exercises of the discipline. Textual hermeneutics itself becomes the broad interpretive system that subsumes the various approaches in just that way. The various approaches constitute a structure of differential relations, each approach being defined by its position with respect to all the others. Had I chosen to look at interpretation from some other perspective (for example, the perspective of the biologist, or of the Marxist, or of the Freudian psychologist), everything would have looked different. But in this chapter, I want to draw out some further implications of the perspective I have chosen. I want to make clearer some of the practical consequences of thinking of textual hermeneutics as an ascetic discipline.

If for no other reason, I want to do that because I am trying to be a good Peircean pragmatist. An early formulation of Peirce's pragmatism appeared in his essay "How To Make Our Ideas Clear" (*Popular Science Monthly*, 1878). Peirce gives the following rule for attaining "clearness of apprehension": ". . . consider what effects, which might conceivably have practical bearings, we conceive the object of our conception to have. Then, our conception of these effects is the whole of our conception of the object" (*W*, 124). Peirce repeated this definition in a 1905 essay for *The Monist* (*B*, 259). I think the definition will sit better with other things Peirce says if one supposes that by *object* here Peirce means not a Cartesian or a Kantian object, but instead a particular place in the triadic sign relation. The definition implies that if I want to understand what it means to conceive textual hermeneutics as an ascetic discipline, I need to consider the practical effects of conceiving textual hermeneutics that way. What particular behaviors would the ascetic discipline of textual hermeneutics bring about?

It also seems inevitable that someone who has come this far with me will say, "Yes, we *can* think of textual hermeneutics as an ascetic discipline, but so what? Why would we *want* to think of it that way, to the exclusion of all the other rich, various, and less dour ways of thinking of it?" Talking about practical effects is the only way to meet the pragmatic spirit of such objections.

The practical effects I am interested in here have to do with education, and specifically with so-called higher education. In this culture there is something called reading for pleasure, which most teachers of literature hope that all of their students will do all of their lives. And there is a "literary criticism" (in the form, for example, of book reviews in newspapers) that is considered as an adjunct to this activity of reading for pleasure. For better or for worse, these are thought of as leisure activities for everybody except those who get their livings by producing the books or the reviews.

But there is also a deadly serious reading and a deadly serious criticism. The activities become deadly serious precisely when they are considered as educative in some way—in practice, when these activities feed into or arise out of what is done in the universities. Certainly, literary cultures or cults often arise in the first place in isolation from or in hostility toward the universities. But the way people know that an author is being taken seriously is that the author is being studied, that the author's work has been taken up in the all-important work of education, which is all that stands between civilization and barbarism. And anyway, I am by vocation a college professor of literature. Naturally, I am obsessed by what I do for a living, namely "teaching texts." I want to keep my deadly serious work from becoming deadly in any other sense.

Just because there is something called reading for pleasure, there can also be a thing called teaching texts that sometimes appears to have little or nothing to do with pleasure. Teaching texts is a practical (one might also say "moral" or "ethical") activity with social effects. For the Marxist, for example, who judges every practical activity under its political aspect, teaching texts is political action. John Dewey, one of the philosophers of education whose thought will be important in this chapter, made decisions about education on the basis of what seemed to him right for a democratic society. Richard Rorty, another philosopher whose ideas I examine, in some sense attempts to extend certain of Dewey's insights into the undiscovered realm beyond poststructuralism. Rorty judges the social uses of texts on the basis of a notion of the contemporary liberal, the heir of nineteenth-century liberalism, who has bought out of the foundationalism of traditional Western philosophy and has become what Rorty calls a liberal ironist.

Both Dewey and Rorty think of themselves as pragmatists, but not exactly Peircean pragmatists. As elsewhere in this book, I want to continue to follow the thread of Peirce's thought. That will mean at a certain point confronting Peirce's ideas with the pragmatic tradition that has come to its full development in Rorty's writings. I hope to clarify the notion of textual hermeneutics as an ascetic discipline by contrasting it with different pragmatic notions about the educative uses of texts.

Three sets of opposed terms will come up again and again in what follows. They are (1) the opposition between the text and interpretive statements about the text, (2) the opposition between public and private uses of the text, and (3) the opposition between truth considered as accuracy of representation and truth considered as a property that a proposition has of being socially warranted.

These oppositions are problematic in a discussion of textual hermeneutics and education. The last opposition, for example, is especially important in Rorty's writing. Rorty argues that at least since Plato, Western philosophy has been dominated by a notion of "truth" that depends on a visual metaphor. The mind is a mirror, and its business is to know, which means accurately to reflect the objects before it. Rorty's story of Western philosophy is a story of successive attempts to find some representation that human beings can be certain is accurate, and on which they can then found a philosophy that will adjudicate truth by assessing the accuracy of all other representations. The story ends, in effect, with Nietzsche, Dewey, Heidegger, and the later Wittgenstein. Their reflections eventually produce the conclusion that truth is not a matter of accuracy of representation, but a matter of what people can get away with asserting. Only propositions can be true or false; what is true is what is "warranted assertible" in the language game.

This opposition between the two notions of truth looms large in my discussion, also. To say that the ascetic discipline of textual hermeneutics aims at total absorption in the real might seem to mean lapsing back into the whole melee of philosophical problems associated with the notion of truth as accurate representation. Am I not saying—is Peirce not saying—that the business of the knowing mind is to reflect accurately some "object" that is "before" it? I think this is a very complicated question, but I think the answer is ultimately that Peirce and I are not saying that. Specifically, considering textual hermeneutics as an ascetic discipline is not equivalent to considering the text as substance standing over against the substance of a mind whose business is to represent that object accurately. I shall try to show how Peirce's semiotic avoids that sort of Cartesian talk. Whatever I am doing when I teach texts, I am not making them into objects of knowledge in that sense.

The opposition between private and public is also important to Rorty. He maintains a sharp distinction between the private and the public uses of texts because he wants to like and to talk about the works of authors such as Derrida. Some writers produce works that enlarge the liberal ironist's perspective, extend the range of the "us" as opposed to the "them," and make it harder to be cruel to others. These works obviously have an important public function. But talking about Derrida presents a problem. Does the relativism implied in Derrida and other such authors mean that there is no public function left for their texts to perform? Rorty takes the line that writers such as Derrida and Proust write to achieve private autonomy, to achieve themselves by reshaping the philosophical or autobiographical past. That project is what there is to like and to talk about in their texts.

Rorty's question about the exact relation between private and public uses of texts is also a question for textual hermeneutics considered as ascetic discipline. Some people might want to consider an ascetic discipline as a strictly private matter; but then what can one say about teaching texts? Education is at least normally thought of as a public, social activity. To answer questions such as these, I shall ultimately have to look at the distinction between public and private in a way rather different from Rorty's.

Finally, it is obvious that the work of teaching and studying texts involves hearing, speaking, reading, and writing interpretive statements. Some talented teachers appear to convey a great deal about texts by simply reading them aloud, but nobody stops with that. College courses do not consist in merely handing students books and telling them to read. Vast libraries of interpretive statements come into existence presumably in aid of the "serious" study of texts.

What these interpretive statements are, however, is problematic. What is their relation to the texts they interpret? Some are presented as more or less drab substitutes for the texts. Some are deliberate or unwitting "deconstructive" wrenchings of texts from their original contexts in order to serve some particular purposes of the interpreter. Sometimes for educative purposes no clear distinction is made between texts and interpretive statements. Perhaps the interpretive statements are thought to perform whatever educative function the texts themselves can perform. Only, the interpretive statements perform it more easily, being written in a more up-to-date idiom or a more "ordinary" language. (A "street version" of *Hamlet* advertised some years ago—Hamlet on Yorick, if memory serves: "He my main man, Horatio. He save my ass many times.")

It is obvious, then, that there are texts and interpretive statements. What is not so obvious is exactly how interpretive statements figure in teaching texts when textual hermeneutics is conceived as an ascetic discipline. I have suggested before that reading, writing, speaking, and hearing interpretive statements are the particular exercises of the ascetic discipline. What I want to do in this essay, among other things, is to unfold the practical consequences of that notion for the process of education called teaching texts.

Now I want to examine in more detail the opposition between texts and interpretive statements. There is an account of "teaching texts" that perhaps no one really holds to, or holds to for long, and which I will call the naive account. In this account, the text is supposed to be an object of knowledge; and the method of communicating that knowledge is to translate the text into a more familiar idiom: to provide an interpretive statement in the form of a gloss or a paraphrase. That, the story goes, is what teachers of texts do. Certain interpretive statements can then be used to substitute for the text for various purposes—for example, for purposes of comparing texts: "In *Richard II* Shakespeare shows that self-indulgent aestheticism is ill-suited to the kingly character, and in *Henry V* he shows that a certain emotional coldness is necessary to the ruler." The text and the interpretive statement are related as two different currencies are related. There is the currency of, say, the Elizabethan drama, and there is the currency of modern critical discourse. Exchanging the interpretive statement for the text enables the text to enter, as it were, a foreign economy.

But one confusion in the naive account is already obvious. What is being *communicated*, strictly speaking, is not the text, but the interpretive statement. In fact, teachers of texts who operate on the assumptions of the naive account must give their students multiple-choice examinations or passages to identify to make sure that the students have "read the text" instead of just dutifully noting down the teacher's interpretive statements or relying on a pony. It is hard to say, then, in what sense "teaching texts" is going on. "Teaching interpretive statements" seems more accurate. By the naive account, not the texts but the interpretive statements enter into relations with each other and the contemporary situation, and thus have "meaning."

Considering the language game is instructive here. Speakers of English talk about "studying rocks," "studying plants," "studying stars," and "studying texts," as if texts were self-subsistent objects to be known like other objects. But speakers of English normally do not talk about "teaching rocks," "teaching plants," or "teaching stars." Instead, they talk about "teaching geology," "teaching botany," and "teaching astronomy." That is, what is taught is a system of propositions about rocks, plants, or stars. Speakers of English do, however, talk about "teaching texts," as if texts were now somehow different from rocks, plants, and stars, and like geology, botany, and astronomy. And of course, texts are different from natural objects in the (perhaps trivial) sense that most of them consist mostly of propositions or virtual propositions. So what is taught—interpretive statements—is the same kind of stuff as the presumed object of knowledge. But that is neither here nor there from the perspective of textual hermeneutics. From that perspective, rocks, plants, and stars are also text-like in every crucial respect.

My point about the language game is that it embodies or perhaps creates the confusion that makes the naive account of teaching texts naive. On the one hand, the language game allows "studying texts" on the model of "studying rocks," and so texts appear as legitimate objects of knowledge separate from whatever system of propositions is applied to them. On the other hand, the language game also allows "teaching texts" on the model of "teaching geology," so that texts appear continuous with the system of interpretive propositions. And now one wants to lapse back into all the metaphysical debates about the true ontological status of texts. The naive account of "teaching texts" is marked by its inevitable slide into this question. The question is unanswerable, in the sense that it must be answered, if at all, within some interpretive system, and different interpretive systems imply different answers.

If a distinction between the text and the interpretive statement is preserved, then, the naive account is hard-pressed to give a clear sense to the notion of "teaching texts." By this account, there is really no satisfactory answer to students' perennial question: "Well, if that's what the author meant, why didn't the author *say* it that way?" The only answer that the naive account provides is the answer of cultural differences: "That's how dramatists wrote in the seventeenth century." Students are only sometimes sophisticated enough to take the next logical step, and ask why the seventeenth-century text is still needed, if good modern translations are available. Versions of this argument do tend to arise when students rebel against foreign-language requirements. Why not just keep on producing good modern versions of the old classics, and let the texts themselves repose in libraries for the sole use of the scholars and poets who will keep the translations up to date?

If questions of this sort do come up, the response is usually of the form that Shakespeare's English is richer, more meaningful, and generally better than that of the modern critic, as anyone can see by means of a detailed comparison of Shakespeare's lines with any modern paraphrase. To make this answer abandons the naive account. "Better" in what sense? Surely for contemporary purposes, because these are the only purposes that people have now. But now what is the function of the interpretive statement? It is no longer to be a substitute for the seventeenth-century text in the contemporary economy, because Shakespeare's text is somehow "better" than the interpretive statement in the contemporary economy, too. One would not justify the preservation of the dollar by explaining how it works better than the yen in the Japanese economy.

The interpretive statement now appears to be only a way of helping the student on to the text itself, a gesture toward the text, and the naive account breaks down entirely. The student is not "studying texts" as objects of knowledge, where the knowledge is what is codified in a system of interpretive statements. So much for "studying texts" as one "studies rocks." Nor is the teacher "teaching texts" the way one "teaches geology." It is apparently indifferent what system of interpretive statements is used, so long as the student is helped on toward the text itself.

I am circling back to the position staked out earlier: namely, that textual hermeneutics can be conceived as an ascetic discipline, and that applying some particular interpretive system to texts is an exercise of the discipline. But as I have said before, teaching texts does not consist in handing books to students and observing their rapt contemplation of the representative function of the signs. Interpretive statements are used somehow. The breakdown of the naive account implies that the goal of teaching texts is not just that students get knowledge of texts on the model of getting knowledge of rocks. Knowledge in this sense is something gotten within some particular interpretive system. No more does anyone want to say that the goal is just knowledge of interpretive statements. As much as I admire the critical works of Kittredge, if forced to choose, I would rather read Chaucer and Shakespeare.

What is going on, then? I will argue, once again, that Peirce's insights can help. Here is Peirce, writing in the Johns Hopkins University Circular (1882) on the subject of a "liberal education":

> This is the age of Methods; and the university which is to be the exponent of the living condition of the human mind must be the university of methods....
>
> Now although a man needs not the theory of a method in order to apply it as it has been applied already, yet in order to

adapt to his own science the method of another with which he is less familiar, and to properly modify it so as to suit it to its new use, an acquaintance with the principles upon which it depends will be of the greatest benefit. For that sort of work a man needs to be more than a specialist; he needs such a general training of his mind and such knowledge as shall show him how to make his powers most effective in a new direction. That knowledge is logic. (W, 336–37)

As everywhere in this book, I would here adapt (distort) Peirce's statement by saying, "Not logic, but hermeneutics." I want to connect "method" here with "methodeutic," the third branch of Peirce's theory of semiotic, the branch also called "speculative rhetoric"—the study of how intelligences connect signs.

It is possible to argue that one should not even try to answer the question, When one studies or teaches texts, what is the object of study or teaching? Maybe *object* is misleading here because of its metaphysical freight. But if one has to answer the question, I want to argue, one should say that the object of study or teaching is the method of connecting the signs of the text with the signs of the interpretive statements about the text. In other words, the object of study and teaching is the interpretive system.

But of course, one cannot study or teach interpretive systems just as abstract codifications of interpretive practice. Constructing such an abstract codification means only to apply a second interpretive system to the first. I have argued before that interpretive systems stand in a reciprocal relation with the texts they interpret; and if that is so, then interpretive systems cannot be understood apart from the interpretive practices they underwrite and in which, ultimately, they fail. The interpretive system becomes accessible through the interpretive statements and interpretive problems it produces. Thus, conceiving the teaching of texts as methodeutic clears up the confusion in the naive account about the relation between texts and interpretive statements. One studies the interpretive system by comparing the systems of signs that it connects.

Texts that are taught, moreover, texts that are thought to have an educative function, are texts that the culture privileges. They are the texts that the culture wants to become canonical texts also for the young. Other texts that are taught appear in the service of the canonical texts. Bad poems are read as foils to good poems; dull historical records are read as buttressing some canonical narrative. Even the "ironist" Rorty identifies "heroes" of his book, thus implying that there are philosophical victims of circumstance for the heroes to rescue, if not actually villains for them to defeat. The educative path to ascetic experience of these canonical texts, to their privileging for the individual, is the exercise of the interpretive system. This exercise involves a clear consciousness of the difference between the text and its interpretive statements.

So regarding textual hermeneutics as ascetic discipline eases some of the confusion of the naive account of teaching texts. It offers an answer of sorts to the question about the object of study. But the naive account is, after all, naive. There are other accounts, perhaps less naive, of how and why people might teach texts. Some of these accounts would advertise themselves as pragmatic in the line, though not in the mode, of Peirce. I would like to turn now to some of Dewey's ideas about education.

2. Dewey on Education

Two of Dewey's books concern me here. The first is the influential *Democracy and Education: An Introduction to the Philosophy of Education* (1916); the second is the later *Experience and Education* (1938), in which Dewey attempts to trim back some of the follies and excesses of the "progressive" educators who were influenced by the earlier book. In both books Dewey seems most concerned with education in public elementary and secondary schools. But he does recognize explicitly that different ways of presenting subject matter are appropriate to students of different ages (e.g., *EE*, 87), and he presents his reflections as a general theory of education. In fact, he goes so far as to define philosophy in terms of education: "If we are willing to conceive education as the process of forming fundamental dispositions, intellectual and emotional, toward nature and fellow men, philosophy may even be defined *as the general theory of education*" (*DE*, 383).

For Dewey, to live is to grow, and education is growing: "Since growth is the characteristic of life, education is all one with growing; it has no end beyond itself" (*DE*, 59). Growing, or education, means "that reconstruction or reorganization of experience which adds to the meaning of experience, and which increases ability to direct the course of subsequent experience" (*DE*, 89–90). Dewey connects the notion of "meaning" with the word *means*, as in "a *means* of doing something." He identifies his theory as "pragmatic" (*DE*, 400). His pragmatism emerges especially in his tendency to explain the meaning of a thing in terms of its use:

> . . . it is the characteristic use to which the thing is put, because of its specific qualities, which supplies the meaning with which it is identified. . . . When things have a meaning for us, we *mean* (intend, propose) what we do. . . . To have an *idea* of a thing is thus not just to get certain sensations from it. It is to be able to respond to the thing in view of its place in an inclusive scheme of action; it is to foresee the drift and probable consequence of the action of the thing upon us and of our action upon it. (*DE*, 35–36)

Thus, to add to the meaning of experience—the business of education—is to bring about "the increased perception of the connections and continuities of the activities in which we are engaged" (*DE*, 90; see also *EE*, 43). Mind itself "as a concrete thing is precisely the power to understand things in terms of the use made of them . . ." (*DE*, 39). John E. Smith points out that Dewey's insistence on seeing the human being as "a creature whose life can best be described in terms of public and objective relations with an environing medium, natural as well as cultural," puts Dewey at odds with "the empiricism of the British tradition," its "reliance upon sensation and the private mind in which sensations must reside" (Smith, 119).

So the goal of education is the improvement of experience present and future. The student should get as much as possible from every present experience—extract its "full meaning"—in order to be prepared for "doing the same thing in the future" (*EE*, 51).

Dewey's commitment to democracy depends on his conviction that a democratic society is best suited to improving the quality of experience of its individual members (*EE*, 26; see also *DE*, 305, 369). It is best suited because it is "more than a form of government; it is primarily a mode of associated living, of conjoint communicated experience" (*DE*, 101). Democracy "stands in principle for free interchange" (*DE*, 401). A democratic society best fulfills two ideals of social life: the interests of the group are shared to a large extent by all of its members, and the group interacts fully and freely with other groups (*DE*, 115).

Democracy promotes communication. And "To be a recipient of a communication is to have an enlarged and changed experience" (*DE*, 6). Here is Dewey's vital connection between education and politics. The increment of meaning that accrues when one grows represents an improvement in the quality of present experience and a potential for better experiences in the future. But meaning is not created ex nihilo. It accrues as part of a *situation,* and for human beings that situation is always to some degree a *social* situation. Humans are gregarious animals. Communication, a social phenomenon, makes it possible for individuals to have better experiences, to give things meanings, by cultivating the "power to join freely and fully in shared or common activities. This is impossible without culture," and "there is perhaps no better definition of culture than that it is the capacity for constantly expanding the range and accuracy of one's perceptions of meanings" (*DE*, 144–45).

If study of the humanities is identified with the study of texts, then the closest Dewey comes to discussing the humanities explicitly in these books is to mention "literature." At that, he lumps literature together with the "fine arts," which are "of peculiar value because they represent appreciation at its best—a heightened realization of meaning through selection and concentration" (*DE*, 292). But, Dewey hastens to add, *every* subject of study at some point should have "an aesthetic quality" (*DE*, 292). Literary art in particular "furnishes the supreme successes in stating of experiences so that they are vitally significant to others" (*DE*, 266). But elsewhere, Dewey expresses some residual hostility toward the classical "liberal" (that is, literary) education (e.g., *DE*, 301ff.) and the medieval inculcation of text-based "authority" (e.g., *EE*, 108), and argues that the scientific method, far from being opposed to "humanism," is in fact the highest expression of it: "Whatever natural science may be for the specialist, for educational purposes it is the knowledge of the conditions of human action" (*DE*, 267).

Language itself in Dewey's pragmatism is just a way of getting things done. It has "unrivaled significance as a means of social direction," but it works only because it "takes place upon a background of coarser and more tangible use of physical means to accomplish results" (*DE*, 39). Even reading, writing, and figuring involve the muscles (*DE*, 166–67). The word becomes a "sign of the activity into which it enters," and "its meaning depends upon connection with a shared experience" (*DE*, 18). In other words, for Dewey language is a particularly useful behavior among other behaviors. He does not seem to think that consciousness is linguistic all the way down, though he does think it is situational all the way down, for "mind" has no meaning apart from contexts of possible physical activity.

It might be possible to extrapolate from these remarks a function in Dewey's scheme for the teaching of texts. Texts preserve and communicate experiences of high quality, and the teacher is attempting to improve the students' experiences by helping them appreciate the best that has been said and thought. This Arnoldian project would distinguish the humanities from the sciences, and in fact Dewey sometimes talks as though he wants to do that: "Aesthetic formulation reveals and enhances the meaning of experiences one already has; scientific formulation supplies one with tools for constructing new experiences with transformed meanings" (*DE*, 266).

But if one takes this last statement quite strictly, it is hard to see how it fits with Dewey's general position. To reveal or enhance the meaning of an experience would presumably be to show new uses for the elements of that experience, or to show how that experience considered as a whole might figure in relation to subsequent experiences. How would that be different from supplying "tools for constructing new experiences with transformed meanings"? When I say that understanding a poem by Keats reveals or enhances the meaning of my past experiences, is that not pragmatically just the same as saying that I now see ways in which my subsequent experiences will be different or better? Where Dewey defines his pragmatism, he seems to obliterate the distinction between knowing something about the past and proposing something for the future: "While the content of knowledge is what *has* happened, . . . the *reference* of knowledge is future or prospective. For knowledge furnishes the means of understanding or giving meaning to what is still going on and what is to be done" (*DE*, 397).

In fact, in other places Dewey seems to want to erase any firm line between *studying* the sciences and *studying* anything else:

> I am aware that the emphasis I have placed upon scientific method may be misleading, for it may result only in calling up the special techniques of laboratory research as that is conducted by specialists. But the meaning of the emphasis placed upon scientific method has little to do with specialized techniques. It means that scientific method is the only authentic means at our command for getting at the significance of our everyday experiences of the world in which we live. It means that scientific method provides a working pattern of the way in which and conditions under which experiences are used to lead ever onward and outward. (*DE*, 111–12)

It might be more faithful to the general tenor of Dewey's argument, then, to try to assimilate the studying of texts to the scientific method as Dewey understands it. And anyway, suppose one did think that the teaching of texts consists simply in telling students "what the texts say" about past experiences. Then, the interpretive statements about the texts would appear once again as glosses or paraphrases, substitutes for the text. One would be back in what I have called the naive account of teaching texts, with all of its confusions. Dewey's notion of knowledge as produced by the scientific method is richer and more sophisticated.

In its most general sense, for Dewey, the scientific method is identical with what he calls thinking: "the accurate and deliberate instituting of connections between what is done and its consequences" (*DE*, 177). Thinking includes the following stages, which will be more or less familiar to any parent of a public-school child who has been abused with a rigid codification of Dewey's thought: "the sense of a problem, the observation of conditions, the formation and rational elaboration of a suggested conclusion, and the active experimental testing" (*DE*, 177). Dewey expands the list in explaining how the essentials of educational method are "identical with the essentials of reflection":

> They are first that the pupil have a genuine situation of experience—that there be a continuous activity in which he is interested for its own sake; secondly, that a genuine problem develop within this situation as a stimulus to thought; third, that he possess the information and make the observations needed to deal with it; fourth, that suggested solutions occur to him which he shall be responsible for developing in an orderly way; fifth, that he have opportunity and occasion to test his ideas by application, to make their meaning clear and to discover for himself their validity. (*DE*, 192)

I have the sense here that Dewey is talking mainly about elementary and secondary pupils, but of course the "essentials of reflection" would be the same for anybody.

The consistent application of the scientific method results in "the progressive development of what is already experienced into a fuller and richer and also more organized form, a form that gradually approximates that in which subject-matter is presented to the skilled, mature person" (*DE*, 87). The characteristic of this form of organization is that it is *logical*. A farmer has practical knowledge of when to plant and when to pluck up, a knowledge of the relation of means to ends. But a scientist has knowledge of how things stand in a whole "cognitive system" (*DE*, 261): "The ideal of scientific organization is, therefore, that every conception and statement shall be of such a kind as to follow from others and to lead to others. Concepts and propositions mutually imply and support one another" (*DE*, 224).

I think it is possible to assimilate studying texts to Dewey's notion of the scientific method, to conceive of a science of texts. Then, the teaching of texts would be like the teaching of science. In college courses, for example, there might be some "doing" (like laboratory work) combined with some organized "telling" (lecture). One difficult task of the teacher of texts would be to decide how much of each is appropriate in particular situations. The point of conceiving such a science of texts would be to clear up the confusions of the naive account. In a science of texts, the relation between texts and interpretive statements would be like the relation between rocks and geology, or between stars and astronomy. Instead of being confusingly thought of as substitutes for their texts, the interpretive statements would form a cognitive system of concepts and propositions constituting organized knowledge about the texts. Dewey's pragmatism also avoids the problem of thinking of the meaning of texts as fixed and unitary, something "objective," eternal, and ahistorical set over against the mirroring mind. In Dewey's account, the meaning of a text would be the uses to be made of it. As the cognitive system develops, new goals and purposes appear, and old goals and purposes are seen in a different light. This is clear from the example of science. Getting closer to ends that have already been visualized is a "minor form" of progress. "More important modes of progress consist in enriching prior purposes and in forming new ones" (*DE*, 261). And if the meaning of something is what it is a means to accomplish, then the meaning of texts would be constantly changing, developing in new directions as new purposes were conceived.

The studying and teaching of texts could be matched with the stages in the scientific method, as follows. First, the "genuine situation of experience" must contain a genuine interest in reading texts as part of a "continuous activity" in which the student is interested "for its own sake." Some people might observe that this interest in reading texts seems to be missing from some students, but that point does not tell against the conception of a possible science of texts. A student who is totally uninterested in light bulbs or lightning bolts might lack the "genuine situation of experience" that would make it possible for that student to learn physics. This is only to say that the uninterested are the ineducable.

In the case of texts, the "genuine problem" that develops to serve as a "stimulus to thought" would presumably be the student's sense of failing to understand some particular text. The student is unable to paraphrase the text, or is unable to locate its referent, or is unable to explain how its parts fit together, and so on. The "information" and "observations" needed to deal with the problem might be almost anything, depending on the problem itself and how the student is disposed or directed to approach problems of that general type. Maybe the student looks up words in a dictionary, or consults a biography of the author or an encyclopedia of poetics, or looks for patterns of imagery, or counts metrical feet, or reads a history book, or listens to a lecture. Then, presumably, "suggested solutions" occur in the form of hypotheses about the meaning of the text. Like all hypotheses, these imply methods of verification or falsification. If, for example, a poem is thought to be about some particular love affair, then one would expect the date of composition to be sometime after the beginning of the love affair. Anyone who wants to interpret Shakespeare's sonnets by identifying some particular woman as the "Dark Lady" is obliged to marshal quantities of historical evidence. And so on.

But that sort of test is not the only test that interpretations are put to. Dewey talks about testing ideas by "application, to make their meaning clear." What would it mean to "apply" a hypothesis about the meaning of a text? What would correspond here to applying, say, the hypothesis that oxygen is essential to combustion, by attempting to burn a candle in an atmosphere of carbon dioxide? I think "application" here could mean only trying to get other readers to assent to one's interpretive statement. That is, very simply, one sees whether other readers nod, or make certain sounds or marks denoting agreement, when one speaks or writes the interpretive statement. That is the same as getting others to agree on what use is to be made of the text in question. A group of interpreters—a so-called interpretive community—agrees to use Wordsworth's "Intimations Ode" as an expression of late Christian neo-Platonism, or agrees to use Brecht's *Mutter Courage* as a Marxist manifesto, or agrees to use Descartes's *Meditations* as a crisis in the story of Western philosophy. These agreements can be formulated in technical terminology appropriate to the particular discipline. Agreements that are wide enough and have been around long enough can be put together into a cognitive system of logically connected concepts and propositions, which can then in the case of mature students be served up whole in lectures. Then, there would be a science of texts, consisting of interpretive statements organized in a cognitive system, that did not make the mistake of confusing interpretive statements with texts, or the mistake of thinking that the meaning of texts—the truth about them—is somehow separate from the uses that human beings make of the texts.

So what is wrong with a Deweyan science of texts, from my perspective? In one way, nothing at all. As long as one is operating within the boundaries of a particular interpretive system, and knows it, the notion of a science of texts makes good sense. I have argued that the only way to understand interpretive systems and therefore interpretation is from within, by operating, as it were, some particular interpretive system. It is a ticklish question exactly where in the educative process the teacher of texts should begin asking the students to push beyond the boundaries of the interpretive system and to study interpretive systems as such. It is also true that some interpretive systems themselves regard truth about texts not in a Deweyan way, but instead as accurate representation. In the historical method advocated by E. D. Hirsch, Jr., for example, the "meaning" of a text is distinguished from its "significance." The business of the interpreter is first accurately to represent the author's "willed type" that Hirsch identifies with meaning, and only then, if ever, to discuss the significance of the text as the uses that can be made of it. And some Anglo-American New Critics might say that the business of interpretation is accurately to represent the objective logical or emotional structure of the text without reference to the author's intention (the uses the author made of the text) or the actual effects on audiences (the uses various readers make of the text). Nevertheless, even such interpretive systems can be taken up into the Deweyan conception of a science, just by saying that the distinction between meaning and significance, or the distinction between structure and intention, is useless. The pragmatist simply observes that making such distinctions gets nowhere, since all anybody is ever really talking about anyway is what uses the current interpretive community is going to make of texts. Whatever Hirsch and the New Critics think they are doing, what they are actually doing is to argue for certain uses of the texts as opposed to others.

But let all that be as it may. As long as I am within the boundaries of, developing the implications of, some particular interpretive system, the description I gave above of a science of texts seems to work. I am doing "normal science," in the phrase that Rorty appropriates from Thomas Kuhn. Normal science even sounds in Dewey's description something like the practice of an ascetic discipline. Science

> aims to free an experience from all which is purely personal and strictly immediate; it aims to detach whatever it has in common with the subject matter of other experiences and which, being common, may be saved for *further* use. . . . To formulate the significance of an experience a man must take into conscious account the experiences of others. He must try to find a standpoint which includes the experience of others as well as his own. Otherwise his communication cannot be understood. (*DE*, 264, 266)

There is the public and there is the private, but science as such has nothing to do with the latter. In the science of texts, my hypotheses about meaning are formulated and tested within the interpretive community. To confirm an interpretive statement means to get the interpretive community to agree that it works, that the text can be used for the particular purpose implied in the interpretive statement.

And here, of course, is the rub. Natural scientists at any one time usually have, or think they have, one big interpretive system that everybody agrees about. (I admit to some skepticism about whether the scientists are right; but I am not competent to judge.) Students and teachers of the humanities, on the other hand, are sometimes painfully aware that they do not have any such thing. Every once in a while the big interpretive system called science changes, but not very often. Maybe scientists are slow, or maybe nature is. But many interpretive systems operate at all times in the humanities, even without their practitioners' realizing that their systems are different.

Not long ago I participated in a year-long seminar for faculty at my institution on contemporary theories of interpretation. Most of the participants were trained in literature or the arts, but there were a couple of scientists: a physicist, and a computer scientist who had begun as a physicist. The discussions proceeded much as I was accustomed to hearing discussions in the humanities proceed. I was a bit taken aback, then, when the scientists complained to me about how things were going. They wanted to present a hypothesis and run with it, to see how it turned out, at which point they would be prepared to accept or reject it. But none of the humanities faculty wanted to do that. If anyone put forth a thesis or an interpretation, what normally happened was that each person in turn would restate the thesis or interpretation in a different vocabulary and try to get the original speaker to accept the amendment. Propositions went around and around the table this way, and naturally never "got anywhere" from the point of view of the scientists. I would now describe that process—standard procedure, I think, in the humanities—as a process of struggle or negotiation among competing interpretive systems. Each person was resisting not so much a particular thesis or interpretation as the whole interpretive system implied in the vocabulary being used.

Often, then, arguments in the humanities are not about what conclusion some particular interpretive system produces. Instead, the arguments are, all unawares, about what interpretive system to adopt. This is the crisis of the humanities, if there is a crisis: that people in the humanities are unable to think of themselves as having anything like what the natural scientists think they have. So the humanities cannot be "justified" on the grounds that they produce "knowledge," useful or otherwise, on the model of the sciences. But this model, broadly conceived, in Dewey's thinking is the only game in town.

It is only within an interpretive community that the game can be played, and in the humanities there are indefinitely many interpretive communities. That creates a problem for a Deweyan science of texts. But for textual hermeneutics considered as an ascetic discipline, it is no problem at all. That is the difference between a science of texts and an ascetic discipline. The science of texts aims to construct a cognitive system by testing in an interpretive community interpretive statements considered as hypotheses about the meanings of texts. An ascetic discipline aims at absorption in the real, the representative function of the signs of the text, through the practice of reading, writing, hearing, and speaking interpretive statements considered as exercises. The interpretive statements are underwritten by interpretive systems that sometimes remain implicit. A plurality of interpretive systems might well be helpful, instead of getting in the way of the enterprise. From the perspective of textual hermeneutics, natural science itself is only one of many interpretive systems. It is not that there is no science of texts. There are potentially as many sciences of texts as there are interpretive systems. The success of one ascetic exercise in its own terms does not call into question the value of another.

To say that studying and teaching texts involves constructing an interpretive community, then, means one thing from a Deweyan perspective and something else from the perspective of textual hermeneutics considered as ascetic discipline. A Deweyan science is not transcendent or ahistorical. It is rooted in the goals and purposes of a particular society in a particular time and place. But for that society in that time and place, a Deweyan science is imperialistic. There must be a common goal that is in everybody's best interest, whether everybody knows it or not. Dewey states the goal "in a formal way" by talking about the transformation that education is supposed to cause in the democratic society: "It signifies a society in which every person shall be occupied in something which makes the lives of others better worth living, and which accordingly makes the ties which bind persons together more perceptible—which breaks down the barriers of distance between them" (*DE*, 369). This goal still sounds good to me. But I doubt that I act that way most of the time, or much of the time. Be that as it may. From a Deweyan perspective, constructing an interpretive community by teaching and studying texts would ultimately mean agreeing about how texts should be used to further this common goal.

From the perspective of textual hermeneutics as an ascetic discipline, however, constructing an interpretive community would mean simply operating within one particular interpretive system among others, as the initial stage of an ascetic exercise. It would not be scandalous or destructive of the enterprise if there were other interpretive communities of people on different paths.

But the lack of a common social goal would apparently destroy Deweyan science. And in fact, the anxiety of pluralism is one of the great postmodern anxieties. Many people do not act as though they agree with Dewey's description of the ideal democratic society. Some people would even be willing to say that they do not agree with it. And even if one thinks one agrees with it, Freud would make one skeptical about one's ability to know oneself that well; Nietzsche would make one wonder whether the description as stated were not just a rhetorical ploy to take power from one elite (the capitalists?) and give it to another (the philosophers?); Derrida would make one question whether such a society can be after all anything more than the texts that talk about it.

3. Rorty on Education

One way of looking at the work of Richard Rorty is to see it as an attempt to develop some of Dewey's crucial ideas, in the face of postmodern anxieties.

A strategy opposed to Rorty's for rehabilitating Dewey's thought is that of Thomas M. Alexander's *John Dewey's Theory of Art, Experience, and Nature: The Horizons of Feeling*. This interesting book is a sustained argument that Dewey's aesthetic theory should be placed at the center of his philosophy. This goes contrary to the opinion of some philosophers, including Rorty, who tend to view Dewey's *Art as Experience* as "an arbitrary or sentimental deviation of Dewey's old age from the robust instrumentalism and naturalism of his middle years" (Alexander, xvii, 266). If aesthetic experience is paradigmatic of "experience" in Dewey's rich sense of that term, and if "communication, the basis of all social life, is most fully realized in art" (264), then "we come to realize that we inhabit the world only with and through each other, and this is how it comes to mean and have value. Through the culture of nature the community appropriates itself as art" (267).

In Alexander's view, then, art only does better what science aims at. He quotes Dewey to the effect that "science is an art" (277). Then, art is the "process of imaginatively enlarging experience, thereby establishing communication through education" (271). Philosophy is identified with criticism (275), and it is crucial that aesthetic responses to art can be learned (205, 218).

To accept Alexander's attractive reading of Dewey would introduce a new perspective on the issue of "teaching texts." But I am not sure that this new perspective would enable one to see a way around the postmodern anxieties that seem to elicit Rorty's reworking of Dewey's ideas. Art has the capacity to establish community, but it is not inevitable that art will do so. As Alexander admits, "A community which is threatened with disorganization, which threatens to cease being a genuine community, will have difficulty establishing a significant shared life. Under such circumstances, Dewey suggests, art will become problematic" (190). Alexander is talking here about "industrial bourgeois society" whose "rising influence" in the nineteenth century canceled the traditional "aristocratic justification of the arts." But I can imagine Rorty's saying that the community Alexander describes is precisely *our* precarious community, where the rising influence of pluralism, relativism, and nihilism threatens to cancel all possible justifications. In any case, it seems to be to such a situation that Rorty wants to respond.

I shall refer to three of Rorty's books: *Philosophy and the Mirror of Nature, Consequences of Pragmatism (Essays: 1972–1980)*, and, especially, *Contingency, Irony, and Solidarity*. I shall try to show that Rorty preserves for the postmodern age some of the essentials of Deweyan pragmatism, in part by maintaining more firmly than Dewey does the distinction between public and private. I shall then explain why I think there are some problems with the educational implications of Rorty's approach, and why I think conceiving textual hermeneutics as an ascetic discipline might be a better thing to do.

I will begin by talking about some similarities and differences between Rorty and Dewey. Writing from a post-Wittgensteinian perspective, Rorty says, ". . . it is essential to my view that we have no prelinguistic consciousness to which language needs to be adequate, no deep sense of how things are which it is the duty of philosophers to spell out in language. What is described in such a consciousness is simply a disposition to use the language of our ancestors, to worship the corpses of their metaphors" (*CIS*, 21). The corpse here is the corpse in the title of this chapter. It is the interpretive system taken as final, the dead end, the deadening notion of a fixed truth about texts that can be reached through a method as certain and as dry as cost accounting. To the extent that the humanities try to justify themselves by pretending to produce this kind of knowledge through a science of texts, they are attempting to resuscitate an argument that was not robust for St. Augustine and must certainly be dead by now.

Rorty's position in the quoted passage is Deweyan in that it is "historicist" (Rorty's word). It makes notions of truth and meaning relative to the social purposes of the particular group that speaks the particular language in question. It seems non-Deweyan, however, in the importance attributed to language. For Dewey, language works only because it "takes place upon a background of coarser and more tangible use of physical means" (*DE*, 39), as if to say that there is some prelinguistic or at least nonlinguistic consciousness. For Rorty, human consciousness is linguistic all the way down.

Thus science, which holds a privileged position for Dewey, appears to Rorty to be only one vocabulary among many, another way of getting things done. As Rorty says at the end of his introduction to *Consequences of Pragmatism*, his pragmatism views science as "one genre of literature—or, put the other way around, literature and the arts as inquiries, on the same footing as scientific inquiries. . . . The question of what propositions to assert, which pictures to look at, what narratives to listen to and comment on and retell, are all questions about what will help us get what we want (about what we *should* want)." Thus, Rorty can talk about "the attitude of the literary intellectual towards science . . . : the view of, say, quantum mechanics as a notoriously great, but quite untranslatable poem, written in a lamentably obscure language" (*ConP*, 67). Because of the difficulty of their technical vocabularies, the sciences have receded into the background of the culture, according to Rorty, and have been replaced by "art and utopian politics" as the "areas which *are* at the forefront of the culture, those which excite the imagination of the young" (*CIS*, 52). What the culture needs now is a "redescription of liberalism as the hope that culture as a whole can be 'poeticized' rather than as the Enlightenment hope that it can be 'rationalized' or 'scientized'" (*CIS*, 53). In this redescription the hero of the culture would be Harold Bloom's "'strong poet' rather than the warrior, the priest, the sage, or the truth-seeking, 'logical,' 'objective' scientist" (*CIS*, 53).

Once again, Rorty's view is Deweyan in one sense: it "sees vocabularies as instruments for coping with things rather than representations of their intrinsic natures" (*ConP*, 198). It thus gives up "the notion of science traveling towards an end called 'correspondence with reality,'" and says just that "a given vocabulary works better than another for a given purpose" (*ConP*, 193).

Yet Rorty's shift of emphasis from "epistemology" to "hermeneutics" seems non-Deweyan in moving science out of the center of the culture and replacing it with the study of texts. Rorty's term, at least sometimes, is "literary criticism" (e.g., *ConP*, 66). So far, Rorty's conclusions resonate with my attempt to look at the world from the perspective of textual hermeneutics. But my metaphor of "moving out" and "replacing" is misleading. As Rorty says, for him "hermeneutics is an expression of hope that the cultural space left by the demise of epistemology will not be filled—that our culture should become one in which the demand for constraint and confrontation is no longer felt" (*PMN*, 316).

Rorty's move is made necessary by the lessons of post-Wittgensteinian philosophy of language and the lessons of other "edifying" philosophers such as Nietzsche, Heidegger, and Derrida. For Rorty, an "edifying" philosophy is one that "takes its point of departure from suspicion about the pretensions of epistemology"; such philosophy exists by reacting to mainstream "systematic" or "constructive" philosophy, which "centers in epistemology" (*PMN*, 366). Dewey himself is one of the great edifying thinkers (*PMN*, 368) precisely because he rejected the project of epistemology as an attempt to ground knowledge in the accuracy of privileged representations on the correspondence theory of truth.

But Dewey's whole picture of education (and therefore of philosophy considered as the theory of education) depends crucially on the existence of common social interests, common social problems, and common social goals. The society in which Deweyan education can occur sounds very much like what Rorty, following Michael Oakeshott, calls an *universitas*: "a group united by mutual interests in achieving a common end" (*PMN*, 318). Rorty says, however, that this is how *epistemology* views the social bond. Hermeneutics, on the other hand, views people as united in what Oakeshott calls a *societas*: "persons whose paths through life have fallen together, united by civility rather than by a common goal, much less by a common ground" (*PMN*, 318). Dewey might have rejected the epistemological project, but his theory of education seems to retain at least one feature of that project as Rorty describes it: namely, the picture of society as an *universitas*. To think of contemporary democratic society as a *societas*, to embrace pluralism with its advantages and anxieties, means to shift the emphasis in education from the scientific method to "literary criticism" or "literature" in its broadest sense, "the areas of culture which, quite self-consciously, forego agreement on an encompassing critical vocabulary" (*ConP*, 142).

For Rorty, it seems, the shift in emphasis is necessary in part just because most young people nowadays are more interested in art and utopian politics than they are in natural science, but also at least in part because the shift pays proper respect to the great edifying philosophers who are the makers of the postmodern mind. An illuminating passage occurs in Rorty's discussion of Hans-Georg Gadamer's *Truth and Method*:

> ... one cannot be counted as educated—gebildet—if one knows only the results of the normal Naturwissenschaften of the

> day. . . . [W]e need a sense of the relativity of descriptive vocabularies to periods, traditions, and historical accidents. This is what the humanist tradition in education does, and what training in the results of the natural sciences cannot do. Given that sense of relativity, we cannot take the notion of "essence" seriously, nor the notion of man's task as the accurate representation of essences. The natural sciences, by themselves, leave us convinced that we know both what we are and what we can be—not just how to predict and control our behavior, but the limits of that behavior (and, in particular, the limits of significant speech). Gadamer's attempt to fend off the demand . . . for "objectivity" in the Geisteswissenschaften is the attempt to prevent education from being reduced to instruction in the sense of normal inquiry. (*PMN*, 362–63)

The humanities, studies of texts, show up most clearly the impossibility of maintaining the epistemological project; they demonstrate the relativity of human thought to particular times, places, and languages; they recognize the bankruptcy of the correspondence theory of truth and meaning; and they enforce all of the lessons of Nietzsche, of Heidegger, of Wittgenstein, of Derrida, and of Dewey himself.

I do not necessarily agree that the natural sciences have to be as bad as all that. Theoretical physics, for example, can perhaps be a salutary study in just the way Rorty wants the humanities to be. But I do believe that looking at the world from the perspective of textual hermeneutics means thinking that humanities education can function in just some such role as Rorty describes. Whether that is the whole story is another question. It is not the whole story for Rorty. But my point for the moment is just that it is possible to see Rorty's shifting of emphasis from the sciences to the humanities in education as an attempt to stretch certain crucial ideas of Dewey's to meet the challenges of contemporary social conditions and of postmodern thought.

Rorty's move leads him also to emphasize more strongly than Dewey does the distinction between public and private ends in the enterprise of education. Rorty understands that "textualism," as he calls it, implies a moral problem. Literary criticism has replaced theology and traditional philosophy as the locus of moral reflection: "Novels and poems are now the principal means by which a bright youth gains a self-image. Criticism of novels is the principal form in which the acquisition of a moral character is made articulate" (*ConP*, 66). But literary criticism teaches precisely that no vocabulary is final; that human consciousness, linguistic all the way down, has no essence; and that there is therefore no ahistorical, transcendent moral truth to be discovered in texts. If there is no common final vocabulary, then the best a critic can do is to present "strong misreadings" of the texts important to the critic or the culture. As Rorty puts it in *Consequences of Pragmatism*,

> This moral objection to textualism is also a moral objection to pragmatism's claim that all vocabularies, even that of our own liberal imagination, are temporary historical resting-places. It is also an objection to the literary culture's isolation from common human concerns.... Put in the pragmatist's own preferred cost-accounting terms, it says that the stimulus to the intellectual's private moral imagination provided by his strong misreadings, by his search for sacred wisdom, is purchased at the price of his separation from his fellow-humans. (158)

Thus the wedge is driven between private and public exactly where the emphasis is shifted to postmodern notions of literary criticism. Rorty thinks that the "moral objection states the really important issue about textualism and pragmatism," but in *Consequences of Pragmatism* he says that he has "no ready way to dispose of it" (158).

In the later *Contingency, Irony, and Solidarity*, Rorty seems to be concerned primarily with this moral objection. In that book Rorty wants to "show how things look if we drop the demand for a theory which unifies the public and private, and are content to treat the demands of self-creation and human solidarity as equally valid, yet forever incommensurable" (xvi). Having accepted the contingency of all human vocabularies, including one's own, one becomes an "ironist." One becomes a "liberal" by thinking (according to Judith Shklar's definition) that "cruelty is the worst thing we do" (*CIS*, xv). There is no noncircular argument to show that cruelty is bad, just because there is no common final vocabulary in which to articulate transcendent moral insights. Every individual has his or her own final vocabulary, parts of which are shared with other individuals and parts of which are private. That cruelty is bad is just what liberals happen to think. Furthermore, humans are different from other animals in being capable of experiencing a special sort of pain: namely, humiliation. Sometimes people can be cruel to others by making their victims believe that all the things the victims have thought important are worth nothing.

The split between the "liberal metaphysician" and the "liberal ironist" comes over the question of what makes human solidarity possible. The liberal metaphysician wants to say that there is some common essence of humanity from which the proposition that "Cruelty is bad" can be derived. Human solidarity consists in that common essence. The liberal metaphysician "wants a final vocabulary with an internal and organic structure, one which is not split down the middle by a public-private distinction . . ." (*CIS*, 92). The liberal ironist, on the other hand, the intellectual who adopts the stance Rorty advocates, believes that "human solidarity is not a matter of sharing a common truth or a common goal but of sharing a common selfish hope, the hope that one's world—the little things around which one has woven into one's final vocabulary—will not be destroyed" (*CIS*, 92). So the liberal ironist must become aware of "all the various ways in which other human beings . . . can be humiliated" (*CIS*, 92); the hope is not to be "limited" by one's own final vocabulary when one is "faced with the possibility of humiliating someone with a quite different final vocabulary" (*CIS*, 93).

The liberal ironist avoids cruelty, in other words, by becoming aware of how it is possible to be cruel. This means being aware of how it is possible to humiliate others, and this in turn means being aware of how the others would describe themselves and their world. But it is important to note that being aware of others' final vocabularies does not mean adopting those vocabularies. People want to be described in their own terms, but the liberal ironist distinguishes between "redescription for private and for public purposes":

> . . . for my private purposes, I may redescribe you and everybody else in terms which have nothing to do with my attitude toward your actual or possible suffering. My private purposes, and the part of my final vocabulary which is not relevant to my public actions, are none of your business. But as I am a liberal, the part of my final vocabulary which is relevant to such actions requires me to become aware of all the various ways in which other human beings whom I might act upon can be humiliated. (*CIS*, 91–92)

This might at first sound dishonest. I might privately think that women are less psychologically stable than men or that blacks are intellectually inferior to whites, but I must be careful never to say so in public, and so on. But the liberal ironist could reply here by asking what I mean by "dishonest." I seem to have fallen back into implying that some common final vocabulary exists in terms of which to measure the truth of the propositions I believe. To be a liberal ironist means to remember that my beliefs are all contingent, and that at the same time I have a public responsibility not to be cruel. A more penetrating question, maybe, is whether "private purposes" can be separated from "public actions." I shall obliquely address that question later. My point for now is only that Rorty's extension of Deweyan pragmatism into the context of postmodern ideas about texts forces this sharp distinction between public and private.

The place of texts and the study of texts in the "liberal utopia" is easy to see, as far as public purposes are concerned. Words are all-important in the liberal utopia: "It is central to the idea of a liberal society that, in respect to words as opposed to deeds, persuasion as opposed to force, anything goes. . . . *A liberal society is one which is content to call 'true' whatever the upshot of such encounters turns out to be*" (*CIS*, 51–52). In one way, this sounds like a Deweyan notion of "truth." Texts in their encounters create truth. They can be used to create the liberal truth that cruelty is the worst thing people do. Science, philosophy, theology, social theory, and social science (*ConP*, 41; *CIS*, 79, 81; *ConP*, 203) can all in some sense be assimilated to "literature," which "now covers just about every sort of book which might conceivably have moral relevance" (*CIS*, 82). The texts of the social sciences, for example, are "continuous with literature" in that they help in "interpreting other people to us, and thus enlarging and deepening our sense of community" (*ConP*, 17). Western anthropologists and historians have "made it possible for us—educated, leisured policy-makers of the West—to see any exotic specimen of humanity as also 'one of us'"; sociologists have done the same for the poor, and psychologists for the insane (*ConP*, 203). Texts help liberals see others in such a way as to avoid humiliating them. They help liberals see what public actions are consistent with the assumptions of a liberal democracy.

There is no noncircular justification of liberal democracy, either, but "We have to start from where we are . . ." (*CIS*, 198). *We* here means those with whom Rorty identifies himself and his readers: "something like 'we twentieth-century liberals' or 'we heirs to the historical contingencies which have created more and more cosmopolitan, more and more democratic political institutions'" (*CIS*, 196). Human solidarity is "made rather than found," and the goal of the liberal society is to "create a more expansive sense of solidarity than we presently have" (*CIS*, 195–96). Texts help to do that.

In this picture, the roles of the literary critic and of the philosopher as students of texts tend to fall together. The Platonic philosopher as "cultural overseer" and custodian of the truth is out, and the "polypragmatic, Socratic intermediary between various discourses" is in (*PMN*, 320). Philosophy looks like "culture criticism" (*ConP*, xl), and philosophers are "all-purpose intellectuals" (*ConP*, xxxix) who are qualified to "kibitz" in debates about public projects because they are good at dealing with arguments (*ConP*, 221–22). Similarly, "Ironists read literary critics, and take them as moral advisers, simply because such critics . . . have read more books and are then in a better position not to get trapped in the vocabulary of any single book" (*CIS*, 80–81). So "dialectic" in Hegel's sense turns out to be a name for what is now called "literary criticism," or the playing off of various people's final vocabularies against each other (*CIS*, 78–79). Epistemology, a negative term in Rorty's story of Western philosophy, tries to put an end to discourse by finding the final, common, neutral vocabulary in which to state the transcendent, ahistorical truth (see, e.g., *ConP*, 105). Hermeneutics, on the other hand, tries to keep the conversation going, in spite of being unable to give any conclusive reason why one should keep it going:

> The pragmatists tell us that the conversation which it is our moral duty to continue is merely our project, the European intellectual's form of life. It has no metaphysical nor epistemological guarantees of success. Further (and this is the crucial point) we do not know what 'success' would mean except simply 'continuance'. We are not conversing because we have a goal, but because Socratic conversation is an activity which is its own end. (*ConP*, 172)

To reconcile this passage with the passage about creating a more expansive sense of solidarity—which sounds like a goal—one could say that continuing a conversation presupposes that the interlocutor is, for that long at least, "one of us."

So the public purpose of studying texts is fairly clear. It is to become aware of other people's final vocabularies in order to create an expanded solidarity and a wider conversation that will preclude the liberal horror of committing cruelty. Therefore, the liberal society wants a canon as "rich and diverse as possible" (*CIS*, 81).

Teaching texts, in this picture, seems to be a matter of discoursing about them. Literary critics "spend their time placing books in the context of other books, figures in the context of other figures" (*CIS*, 80). Philosophers as culture critics point out "similarities and differences between great big pictures" (*ConP*, xl). The distinction between texts and interpretive statements about those texts, in other words, is that the interpretive statements are statements about how the texts are related to other texts. In Rorty's pragmatism, the interpretive statements have exactly the same use as the texts themselves have—to keep the conversation going, to expand solidarity. But Rorty does not subscribe to what I have called the naive account of the relation between texts and interpretive statements. It is not that interpretive statements serve as substitutes for their texts. Instead, texts and interpretive statements, like everything else in the culture, are different means to the same end.

This is the public side, then, of the studying and teaching of texts. I am not interested here primarily in showing that Rorty is right or wrong about public or private uses of texts. I want to explain what it means to regard textual hermeneutics as an ascetic discipline. I want to explain that by considering a practical effect of regarding textual hermeneutics that way. Namely, I want to think about what it means to "teach a text" under that assumption. My method is to contrast my notion of teaching texts as Peircean methodeutic with notions derived from two other pragmatists (Dewey and Rorty). Right now, I am more interested in the fact that Rorty finds it necessary to distinguish sharply between public and private than I am in anything he says about particular uses of texts. Nevertheless, before going on to consider Rorty's ideas about the private side, I want to make two remarks about his discussion of the public side.

First, and quickly dealt with, is the obvious remark that it seems possible to read the story of Western philosophy another way. That is, Rorty suggests that it is the ambition of epistemology and "systematic" philosophy to close down discourse by finding the final, absolute vocabulary that will accurately represent what is "out there," independently of what anybody happens to think. The ambition of hermeneutics and "edifying" philosophy, however, is to keep the conversation going—in part, at least, by pointing out problems in the systems of the epistemologists. But one could perhaps argue that it works just the other way. Maybe the story of Western philosophy itself demonstrates that the way to keep conversation going is to write *systematic* philosophy. As Rorty often admits, edifying discourse is parasitic on systematic discourse. People want to reply and usually have some reply when I first tell them that they have gotten everything wrong, and then present my system, which I say has gotten everything right. If I tell them, however, that I think nobody has ever gotten anything right or ever will, but that I do not know how to argue about whether that is so, they might be distressed, but they would surely be at something of a loss about what to say to me next. An academic version of this spectacle is perhaps played out whenever someone experiences the frustration of trying to enter into conversation with the writings of Derrida. What does "continuing the conversation" mean in such a situation, which resembles nothing so much as getting one foot caught on the tarbaby? But pressing this kind of objection to Rorty would involve a long discussion of Western intellectual history and perhaps a longer discussion of what the analytic philosophers think they are doing. This is a conversation that I am not competent to continue, even if I wanted to.

My other remark is that I am not sure Rorty hews firmly enough to his own line when it comes to talking about education. Here is an explicit statement about colleges:

> ... the only way in which institutions of liberal learning can justify their existence is to be places in which students can find practically any book in the library—Gadamer or Kripke, Searle or Derrida—and then find somebody to talk with about it. When all the jockeying to decide which department's budget will bear the freight is over, we have to make sure that the result has not been to limit the possibilities open to the students. (*ConP*, 225)

Of course, there is the obvious practical objection that very few institutions can afford to maintain libraries where students can find "practically any book," or faculties with people competent to discuss practically any book. The practical objection leads quickly into the extremely thorny questions of which books are or should be canonical, and which noncanonical books the library should have. But this is a quibble if one thinks of Rorty as describing only the universities of his liberal utopia. When the quibble has been disposed of, I see very little in Rorty's statement to take exception to.

But what kind of talk should go on? Under the assumption that issues of canon are settled or will be settled, that is the remaining question of real educative concern. Rorty leaves room for epistemology in education. The difference between the "domains" of epistemology and hermeneutics is, he says, "purely one of familiarity. We will be epistemological where we understand perfectly well what is happening but want to codify it in order to extend, or strengthen, or teach, or 'ground' it. We must be hermeneutical where we do not understand what is happening but are honest enough to admit it" (*PMN*, 321). The crucial word here is *teach*. It is all right to be epistemological where conventions have been in place long enough for people to talk as though they understand what is going on. Rorty maintains that "education has to start from acculturation," and "needs to begin with . . . conformity" (*PMN*, 365). That is because the "hermeneutic point of view" he advocates "is possible only if we once stood at another point of view" (*PMN*, 365). The other point of view is epistemological, the "search for objectivity and the self-conscious awareness of the social practices in which objectivity consists" (*PMN*, 365). From the hermeneutic point of view, "the acquisition of truth dwindles in importance, and is seen as a component of education"—presumably, then, not the whole of education, but only the "first step" (*PMN*, 365).

So far, then, Rorty's *epistemological* seems to refer to something like discourse within a particular interpretive system, or a Deweyan science of texts insofar as that is possible. Rorty does not say that teaching *always* means being epistemological. But I want to press this point by juxtaposing another passage (from a later book) with the ones above:

> . . . even if I am right in thinking that a liberal culture whose public rhetoric is nominalist and historicist is both possible and desirable, I cannot go on to claim that there could or ought to be a culture whose public rhetoric is *ironist*. I cannot imagine a culture which socialized its youth in such a way as to make them continually dubious about their own process of socialization. Irony seems inherently a private matter. (*CIS*, 87)

I might say in passing that "dubious about their own process of socialization" seems in fact a pretty good description of many students. I do not know where or how it begins, but there it is. My point, however, is that this passage seems to imply that education, and therefore teaching texts insofar as it is a matter of public rhetoric, *must* always be to some degree epistemological. To teach texts otherwise would be to undermine the process of education (socialization) itself, Rorty seems to be saying.

But what about those edifying texts written by ironists? How shall one teach those? What sort of talk about those texts is appropriate? Does a teacher have to behave like an encyclopedist and write Nietzsche and Heidegger into some standard story of Western philosophy? Does one have to treat Derrida by formulating his "method" of deconstruction so that students can apply it to arbitrarily chosen texts?

Now, obviously I am pushing Rorty's language much too hard and unfairly. But it becomes very clear here why Rorty wants to separate public from private in a way that Dewey's theory of education does not. In discussing the work of Habermas, Rorty mentions the

> ironists whom Habermas distrusts: Nietzsche, Heidegger, Derrida. Habermas looks at these men from the point of view of public needs. I agree with Habermas that as *public* philosophers they are at best useless and at worst dangerous, but I want to insist on the role they and others like them can play in accommodating the ironist's *private* sense of identity to her liberal

hopes. All that is in question, however, is accommodation—not synthesis. (*CIS*, 68)

Dewey's pragmatism might seem to lead to the conclusion that texts with no social function or texts damaging to social goals should have no place in the educational enterprise. To make room for the texts he likes, therefore, Rorty opens up the territory of the private and gives those texts what sounds like an educative function in that realm.

Rorty describes the good and the goal of writers such as Nietzsche, Heidegger, and Derrida as "private perfection," "self-creation," or "private autonomy" (*CIS*, xiii–xiv). For Nietzsche,

> . . . to fail as a human being . . . is to accept somebody else's description of oneself, to execute a previously prepared program, to write, at most, elegant variations on previously written poems. So the only way to trace home the causes of one's being as one is would be to tell a story about one's causes in a new language. . . . With luck—the sort of luck which makes the difference between genius and eccentricity—that language will also strike the next generation as inevitable. (*CIS*, 29)

Proust writes a novel redescribing the events of his private past so as to make it really his own. Similarly, philosophers such as Nietzsche and Heidegger redescribe "a particular, rather narrowly confined, literary tradition—roughly, the Plato-Kant canon." They want to cause the canon "to lose the power it has" over them (*CIS*, 97). And just as Proust's novel makes no epistemological claim on anyone else to accept his redescriptions of his world, so "ironist theory" is almost a contradiction in terms. The intellectual who is trying to win free of the philosophical tradition cannot make logical, theoretical claims on anybody else to accept the redescription offered. To try to make such claims would be to play the Plato-Kant game, after all. If others accept the redescription—the function of which is in the first place just private—it is because of the merely "accidental coincidence of a private obsession with a public need" (*CIS*, 37).

For Rorty, the exemplary ironist theorizer is Derrida. Derrida has no arguments or theses. He begins by trying to show why there should be no "philosophy of language" on the Kantian model, a philosophy that by getting it right once and for all renders all further writing about writing unnecessary (*ConP*, 90ff.). Derrida "*is suggesting how things might look if we did not have Kantian philosophy built into the fabric of our intellectual life*" (*ConP*, 98). Finally, Derrida "privatizes" his thinking: "He simply drops theory—the attempt to see his predecessors steadily and whole—in favor of fantasizing about those predecessors, playing with them, giving free rein to the trains of association they produce" (*CIS*, 125). In "Envois," Derrida has "done for the history of philosophy what Proust did for his own life story," by playing off all the great authority figures against each other until the "very notion of 'authority' loses application in reference to his work. He has achieved autonomy in the same way that Proust achieved autonomy" (*CIS*, 137). This is "a kind of book which nobody had ever thought of before" (*CIS*, 137).

Such fantasizing is, for Rorty, "the product of ironist theorizing." If one were to argue with one's predecessors, show how they got things wrong, one would be simply repeating their mistake of thinking that there was some way to tell when one had gotten things right. Fantasizing is what is left after the Kantian dream of writing the last book has been dispelled. Derrida is important precisely because he has "had the courage to give up the attempt to unite the private and the public, to stop trying to bring together a quest for private autonomy and an attempt at public resonance and utility" (*CIS*, 125).

This, then, is the terminus of Rorty's branch of Deweyan pragmatism. The anxieties of pluralism and the texts of postmodern writers are dealt with by sharply dividing the private from the public and relegating certain concerns and texts to the former realm. This line of thought is seductive, not least because it seems to leave room for everything that intellectuals want to do: be epistemological sometimes, and be hermeneutical sometimes; engage in normal discourse, and engage in abnormal discourse; realize private ends, and fulfill public responsibilities; be committed to one's own "final" vocabulary, and be tolerant of other people's. Nevertheless, I think that there are some problems involved in attempting to split off the private from the public in this way. A couple of these problems are general concerns about big issues that go well beyond my main concern here—namely, the teaching of texts—so I shall mention these problems only briefly.

First, and most general, is the moral problem that Rorty recognizes already in *Consequences of Pragmatism*—namely, the objection to "textualism" that says that "the stimulus to the intellectual's private moral imagination provided by his strong misreadings . . . is purchased at the price of his separation from his fellow-humans" (*ConP*, 158). Rorty's answer in *Contingency, Irony, and Solidarity* seems to be that since there is not going to be a theory that unifies public and private aims, liberal intellectuals will have to solve the moral problems that inevitably result from this split by muddling through, as it were, on an ad hoc basis:

> The existence of these two sides . . . generates dilemmas. Such dilemmas we shall always have with us, but they are never going to be resolved by appeal to some further, higher set of obligations which a philosophical tribunal might discover and apply. . . . All we can do is work with the final vocabulary we have, while keeping our ears open for hints about how it might be expanded or revised. (*CIS*, 197)

Thus, if one sees the later book as in part an exploration of the moral problem recognized in the earlier one, then one would have to see the later book not as presenting a solution to the moral problem, but only as situating it within a particular form of life (that of the liberal intellectual) in such a way as to show why a blanket solution is not going to be forthcoming.

Rorty says that "the aim of a just and free society" ought to be "letting its citizens be as privatistic . . . as they please so long as they do it on their own time—causing no harm to others and using no resources needed by those less advantaged" (*CIS*, xiv). The question here, ultimately, is, How can I sit in my comfortable office at a wealthy university and read Derrida, without in some sense using resources needed by those less advantaged? Who pays for my leisure? This sort of guilt is not very productive unless I am prepared seriously to consider resigning my professorship to work for the homeless and the hungry, or unless I can persuade myself that somehow my reading (and teaching) of Derrida might, however indirectly, improve their lot. But if I separate public from private, and relegate Derrida's writings to the realm of purely private concerns, I am precluded from thinking that Derrida might have any public use. As Rorty himself says, "irony is of little public use" (*CIS*, 121). But surely, one wants to reply, a public use can be found even for the works of Derrida; and if not, then perhaps no public resources at all ought to be devoted to the reading, writing, and teaching of such texts.

A second problem that interferes with maintaining a sharp distinction between public and private is that Derrida after all writes books that other literary intellectuals read or pretend to read. Achieving private autonomy or self-creation apparently involves public action, then, since one could hardly imagine an action more public than publishing. Nor does it seem that one could say that Derrida (or Proust) first achieves private autonomy "inside," as it were, through some mental redescription, and then writes just in order to provide others with directions along the same route or a record of the journey. That kind of talk would lapse back into a pre-Wittgensteinian picture of language as a sign for some private, internal reality. Instead, it seems necessary to say that the achieving of private autonomy is identical with the public action of writing, and further that taking Derrida's writing as exemplary of private self-creation is identical with the public activity of reading it. Precisely where private redescription becomes a category, it is identical with public action.

I shall glance at these big problems again later. But the crucial problem with Rorty's account for my project here is that the account seems to provide no sense for the notion of "teaching texts," if the texts in question are edifying texts such as Derrida's. As Rorty says of "Envois," "There is no moral to these fantasies, nor any public (pedagogic or political) use to be made of them; but for Derrida's readers, they may nevertheless be exemplary—suggestions of the sort of thing one might do, a sort of thing rarely done before" (*CIS*, 125). Literature faculties of some universities might challenge Rorty's statement that there is no political use to be made of Derrida's fantasies. My concern, however, is with the statement that there is no pedagogic use to be made of them. Again, I want to push Rorty's words rather hard, but this time, I think, with more warrant. For if one buys into Rorty's general view, I think this statement is precisely correct. There *is* no pedagogic use to be made of Derrida's text conceived as Rorty conceives it, no meaning that can be attached to the notion of "teaching" such a text.

In the first place, as Rorty himself points out, it is misleading to say that Derrida "has demonstrated anything or refuted anybody" or that he has developed a "deconstructive method": "there is no *method* involved, if a method is a procedure which can be taught by reference to rules" (*CIS*, 134). To the extent that deconstruction is the name of a particular procedure, it is just the procedure of "recontextualization," which has been around since Socrates. Nor should Derrida's writing be "judged by 'literary' rather than 'philosophical' criteria," since there are no "antecedently available criteria of *either* sort" (*CIS*, 135). If a teacher cannot abstract arguments from what looks like a philosophical text, cannot derive a method from it, and cannot judge it, what is there left to do? What kinds of interpretive statements would be left to make, and what would their relation be to the text in question?

One possible answer might be that the teacher could paraphrase the difficult text, to make it more accessible to the student. There are two difficulties here, however. One is that the answer might fall back into the naive account where interpretive statements are seen as substitutes for the text, in some sense. I would venture to guess that this is how Derrida is most often "taught." Certainly this is how his texts are most often written about in handbooks. Derrida's texts are usually fairly successful in resisting this kind of "teaching," however. Sooner or later, the paraphraser finds it necessary to repeat Derrida's own language. Another difficulty here, of course, is that such "teaching," if it "succeeds," necessarily succeeds precisely by *removing* Derrida's text from the realm of the private and relocating it in the realm of the public. To say that there can be a paraphrase means to deny the existence of the private realm where Derrida's text supposedly operates.

Another possible answer might come from looking at what Rorty does with Derrida's text. Rorty makes statements that look like interpretive statements; could these statements not be seen as implying a way of "teaching" Derrida's text? Is Rorty not, in some sense, "teaching" Derrida's text to Rorty's readers? In general, Rorty's interpretive statements place Derrida's text within the story of Western philosophy that Rorty is telling. Maybe that is what "teaching a text" means? But if so, the distinction between public and private cannot be maintained, so far as education is concerned. In its teaching, Derrida's text is not being used as an exemplum of self-creation. It is being used as a commentary on the Western philosophical tradition. Similarly, one might guess, in a course about novels *The Remembrance of Things Past* might be used as a study in novelistic technique, or in the representation of consciousness, or something of the sort. But it could not be simply an exemplum of the achievement of private autonomy. There would be in that case nothing to teach. The only thing to do would be to hand the student the book and urge the student to read it.

Rorty says that texts such as Proust's and Derrida's are special in that neither "fits within any conceptual scheme previously used to evaluate novels or philosophical treatises" (*CIS*, 137). He suggests that with such a text readers are in the position of trying to "see whether we can find a use for it" (*CIS*, 135). To find a use is to find a meaning; to write an interpretive statement requires finding a meaning. But finding uses, finding meanings, and finding interpretive statements are all public activities. In short, education is a social—i.e., public—activity. "Teaching a text" implies public action. Where a text is simply the achievement of someone's private autonomy, there is nothing about it to teach. Even to discuss with students why a text *cannot* be fitted into familiar conceptual categories is to place the text within a public context.

Rorty's move means to save the "abnormal" texts that literary intellectuals such as Rorty find fascinating, and that other literary intellectuals hate, by distinguishing between public and private uses of texts. But the move has a price. The price is to remove those texts from the public realm where teaching and learning happen. Rorty's move seems to deprive the notion of teaching such texts of any clear meaning.

4. Literary Education as Ascetic Discipline

People in colleges and universities do at least have the illusion that they are teaching Proust's and Derrida's texts, and sometimes they have the further illusion that they are teaching these texts "in just the same way" as they teach other, more "normal," texts. What is going on? No doubt in many cases what is going on is that people are teaching these texts in one or more of the misleading ways that Rorty criticizes. But the question is whether it is possible, after all, to give a nonmisleading sense to the notion of teaching these texts. I want to see whether conceiving textual hermeneutics as an ascetic discipline can be helpful here.

In the ascetic discipline of textual hermeneutics, the goal is total absorption in the reality of the text—that is, in the representative function of the signs. That representative function is what constitutes the part of human consciousness (Peirce's "man-sign") that is real, that can survive for the indefinitely future community. It is not possible to generalize about the object of the signs of the text. Different texts might have different sorts of objects. It is possible only to say that the object of the signs of a text is whatever is at the limit of the chain of signification through which the text exists for the indefinitely future community. Maybe in the fully developed sign of the indefinite future the text will appear to be a sign of its author's consciousness. Or maybe it will appear to be a sign of a class of emotional responses in its readers. Or maybe it will appear to be a sign of some material or immaterial object. And so on. Meanwhile, the object of the text for fallible human consciousness is simply a place in the triadic sign relation. Now, one can imagine that a feeling of enlightenment about a text could occur naturally and without effort, with the unshakable conviction of a nonparaphrasable experience. In that case, no teaching or further learning about the text would seem necessary or possible.

But textual hermeneutics as a discipline exists because such feelings of instant enlightenment occur rarely or not at all. If they do occur, one wants to repeat them with other texts. If they do not occur, one believes or at least suspects that other people, somehow, are able to "get more out of" texts, and one wants to acquire that power for oneself. Textual hermeneutics consists of the exercises that one undertakes in order to achieve such experiences of texts. In the educational context, those exercises consist of reading, writing, speaking, and hearing interpretive statements that are underwritten by the various interpretive systems applied to texts. In the ascetic discipline, however, the production of interpretive statements is not the goal. The goal is to be totally absorbed in the signs of the text.

But in the discipline the text and the interpretive system stand in a reciprocal relation. Each is known only as one pole of the interpretive act in which they are united. It is necessary, then, to consider not just the interpretive statements produced by any particular interpretive system, but also the relation between the text and the interpretive system. This means studying the interpretive system as such, considering what sorts of questions and answers it is blind to.

An analogy might be the following. People sit in the lotus posture or chant a mantra as exercises to help them achieve enlightenment. But the use of the lotus posture or the mantra in achieving enlightenment is not just to understand these exercises. It is also to understand that sitting for hours in the lotus posture or chanting the mantra for hours is not equivalent to enlightenment. The ascetic discipline is an exercise, and must be understood as such. Otherwise, it blocks the path. Similarly, each interpretive system of textual hermeneutics is a method, and must be understood as such. It happens that the only way to understand an interpretive system is in its practice (as maybe also with the lotus posture or the mantra)—that is, as I have said before, "from the inside." In this sense it is pointless to talk about a distinction between "truth" and "method." But whatever teaching and learning go on are teaching and learning about the interpretive system. The texts are not the objects of study, if one thinks that to be an "object of study" means to be something that knowledge is produced about. There is no knowledge about texts except within the boundaries of some interpretive system. The teaching and learning are thus more properly called by Peirce's name of "methodeutic."

Now, why is this a better way than Rorty's to think about textual hermeneutics? It is better because it avoids the problems associated with distinguishing sharply between public and private. Some experiences with texts might feel like enlightenment that is sui generis and incommunicable. But if these experiences are real, in the picture I have been extrapolating from Peirce, then *incommunicable* means only "incommunicable in the currently available interpretive vocabulary." In fact, the feeling of genuine enlightenment consists precisely in the belief that the experience *will* be communicable in some future community—that is, that the experience is real.

But more to my point here, it is impossible to conceive of an ascetic discipline that is purely private. If one tries to do so, as I argued in an earlier essay, the concept of an ascetic discipline becomes vulnerable to the devastating force of Wittgenstein's private-language argument. The notion of a private discipline is just as nonsensical as the notion of a private language. To put it crudely, disciplines involve rules, and rules are a matter of social practice, of a particular form of life. Even if one should persist, in a non-Peircean way, in thinking of enlightenment about texts as ultimately a private matter, still one would have to think of the reading, writing, speaking, and hearing of interpretive statements that occur on the way to that enlightenment as public matters, rule-governed exercises of a discipline.

Let me try to show more concretely how considering textual hermeneutics as an ascetic discipline would ease the problems created by Rorty's insistence on the distinction between public and private. The first big problem I mentioned above is the moral problem. How can one justify the preciosity of the literary intellectual who consumes public resources to study texts that remove the reader further and further from the concerns of the common human being, while some of those common human beings are starving in the streets? Rorty's distinction between public and private sacrifices the traditional arguments for the social utility of the study of literature, insofar as one might try to apply those arguments to the study of texts that aim only at private autonomy. Even if I sit in a comfortable office at an elite liberal-arts college, I might be able to justify studying the novels of Upton Sinclair, because I can tell myself that I will use these novels to raise the social consciousness of my students, who as the children of the wealthy are destined to be the leaders of tomorrow. Then *they* can work to improve the lot of the poor. I will have done my part by helping them see what that lot is. This line of argument can easily be made into a cruel parody, but I think it is not far from a line that is often taken in attempting to justify the study of literature. But I cannot use a similar justification for studying Derrida, if Derrida's text is what Rorty says it is: namely, an exemplum of (and not even a recipe for) the attaining of autonomy from the authority of a narrow and musty philosophical tradition.

But suppose I regard textual hermeneutics as an ascetic discipline. Then I could say something like the following about studying Derrida. Derrida's texts, even the late ones that are frankly fantasizing about other texts, represent one sort of ascetic exercise. Even fantasy has its rules, as Freud would agree. And so even if it is misleading to talk about "Derrida's deconstructive method," it makes sense to talk about the interpretive system that underwrites Derrida's remarks in "Envois" about the philosophers he discusses. Derrida offers one (or more than one) interpretive system that can take its place among all the interpretive systems currently operating, one more way of getting at texts. In fact, I could apply the rules of Derrida's fantasizing—or my own—as an exercise for the study of Upton Sinclair. So whatever social utility there might be in studying Plato, Kant, or *The Jungle* can also count in favor of studying a text of Derrida's that might help me study Plato, Kant, or *The Jungle*.

Or, suppose that Derrida's text is itself elevated to the status of canonical literature, something people read not just as a commentary on other philosophers, but "for its own sake." Then, it seems, one could argue that studying Derrida's text (that is, reading, writing, speaking, and hearing interpretive statements about it) has no less social utility than studying *The Dunciad* or *Mac Flecknoe*, where Pope or Dryden puts other literary intellectuals in their places.

Now, maybe someone will say that there in fact is not much social utility in studying Dryden, Pope, *or* Derrida. I do not want to minimize the problem of giving social justifications for the study of texts. Regarding textual hermeneutics as an ascetic discipline does not necessarily help with that. The canonical texts of a culture are just those for the study of which social justifications are available. I do not believe that my reflections have made the problem of canon any less important or any less difficult. My point here is only that conceiving textual hermeneutics as an ascetic discipline makes available for texts such as Derrida's the same sorts of social justification, whatever they may be—that is, whatever works—as are available for other texts that are already in the canon. Rorty separates public and private because in his account he has to give up on justifying the study of Derrida's texts in terms of common social goals. Rorty's problem does not disappear in my account, but its locus is shifted. Instead of the moral problem of using public resources to support a favored few while they study texts that have only private uses, there is now the political problem of deciding what is going to count as social justification for the study of texts. This problem seems inevitable as long as the educational enterprise asks people to support studying of texts.

The second big problem with Rorty's account that I mentioned above is that it seems at least counterintuitive to say that Derrida, Proust, and others achieve private autonomy only through the most public activity of writing books for which, presumably, they expect to have readers. They do not put their manuscripts in bottles and bury them. The apparent paradox disappears in the account of textual hermeneutics as an ascetic discipline. *The Remembrance of Things Past*, one might say, is an interpretive statement about a text—namely, the events of Proust's life rendered as a text. The writing of the novel is an exercise designed to help Proust and his readers get at the reality of those events. Carrying out the exercise means submitting to the rules of the discipline—refiguring, in this case, human experiences by means of the French language, according to its lexicon, its grammar, its syntax, and its novelistic conventions both old and new. Such an exercise has no meaning—is inconceivable—apart from the linguistic community Proust addresses. Similarly, Derrida's "Envois" is an interpretive statement about the old philosophers, an exercise that, if Rorty is right, refigures their discourse according to the rules of Derrida's own fantasy, rules that might have been accessible earlier to Derrida's analyst, and that become accessible to the reader now through the writing of the text. Again, the exercise has no meaning apart from the community of literary intellectuals whose concerns and whose discourse make the reconfiguring possible.

Finally, the crucial problem with Rorty's sharp distinction between public and private is that it seems to make it impossible to give a meaning to the notion of "teaching" a text such as Derrida's, a text whose value is only that it exemplifies the achieving of private autonomy. But "teaching the text" has a clear meaning if textual hermeneutics is conceived as an ascetic discipline. Teaching the text means first teaching the exercises of the discipline. That is, teaching students how to apply interpretive systems to texts. It means also teaching the students how the exercises are exercises—that is, it means studying interpretive systems as such. Teaching texts means methodeutic, pointing out how the interpretive systems work and what it means to say that they are interpretive systems. If teaching a text means methodeutic, then it makes sense to say that Derrida's text can be taught in "just the same way" as other texts.

After all, then, I am making a move that has at least a kind of Rortyan spirit about it. Rorty picks up Wittgenstein's theme that people ought to give up the vocabularies that are not getting them anywhere or are confusing them. I am arguing that it might be a good idea to stop talking about "teaching texts." It is too easy to take that phrase as implying that in the humanities one gets knowledge of poems, for example, the way an astronomer gets knowledge of celestial objects, and that accumulating this knowledge is the goal and justification of the humanities. That view, I think, is mistaken. "Teaching the humanities" does not mean "teaching texts." It means, instead, methodeutic.

The social justification for the humanities is as it may be. I suspect that whether the humanities survive as disciplines will depend on whether human beings continue to be fascinated by what the humanities call texts, and whether the lives of the people who teach the humanities seem to other people to be in some sense exemplary lives. This is the criterion for the survival of any ascetic discipline—namely, whether it appeals to enough people as a satisfactory way of being in the world. Since I have been old enough to think in such terms, the humanities have not seemed to me to be doing particularly well on this score. Maybe what appears now to be a crisis for the humanities is only healthy ferment, or maybe it is the last convulsion. My experience is limited. It is one thing to be Kant in Königsberg. It is another thing entirely to feel stupid in Königsberg as the anxieties of pluralism become more acute and its problems more intractable. From the perspective of textual hermeneutics, textual hermeneutics itself naturally appears to be the inevitable way of being in the world. I have adopted that perspective from the beginning because I think it is the necessary perspective from which to see through whatever crisis the humanities may be facing. But there are other perspectives, and I cannot see that textual hermeneutics or the humanities make any absolute claim, any more than any other ascetic discipline does.

Besides easing some of the problems created by Rorty's opposition of public and private, an account of textual hermeneutics as an ascetic discipline has some other positive results for the theory of humanities education. I shall briefly outline those results.

First, this account helps to address the problem of "literary theory." The problem of "literary theory" has two aspects, as I see it: (1) the question of what literary theory is or should be, and (2) the question of what place, if any, literary theory should have in the curriculum. One big issue in the debate about the nature of literary theory is whether it is prescriptive or only descriptive: whether it should aspire to give the rule to writers about what does and does not count as literature or as criticism; or whether it merely attempts to codify practice, which is always one or more steps ahead of it. Another big issue is the domain of literary theory. Does it explain poems, plays, and novels, or should it modestly confine itself to the role of metacriticism? Or should it imperialistically expand into a general criticism of culture? Another issue is the disciplinary home of literary theory. Is it philosophy commenting upon literature? Or is it literature commenting upon philosophical, historical, and religious texts? And so on.

The big question about the place of literary theory in the curriculum is whether literary theory should be reserved to inform the teacher's teaching while students are more or less cloistered in innocence of its complexities, or whether literary theory should become an explicit subject of instruction and a specialty in its own right.

On the account of textual hermeneutics as ascetic discipline, literary theory is one branch of methodeutic. It is the study of how hermeneutic intelligences connect signs—specifically, connect the signs of a literary work with the signs of an interpretive statement by means of some interpretive system. Literary theory belongs wherever texts are studied that people are willing to call literature. It may or may not evolve into a general criticism of culture, depending upon how broad a range of texts is considered to constitute "literature." But literary theory cannot be a theory about how to write "literature." It is only a theory about how interpretive statements get written. It might begin as description of critical practice, and then produce an explicit statement of an interpretive system in the form of rules that can be applied to new texts. But when the system is so applied, it must be applied in the awareness that the application is an exercise and not a method of articulating absolute truth. Literary theory can codify a method or methods of writing criticism, but it cannot give the rule to criticism in the sense of excluding other possible methods.

In a sense, literary theory always begins in the mode of an *apologia*. Somebody asks me why I have written an interpretive statement as I have, and I try to explain myself. Literary theory arises only in the context of the reading, writing, hearing, and speaking of conflicting interpretive statements. But for that very reason, explicit literary theory does belong in the curriculum, since the business of the humanities is methodeutic. Whether literary theory should be made explicit in introductory literature courses, whether it should be segregated in a group of special courses all its own, and whether it should form part of every course in any literature major, are all prudential questions whose answers would depend on many variables. But to practice textual hermeneutics as an ascetic discipline means at some point to study interpretive systems as such—that is, methodeutic. This quickly translates into various practical, political consequences for humanities departments. In a sense, literary education means causing the students to repeat the agonies of the teachers. Literary education recapitulates its phylogeny, beginning with the textual problems solved by means of interpretive systems and ending with the problems created by the deconstruction of the interpretive systems.

The remaining difficulty—that is, saying which discipline literary theory belongs to—brings me to my second point. It is a point about "interdisciplinary study." This catchphrase is much abused by being employed in academic debate to bring about desired ends while deliberately allowing the meaning of the term to remain vague. I recently sat in a seminar of humanities faculty from several colleges, all of whom had expressed some sort of commitment to "interdisciplinary study" and all of whom had had considerable experience with courses described as "interdisciplinary." The question was posed, What is interdisciplinary study, anyway? The ensuing discussion was far from lucid.

But if I had to summarize it, I would say that there were almost as many different notions of interdisciplinary study as there were speakers, and that at least the following definitions were explicitly or implicitly invoked:

1. *Interdisciplinary study* refers to a particular method of study, and that method is the method that is also referred to as "intellectual history."
2. *Interdisciplinary study* refers to any study that helps students address the genuine major concerns of their lives—such as their maturation, their relationships with members of the opposite sex, their anxiety about making a living, and so on.
3. *Interdisciplinary study* refers to the application of several different methodologies—e.g., psychological, sociological, anthropological, narratological—to a single text.
4. *Interdisciplinary study* refers to the study of some problem of grave social concern—e.g., ecological crisis, the threat of nuclear war, the oppression of women—that cannot be solved or exhaustively studied within the boundaries of a single discipline.
5. *Interdisciplinary study* refers to team-teaching, where the members of the team are from different departments.
6. *Interdisciplinary study* is an administrative designation for the convenience of deans and the writers of college catalogs who want to list courses that for one reason or another will not fit under any existing department.

The answer to the question by my account, of course, is that interdisciplinary study is methodeutic. Even a single branch of methodeutic, no matter how methodeutic may be divided, is interdisciplinary study. One cannot understand that something is a branch of something else without understanding at least that there are other branches with which this branch stands in a certain relationship. Studying an interpretive system as such implies understanding that it is one interpretive system among others.

On this account, it is not the concept of "interdisciplinary study" that is confused. Instead, what is confused is the concept of "discipline" defined in terms of "proper subject matter." The confusion becomes more and more obvious as it happens more and more often that people in different disciplines, so-called, find themselves studying the same texts. Thus, the difficulty of placing literary theory under any particular discipline shows, as I think most teachers of literature already suspect, not that there is something funny about the concept of "literary theory," but that there is something funny about the traditional division of the departments of the humanities. To be committed to the account of textual hermeneutics as ascetic discipline is to be committed to interdisciplinary study. That commitment would translate into practical consequences differently in different situations. But in my experience, at least, the traditional departmental structure of humanities faculties makes it too easy to devote full time to operating particular interpretive systems, at the cost of ignoring the crucial step of methodeutic. Interdisciplinary study, which is methodeutic, means to study interpretive systems as such.

5. *Kinds of Pragmatism*

I want to finish by speculating about a difference. Peirce, Dewey, and Rorty all advertise themselves as "pragmatists." Peirce did coin the term *pragmaticism* to distinguish his doctrine from other versions of pragmatism, in the essay "What Pragmatism Is" in *The Monist* for 1905 (*CP*, 5.411–36; *W*, 180–202; *B*, 251–67). But it is reasonable to ask why Rorty's extension of Dewey's pragmatism produces such different conclusions about literary education from my extension of Peirce's pragmatism. I think the differences can be explained by considering two topics: the notion of philosophical justification and the notion of the rational community.

Rorty sometimes speaks as though there were two and only two ways of regarding philosophical justification. One is the traditional, metaphysical, epistemological, foundational way of Plato, Descartes, and Kant. In this view, philosophical justifications are to be founded on the indubitable accuracy of some privileged representation. The only problem is to decide what representations to privilege—rational apprehension of the Ideas, intuitive knowledge of the self, formal categories of experience, sense impressions, grammatical categories, or whatever. This view is dominated by an optical metaphor, the metaphor of the mind as a mirror that reflects something "out there." Thus Rorty's title *Philosophy and the Mirror of Nature*. In this book, he argues that the metaphor has outlived its usefulness. By this metaphor, the task of the philosopher is to attain rational certainty by polishing the mirror to remove distortions and make sure that the privileged representations are accurate. Polishing the mirror means finding the final, neutral vocabulary that really corresponds with "the way things are," and the search for such a vocabulary is the defining characteristic of philosophers who are captured by this picture.

The other way of regarding justification is the Deweyan, post-Wittgensteinian way—namely, as a social practice, the playing of a particular language game. In this view there is no special reason to distinguish philosophical justification from any other kind, and no reason to think of the philosopher as the custodian of truth. Absolute certainty is not attainable, since there are no culture-neutral privileged representations. Every justification is, as it were, a local matter. What replaces the mirror in this picture is the conversation. Justification is conversational, and therefore complicated, unpredictable, and limited to a particular time and place. Philosophers who accept this picture have given up on the search for a final, context-free, neutral vocabulary.

The following passage from *Consequences of Pragmatism* is one of those in which, it seems to me, Rorty implies that these two competing views of justification are the only meaningful ones. The context of this passage is Rorty's list of some characteristics of pragmatism. The passage contains his third characterization, which he says is a summary. Pragmatism

> is the doctrine that there are no constraints on inquiry save conversational ones—no wholesale constraints derived from the nature of the objects, or of the mind, or of language, but only those retail constraints provided by the remarks of our fellow-inquirers. . . . The only sense in which we are constrained to truth is that, as Peirce suggested, we can make no sense of the notion that the view which can survive all objections might be false. But objections—conversational constraints—cannot be anticipated. There is no method for knowing when one has reached the truth, or when one is closer to it than before. (*ConP*, 165–66)

Rorty goes on to say that this characteristic of pragmatism focuses on

> a fundamental choice which confronts the reflective mind: that between accepting the contingent character of starting-points, and attempting to evade this contingency. To accept the contingency of starting-points is to accept our inheritance from, and our conversation with, our fellow-humans as our only source of

guidance. To attempt to evade this contingency is to hope to become a properly-programmed machine. (*ConP*, 166)

To become a machine would be to have a well-polished mirror: the mirror cannot choose what it reflects, and the image in it is determined by the object "out there."

Rorty thinks Peirce is right in his suggestion that there is no sense in "the notion that the view which can survive all objections might be false." But Rorty also implies that Peirce's suggestion is trivial. In practice there is no way of knowing what objections might come up. Therefore, Peirce's suggestion is of no help in knowing whether any particular view is right. In other words, it provides no way of justifying any particular view. Rorty's submerged argument seems to go something like this: Peirce's suggestion, though right, is trivial from the perspective that regards justification as the name of the game. From this perspective, justification is what philosophers do, and the only question is which of the two possible kinds of justification one is going to plump for. One can be a mirror reflecting accurate representations, or one can be an interlocutor in many ongoing conversations. Even though Peirce sounds as though he is talking about future conversations, as a philosopher he could not *really* be choosing the metaphor of conversation. If he were choosing it, he would come up empty of justifications. He cannot predict what is going to happen in future conversations. Therefore, since justification is what philosophers do, Peirce as a philosopher is not really choosing that metaphor. When philosophical push comes to philosophical shove, Peirce chooses the old metaphor from the tradition, the mirror of accurate representation.

Now, I am obviously doing some heavy between-the-lines reading of Rorty's text in this spot. But this reconstruction seems to me the simplest way of explaining what he says in a passage a little earlier: "Peirce himself remained the most Kantian of thinkers—the most convinced that philosophy gave us an all-embracing ahistorical context in which every other species of discourse could be assigned its proper place and rank" (*ConP*, 161). The implication here is clearly that Peirce ultimately chose option A: to "attempt to evade the contingency" of starting points. On the face of it, that might seem a strange thing to say about a philosopher who argued against Descartes that "No cognition not determined by a previous cognition . . . can be known" ("Questions Concerning Certain Faculties Claimed for Man," *W*, 37). Rorty might have in mind here the undoubted influence of Kant on Peirce, Peirce's insistence on the importance of logic as a normative science, and Peirce's obsession with classifying the sciences. As is always possible in disagreements about Peirce, maybe the disputants are just reading different passages from the bewildering store. Nevertheless, Rorty's classification of Peirce as "Kantian" seems to depend crucially on Rorty's notion of the "fundamental choice which confronts the reflective mind." It is a fundamental choice of ways of justification. If one does not get one's justifications conversationally, then one must be doing the other thing. Where Peirce seems to be talking conversationally, he comes up empty of justifications; the one thing philosophers cannot lack is justifications; so Peirce must be a Kantian, after all.

In exploring this structure of Rorty's thought (or at least, my unsympathetic reconstruction of it), I want to begin with a quibble. Throughout *Philosophy and the Mirror of Nature*, Rorty uses the phrase "Glassy Essence" to denote the mirror that stands for the knowing human soul in the optical metaphor that has so far dominated Western philosophy. The "essence" of the soul is to know, and to know means to be "glassy" in the sense of mirroring that which is represented. Rorty gets the phrase from Shakespeare via Peirce. Rorty quotes *Measure for Measure*, II.ii.117–23:

> but man, proud man,
> Drest in a little brief authority,—
> Most ignorant of what he's most assured,
> His glassy essence,—like an angry ape,
> Plays such fantastic tricks before high heaven
> As makes the angels weep; who, with our spleens,
> Would all themselves laugh mortal.

Rorty identifies the "glassy essence" with the "'intellectual soul' of the scholastics," and quotes a passage from Bacon that compares the "mind of man" with a "glass" or mirror (*PMN*, 42).

Here Rorty is following an article by J. V. Cunningham, "'Essence' and *The Phoenix and the Turtle*." Cunningham examines the word *essence* in Shakespeare, arguing that Shakespeare uses it with overtones of its technical scholastic sense to refer to the soul of man, which Shakespeare describes as "glassy" because it mirrors the image of God. Citing Peirce (*CP*, 6.270–71), Rorty says, "The phrase *man's glassy essence* was first invoked in philosophy by C. S. Peirce in an 1892 essay of that title on the 'molecular theory of protoplasm,' which Peirce strangely thought important in confirming the view that 'a person is nothing but a symbol involving a general idea'" (*PMN*, 42n). My quibble has to do with Cunningham's and Rorty's interpretation of the passage in Shakespeare.

The speech in question is Isabella's. She has just been begging Angelo to have mercy on her brother, and she has been treated to a pompous self-advertisement from Angelo on the subject of how punctiliously just he is. Isabella's point seems to be that Angelo exhibits hubris. Perfect justice might be possible for a god, but Angelo's posturing makes the angels weep. If they were human and therefore crueler, the angels would laugh at his pretensions. By pretending to be more than a man can be, Angelo makes himself less—an "angry ape." In short, Angelo does not know himself. Now, it seems to me at least possible that Isabella is not saying that Angelo mirrors the image of God without knowing it. The point of the phrase "glassy essence" could well be that Angelo cannot perceive his own nature, which is considerably less than godlike. He is transparent to himself. If he knew himself, he would stop playing the fool and would speak and act more humbly in accordance with his true human nature. In this interpretation, "glassy" would mean something like "transparent," instead of "mirroring."

Arguments could be mustered on either side. I do not want to spend any more time with this quibble. The issue becomes a little more serious and a little more germane to my purposes, however, when it becomes a question of how Peirce interpreted the passage from Shakespeare. In fact, Peirce had used this passage earlier than 1892. He uses lines 117 and 119–20 in 1868, to conclude his refutation of Cartesianism in two essays in the *Journal of Speculative Philosophy*. I quote the last paragraph of "Some Consequences of Four Incapacities":

> The individual man, since his separate existence is manifested only by ignorance and error, so far as he is anything apart from his fellows, and from what he and they are to be, is only a negation. This is man,
>
> > "proud man,
> > Most ignorant of what he's most assured,
> > His glassy essence."
>
> (*W*, 72)

So the context of this passage in Peirce is his argument against Descartes's attempt to evade the contingency of starting points. The point of Peirce's pair of essays is to demolish Descartes's candidate for a noncontingent starting point, namely the intuitive self-presence of the *cogito*. The essence of the individual human, then, considered in isolation from others and from the future community, is so transparent that it is completely invisible—a negation. Like Angelo, the Cartesian philosopher is unaware of what human beings are not. They are not substantial souls susceptible to direct self-inspection. They are chains of signification that exist only insofar as they are taken up in further chains of signification. They are, as it were, windowpanes through which the future looks back into the past. Peirce talks about the "glassy essence" not as an image of some noncontingent starting point, but as an image of the error involved in thinking that self-presence is one.

The position is in accord with Peirce's general "doctrine of fallibilism" (*CP*, 1.148), which says that "We can never be absolutely sure of anything, nor can we with any probability ascertain the exact value of any measure or general ratio" (*CP*, 1.147). This amounts to saying that there is no justification available that starts from indubitable premises and proceeds by valid reasoning to indubitable conclusions. At least sometimes, then, Peirce refuses to place himself in the company of those who think they can evade the contingency of starting points.

On the other hand, Peirce does not place himself in the company of those who accept current conversations as providing the last word about themselves. In the penultimate paragraph of "Some Consequences of Four Incapacities," he says,

> Finally, as what anything really is, is what it may finally come to be known to be in the ideal state of complete information, so that reality depends on the ultimate decision of the community; so thought is what it is only by virtue of its addressing a future thought which is in its value as thought identical with it, though more developed. In this way, the existence of thought now depends on what is to be hereafter; so that it has only a potential existence, dependent on the future thought of the community. (*W*, 72)

Current conversations depend on future conversations, current thought on future thought. So current conversations and current thought cannot justify themselves by themselves. But there is also no question of justifying current thought in terms of future thought of the community, because future thought does not yet exist. Philosophical justification for Peirce consists in logical argument. But valid arguments themselves are only signs, patterns of inference that have become so habitual that they seem to constrain thought forcefully. Justification in this sense does depend on the contingent decisions of the current community of sign users about what counts as valid argument. But justification is not the primary business of the thinking human being. The primary business is to get at the truth.

Nor does one have to fall into the trap of the optical metaphor. For Peirce it does not make sense to say that the truth is something "out there" that has to be accurately reflected by something "in the mind." His notion of representation is more complex than that. One does not get at the truth by reasoning from noncontingent starting points, nor does one do it by trying to force consensus with one's fellows. One does it by remaining always in the empirical position, with a cheerful faith (not certainty) that true representations will prevail in the indefinite future community. These representations are not mirror images, but signs—with all that implies for Peirce.

So Peirce will not fit either of Rorty's categories. He does not attempt to evade the contingency of starting points, nor does he accept current conversations as the only source of guidance. Peirce eludes this categorization because he does not think that justification is the primary concern of the reflective mind. Rorty does seem to think that. If the truth is just whatever survives verbal encounters in the current conversation, then the truth reduces to what can be justified. Then one can classify thinkers according to their views on justification, as opposed to their views on epistemology. Peirce, as it seems to me, eludes Rorty's classification by denying its premise. Peirce gives up, with Dewey and Rorty, the traditional notion of certainty and the Cartesian ambition of justifying propositions by building on the foundation of privileged, indubitable representations. But Peirce wants to hold onto the notion of truth and the real as possibly independent of whatever anybody says right now. Whether Peirce can get away with that, whether he can consistently give up the one and hold onto the other, is a deep question. But his attempt to pull off this feat nudges philosophical justification out of its familiar position at the center of philosophical discourse—a position that it seems still to occupy, at times, in Rorty's writing. That Peirce thinks he can accomplish this feat is what distinguishes his pragmatism from Dewey's and Rorty's, for my purposes. For all three pragmatists, truth is a communal matter. But Dewey and Rorty are concerned with the actual present community. Peirce is concerned with the virtual future community.

Of course, if Peirce is all wrong, then he and those who pursue textual hermeneutics as an ascetic discipline are of all humans the most to be pitied. The objections to Peirce's view are obvious. Nobody has any warrant for supposing that "truth is fated to win" or that "truth will win" (*ConP*, 203). And "Peirce's identification of 'the truth' with 'the opinion fated to be ultimately agreed to by all' makes it seem that the very existence of truth and reality depends upon such hazardous matters as the continuation of the race and of the Enlightenment's notion of rational inquiry" (*PMN*, 297). The solar system could be destroyed or the universe suffer heat-death before the virtual future community visualized by Peirce comes to pass, and where would truth and reality be then? The reality of what has happened in the past and of what is happening right now depends upon the existence of that future community. If that community never exists, is everything nothing?

I think this line of argument is mistaken. The long answer to the argument is perhaps that of Christopher Hookway, whose major project in *Peirce* is to show how Peirce could have thought that the community of scientific inquirers would approach closer and closer to the truth as the limit of inquiry. But there is also a shorter answer to the argument. It is to say that Rorty's argument amounts to asking Peirce to *justify* his assertions about truth and reality by demonstrating in current conversation that the future community he envisions will exist. But that demand misses the point. The point is not whether such a community will exist. The point is whether the projection of such a community is crucial to the semiosis, and therefore the behavior, that is going on right now. By analogy, one might say that it is not crucial to the science of astronomy whether the sun will rise tomorrow. This is a prediction that can be verified in due time. If it is not verified, *then* it becomes crucial to the science of astronomy as an anomalous fact. What is crucial to the science of astronomy right now is whether and how the ability to make such predictions constrains the science. People seem to think that some of their thoughts, at least, are somehow constrained. To reject Plato or Descartes means to think that cognitions are not constrained solely or primarily by the nature of their objects; to reject Kant means to think that cognitions are not constrained solely or primarily by the constitution of the thinking subject. To reject Rorty's pragmatism means to think that cognitions are not constrained solely by the language game of the current community. To embrace Peirce's pragmatism means to think that cognitions are constrained by the projection (often wrong and therefore unreal) of what the virtual future community will think.

I think even Rorty sometimes flirts with this tenet of Peirce's pragmatism. In an interesting passage in *Philosophy and the Mirror of Nature*, Rorty discusses whether babies before they have language know that they have pains. Philosophers think that this question is important in the debate about Wittgenstein's private-language argument. Rorty concludes,

> The child *feels* the same thing, and it feels just the *same* to him before and after language-learning. Before language, he is said to *know* the thing he feels just in case it is the sort of thing which in later life he will be able to make noninferential reports about.

That latent ability is what sets him apart from the photoelectric cell, not his greater sensitivity. (*PMN*, 184–85)

The acquisition of language means the entry into a "community whose members exchange justifications of assertions, and other actions, with one another" (185). Rorty continues,

> Having reverted yet again to the community as source of epistemic authority, I shall end this section by reemphasizing that even the nonconceptual, nonlinguistic knowledge of what a raw feel is like is attributed to beings on the basis of their potential membership in this community. (188–89)

Rorty observes that anything that looks "humanoid" (that is, has something like a human face, with a mouth that can be imagined as talking) is "usually credited with 'feelings'" (189). Thus, human beings are more likely to sympathize with koala bears than with pigs, because koala bears look more human (190). Rorty views "the attribution of prelinguistic awareness . . . as a courtesy extended potential or imagined fellow-speakers of our language" (190).

But babies have only "potential" membership in the community. Some of them will not survive to the age of linguistic awareness; some of them will grow up but will never speak. Attributing nonlinguistic knowledge of raw feels to babies is a linguistic practice of the actual present community, but it is a "courtesy" constrained by that community's projection of what the future community will be like. People are constrained to think about babies a certain way now on the basis of a projection of what is going to be thought later about what those babies were.

Now, in one sense, the point seems trivial. People have experiences of babies' growing up and learning to talk; but nobody has an experience of a future community, existing before the heat-death of the universe, where everybody agrees about everything. (For any *particular* infant, of course, there is no experience that will guarantee that it will learn to talk.) But my point is rather about the structure of Rorty's argument. Suppose someone were to ask, "Why do you attribute nonlinguistic knowledge of raw feels to *this* baby, who does not talk yet? Why not wait until the baby learns to talk, and at *that* point attribute the knowledge retroactively?" It would seem that a sufficient answer, in Rorty's account, would be, "That is just how we talk. That is how we play the language game about raw feels—we attribute nonlinguistic knowledge of them to anything that looks sort of like us and does not talk."

But Rorty does not stop there. He attempts, in fact, to *justify* this language game, by appealing to something that is going to (or only might) happen. There is a further explanation underneath the "epistemic authority" of the current community. The linguistic community is constrained to think of babies in a certain way because of their projection of the future linguistic community that includes the people those babies will become.

This further attempt at justification of the language game seems to me to involve a momentary lapse into Peircean pragmatism, a gesture toward an indefinitely future community. If Peirce is right, such lapses are inevitable no matter where one starts, since human activity is semiotic activity, and since every sign necessarily involves a reference to an infinite chain of future signification.

In this final chapter I have tried to explain further what it means to conceive of textual hermeneutics as an ascetic discipline, defined according to certain of Peirce's notions. My strategy has been to outline the consequences of that conception for humanities education, since in Peirce's pragmatism the meaning of a conception is the practical effects its object is conceived to have. My tactic has been to contrast some of these consequences with the educational consequences of Dewey's and Rorty's pragmatism. If some of the things I have said seem to canonize the teachers of the humanities by making them into masters of the discipline or unimpeachable gurus, I can only remind those teachers of what they know already from their experiences with their own teachers—that the best masters are those who are most aware of continuing to learn with their disciples. The sacrifice of certainty prepares the way for humility and for faith.

Bibliography

Alexander, Thomas M. *John Dewey's Theory of Art, Experience, and Nature: The Horizons of Feeling*. Albany: State University of New York Press, 1987.
Altieri, Charles. *Self and Sensibility in Contemporary American Poetry*. Cambridge: Cambridge University Press, 1984.
Ashbery, John. *Self-Portrait in a Convex Mirror: Poems*. New York: Viking, 1975.
Bloom, Allan. *The Closing of the American Mind*. New York: Simon & Schuster, 1987.
Bloom, Harold. *The Anxiety of Influence*. New York: Oxford, 1973.
Boler, John F. *Charles Peirce and Scholastic Realism: A Study of Peirce's Relation to John Duns Scotus*. Seattle: University of Washington Press, 1963.
Brower, Reuben A. *The Poetry of Robert Frost: Constellations of Intention*. New York: Oxford University Press, 1963.
Burnshaw, Stanley. *Robert Frost Himself*. New York: George Braziller, 1986.
Chun, Richard, with Paul Hastings Wilson. *Tae Kwon Do: The Korean Martial Art*. New York: Harper & Row, 1976.
Cunningham, J. V. "'Essence' and the *Phoenix and the Turtle*." *ELH* 19 (1952): 265–76.
Derrida, Jacques. *Margins of Philosophy*. Trans. Alan Bass. Chicago: University of Chicago Press, 1982.
———. *Of Grammatology*. Trans. Gayatri Chakravorty Spivak. Baltimore: Johns Hopkins University Press, 1976.
Descartes, René. *Meditations on First Philosophy*. Trans. Laurence J. Lafleur. Library of Liberal Arts. New York: Macmillan, 1951.
Dewey, John. *Democracy and Education: An Introduction to the Philosophy of Education*. New York: Macmillan, 1916. [*DE*]
———. *Experience and Education*. New York: Macmillan, 1938. [*EE*]
Dilthey, Wilhelm W. *Dilthey: Selected Writings*. Trans. H. P. Rickman. Cambridge: Cambridge University Press, 1976.
Draeger, Donn F., and Robert W. Smith. *Asian Fighting Arts*. New York: Berkley, 1974.
Eagleton, Terry. *Literary Theory: An Introduction*. Minneapolis: University of Minnesota Press, 1983.
Egami, Shigeru. *The Heart of Karate-do*. Tokyo, New York, and San Francisco: Kodansha International, 1976. Originally published as *The Way of Karate*.

Feibleman, James K. *An Introduction to the Philosophy of Charles S. Peirce, Interpreted as a System*. Cambridge: MIT Press, 1970.
Fisch, Max. *Peirce, Semeiotic, and Pragmatism: Essays by Max H. Fisch*. Ed. Kenneth Laine Ketner and Christian J. W. Kloesel. Bloomington: Indiana University Press, 1986.
Freud, Sigmund. *The Freud Reader*. Ed. Peter Gay. New York: W. W. Norton, 1989.
Frost, Robert. *Robert Frost: Poetry and Prose*. Ed. Edward Connery Lathem and Lawrance Thompson. New York: Holt, Rinehart & Winston, 1973.
Funakoshi, Gichin. *Karate-Do Kyohan: The Master Text*. Trans. Tsutomu Ohshima. Tokyo, New York, and San Francisco: Kodansha International, 1973.
―――. *Karate-do Nyumon*. Trans. John Teramoto. Tokyo and New York: Kodansha International, 1988.
Gadamer, Hans-Georg. *Truth and Method*. New York: Seabury, 1975.
Greenlee, Douglas. *Peirce's Concept of Sign*. Approaches to Semiotics, no. 5, ed. Thomas A. Sebeok. The Hague: Mouton, 1973.
Halliburton, David. *Poetic Thinking: An Approach to Heidegger*. Chicago: University of Chicago Press, 1981.
Hamilton, A. G. *Logic for Mathematicians*. Cambridge: Cambridge University Press, 1978.
Heidegger, Martin. *Poetry, Language, Thought*. Trans. Albert Hofstadter. New York: Harper & Row, 1975.
Hirsch, E. D., Jr. *The Aims of Interpretation*. Chicago: University of Chicago Press, 1976.
―――. *Cultural Literacy: What Every American Needs to Know*. New York: Vintage Books, 1988.
―――. "Meaning and Significance Reinterpreted." *Critical Inquiry* 11 (1984): 202–25.
―――. *Validity in Interpretation*. New Haven: Yale University Press, 1967.
Hookway, Christopher. *Peirce*. London: Routledge & Kegan Paul, 1985.
Jakobson, Roman. "Linguistics and Poetics." In *Style in Language*, ed. Thomas A. Sebeok, 350–77. Cambridge: MIT Press, 1960.
Kalstone, David. *Five Temperaments*. New York: Oxford University Press, 1977.
Kant, Immanuel. *Immanuel Kant's Critique of Pure Reason*. Trans. Norman Kemp Smith. New York: Humanities Press, 1950.
Kockelmans, Joseph J. *Heidegger on Art and Art Works*. Dordrecht, Boston, Lancaster: Martinus Nijhoff, 1985.
―――, ed. and trans. *On Heidegger and Language*. Evanston: Northwestern University Press, 1972.
Kripke, Saul A. *Wittgenstein on Rules and Private Language: An Elementary Exposition*. Cambridge: Harvard University Press, 1982.
Lehman, David, ed. *Beyond Amazement: New Essays on John Ashbery*. Ithaca: Cornell University Press, 1980.
Lotman, Jurij. *Analysis of the Poetic Text*. Ed. and trans. D. Barton Johnson. Ann Arbor, Mich.: Ardis, 1976.
―――. *The Structure of the Artistic Text*. Trans. Ronald Vroon. Ann Arbor: Michigan Slavic Contributions, no. 7, 1977.
McKnight, Edgar V. *Meaning in Texts: The Historical Shaping of a Narrative Hermeneutics*. Philadelphia: Fortress Press, 1978.

———. *Postmodern Use of the Bible: The Emergence of Reader-Oriented Criticism.* Nashville: Abington Press, 1988.
Maliszewski, Michael. "Meditative-Religious Traditions of Fighting Arts and Martial Ways." *Journal of Asian Martial Arts* 1 (July 1992): 1–104.
Nietzsche, Friedrich. *A Nietzsche Reader.* Selected and trans. R. J. Hollingdale. New York: Viking, 1977.
———. *Twilight of the Idols and The Anti-Christ.* Trans. R. J. Hollingdale. New York: Viking, 1968.
Peirce, Charles S. *Charles S. Peirce: Selected Writings (Values in a Universe of Chance).* Ed. Philip P. Wiener. New York: Dover Publications, 1966. [*W*]
———. *Collected Papers of Charles Sanders Peirce.* 6 vols. Ed. Charles Hartshorne and Paul Weiss. Cambridge: Harvard University Press, 1931–35. [*CP*]
———. *Philosophical Writings of Peirce.* Ed. Justus Buchler. New York: Dover Publications, 1955. [*B*]
———. *Writings of Charles S. Peirce: A Chronological Edition.* Ed. Max H. Fisch. Bloomington: Indiana University Press, 1982– .
Peirce, Charles S., and Victoria Lady Welby. *Semiotic and Significs: The Correspondence Between Charles S. Peirce and Victoria Lady Welby.* Ed. Charles S. Hardwick. Bloomington: Indiana University Press, 1977. [*SS*]
Poirier, Richard. *Robert Frost: The Work of Knowing.* New York: Oxford University Press, 1977.
Putnam, Hilary. *Mind, Language and Reality: Philosophical Papers, Volume 2.* Cambridge: Cambridge University Press, 1975.
Quine, Willard Van Orman. *From a Logical Point of View: 9 Logico-Philosophical Essays.* 2d ed. New York: Harper & Row, 1963.
Reid, Howard, and Michael Croucher. *The Way of the Warrior.* New York: Simon & Schuster, 1987. Originally published as *The Fighting Arts.*
Ricoeur, Paul. *The Conflict of Interpretations: Essays in Hermeneutics.* Ed. Don Ihde. Evanston: Northwestern University Press, 1974.
———. *Essays on Biblical Interpretation.* Ed. Lewis S. Mudge. Philadelphia: Fortress Press, 1980. [*EBI*]
———. *Hermeneutics and the Human Sciences.* Ed. and trans. John B. Thompson. Cambridge and Paris: Cambridge University Press and Éditions de la Maison des Sciences de L'Homme, 1981. [*HHS*]
———. *Interpretation Theory: Discourse and the Surplus of Meaning.* Fort Worth: Texas Christian University Press, 1976. [*IT*]
———. *The Rule of Metaphor: Multi-disciplinary Studies in the Creation of Meaning in Language.* Trans. Robert Czerny, with Kathleen McLaughlin and John Costello, S.J. Toronto: University of Toronto Press, 1977. Originally published in 1975 as *La métaphore vive.*
———. *The Symbolism of Evil.* Trans. Emerson Buchanan. New York: Harper & Row, 1967. Originally published in 1960 as *La Symbolique du mal.*
———. *Time and Narrative.* 3 vols. Vols. 1 and 2 trans. Kathleen McLaughlin and David Pellauer. Vol. 3 trans. Kathleen Blamey and David Pellauer. Chicago: University of Chicago Press, 1984–88. Originally published in 1983–85 as *Temps et Récit.*
Roberts, Don D. *The Existential Graphs of Charles S. Peirce.* The Hague: Mouton, 1973.
Rorty, Richard. *Consequences of Pragmatism (Essays: 1972–1980).* Minneapolis: University of Minnesota Press, 1982. [*ConP*]

———. *Contingency, Irony, and Solidarity*. Cambridge: Cambridge University Press, 1989. [*CIS*]
———. *Philosophy and the Mirror of Nature*. Princeton: Princeton University Press, 1979. [*PMN*]
Saussure, Ferdinand de. *Course in General Linguistics*. Trans. Wade Baskin. New York: McGraw-Hill, 1966.
Scheffler, Israel. *Four Pragmatists: A Critical Introduction to Peirce, James, Mead, and Dewey*. New York: Humanities Press, 1974.
Sebeok, Thomas A., ed. *Style in Language*. Cambridge: MIT Press, 1960.
Shapiro, David. *John Ashbery: An Introduction to the Poetry*. New York: Columbia University Press, 1979.
Shapiro, Michael, and Marianne Shapiro. *Hierarchy and the Structure of Tropes*. Studies in Semiotics. Bloomington and Lisse: Indiana University and The Peter de Ridder Press, 1976.
Smith, John E. *The Spirit of American Philosophy*. Rev. ed. SUNY Series in Philosophy. Albany: State University of New York Press, 1983.
Staton, Shirley F., ed. *Literary Theory in Praxis*. Philadelphia: University of Pennsylvania Press, 1987.
Studies in the Philosophy of Charles Sanders Peirce. Second Series. Ed. Edward C. Moore and Richard S. Robin. Amherst: University of Massachusetts Press, 1964.
Thompson, Lawrance. *Robert Frost: The Years of Triumph, 1915–1938*. New York: Holt, Rinehart & Winston, 1970.
Westbrook, A., and O. Ratti. *Aikido and the Dynamic Sphere*. Rutland, Vt.: Charles E. Tuttle, 1970.
Williams, Barbara. *Albert's Toothache*. Illus. Kay Chorao. New York: E. P. Dutton, 1974.
Wittgenstein, Ludwig. *Philosophical Investigations*. 3d ed. Trans. G.E.M. Anscombe. New York: Macmillan, 1958. [*PI*]
———. *Tractatus Logico-Philosophicus*. Trans. D. F. Pears and B. F. McGuinness. London: Routledge & Kegan Paul, 1974.
World Taekwondo Federation. *Taekwondo (Poomse)*. Seoul: Shin Jin Gak, 1975.

Index

abduction, 39–41
acoustic image, 29–30, 32
aikido, 100, 102, 104, 105
Alexander, Thomas M., 197–98
Argument, 25
Aristotle, 7, 23, 27, 41, 85, 143, 167
Ashbery, John
 "Grand Galop," 77
 "Self-Portrait in a Convex Mirror," 65–98
audience, 48, 50, 54–56, 105, 161, 194
Aufhebung, 10, 21
Augustine, Saint, 9, 11, 18, 113–14, 173, 198
author, 48–55, 67–71, 79–80, 105, 108, 132, 142–44, 154, 194
authority, 189, 210, 216, 225, 230–31
autonomy, 142, 146, 182, 209–13, 216–18

Baygents, Jeff, 100
Bible. *See* scripture
Bloom, Allan, 2
Bloom, Harold, 59, 199
Brower, Reuben, 60
Burnshaw, Stanley, 60

canon, 2, 139–77, 186–87, 205, 207, 209, 217
Catullus, 60
causality, 28, 36
Chun, Richard, 111–12
correctness, 46, 64, 94, 118–19, 176
Croucher, Michael, 105, 111
cruelty, 202–5
culture criticism, 204, 219–20
Cunningham, J. V., 225

deconstruction, 6–7, 19–20, 46, 65–66, 74, 81, 94, 208, 212
deduction, 28, 39–41, 64, 156, 161–62
definition, 5–6, 21–22
democracy, 181, 188, 196–97, 200, 204
Derrida, Jacques, 5–10, 13, 16, 18–19, 22, 29, 64, 182, 197, 200–201, 206–18
Descartes, René, 16, 48, 193, 222, 224, 226, 229. *See also* Cartesianism *under* Peirce, Charles Sanders
Dewey, John, 4, 180–81, 187–201, 204, 206, 208–10, 223, 228
Dicent Sign, 25
diction, 50, 61–63, 76–77
différance, 58
Dilthey, Wilhelm, 145
Dryden, John, 217

Eagleton, Terry, 166
edifying philosophy, 200, 206, 208, 212
education, 179–231
Egami, Shigeru, 133–34
empiricism, 6, 177, 188, 228
epistemology, 57, 159, 199–200, 205–7, 228

fiction, 143–44, 146, 157–62, 175
final vocabulary, 202–3, 211
Firstness, 23–26, 31–34, 37–38, 40, 42, 128
Fisch, Max, 2, 15, 39, 124
form (*kata, poomse*), 104–6, 111–12, 133
form (poetic), 50, 59–61, 74–76, 79
form of life, 117, 123, 126, 131, 205, 211, 216
Freedberg, Sydney, 71–72, 74–76

Frege, Gottlob, 142
Freud, Sigmund, 58, 62–63, 155, 167–68, 197, 216
Frost, Robert
    "Design," 63
    "The Figure a Poem Makes," 52
    "For Once, Then, Something," 47–65
Funakoshi, Gichin, 132–33

Gadamer, Hans-Georg, 142, 144, 153–55, 157, 200–201, 207
Greimas, A.-J., 159

Habermas, Jürgen, 208
Hankil, 106
Hegel, G. W. F., 205
Heidegger, Martin, 5–10, 13, 22, 28, 34, 36, 78, 137, 143, 147, 181, 200–201, 208–9
hermeneutic circle, 155, 172
Hirsch, E. D., Jr., 2, 146, 194
historicism, 142, 198, 208
historiography, 159–62
history, 142–44, 151–54, 157–65, 171, 177, 194, 204
Hookway, Christopher, 15, 23, 26, 40, 124, 229
hsing-i, 105
human sciences, 153–54, 157
humanities, 2, 4, 20, 42–43, 46, 97–98, 136–37, 189, 195–96, 198, 201, 218–22, 231
Hung, I-hsiang, 105, 111
Husserl, Edmund, 142

I-Ching, 105
icon, 25, 124
Ilyo, 112
index, 25, 30, 34–36, 124
induction, 39–42, 130
inerrancy, 171
infinite regression, 13–16
interdisciplinary, 220–22
interpretant, 11–15, 24–27, 31–32, 128, 144, 167–69, 171–74, 176–77
interpretive system (definition), 21
ironist, 181–82, 186, 202–3, 205, 208–10
irony, 49–53, 64–65, 79–80, 208, 211

Jakobson, Roman, 48–50, 54, 66, 78–81
Joo-yeok, 106

judo, 100, 104
justification, 49, 115–19, 122–25, 151, 154, 156, 159, 161–63, 175–77, 198, 204, 216–18, 222–28, 230–31

Kant, Immanuel, 7, 23, 25, 27–29, 34, 38, 64, 167, 180, 209–10, 216, 217, 219, 222, 224–25, 229
karate, 132–33
kata. See form
Keats, John, 64
Keumgang, 106, 112
ki, 100
Kripke, Saul, 113, 131, 207
Kuhn, Thomas, 194

Labanotation, 99
language game, 114–31, 181, 184, 223, 229–31
langue, 7, 11, 30
Legisign, 25
liberal education, 185, 189, 207, 216
liberalism, 181–82, 199, 202–5, 207–8, 210
literary criticism, 18, 50, 165, 180, 199–205
literary theory, 18, 219–21
literature, 3, 139–77, 189, 199–200, 204, 216–17, 219–20
Lotman, Jurij, 61

martial arts, 99–137
Marvell, Andrew
    "The Garden," 166–67, 169–70
Marxist, 155, 166–70, 180
meaning, 16, 19, 21, 42, 50, 55–56, 58, 62–63, 64, 67–68, 76–77, 82, 95, 103–5, 112, 114, 117, 120, 123, 132, 134–36, 142–51, 158, 165–77, 183, 187–94, 198, 201, 213. *See also* meaning under Peirce, Charles Sanders
Melville, Herman, 62
metaphor, 80–85, 93–97, 143, 152–53, 155, 165–66
Metaphysical, 83
metaphysics, 6, 15, 23, 25, 27–28, 34, 39, 43, 64, 83, 127, 202–3, 205, 222
mimesis, 143
Moore, Edward C., 124
Mudge, Lewis S., 148, 150–51, 156

INDEX

Nabert, Jean, 150–51
narratology, 159–61
New Criticism, 84, 139, 166–70, 194
Nietzsche, Friedrich, x, 8–9, 13, 23, 27, 181, 197, 200, 201, 208–9
nominalism, 15, 22, 33, 124, 208
nonsense, 127, 131, 135

Oakeshott, Michael, 200

pa-kua, 105–6, 111–12
Palgwe, 105, 111–12
paradigmatic relation, 29, 37–38, 42, 82
Parmigianino, Francesco, 66–97
parole, 7, 35
Peirce, Benjamin, 27
Peirce, Charles Sanders
 attention, 24, 25, 26, 127, 129–30, 132
 Cartesianism, 14, 15, 23, 124–30, 162, 180, 182, 226–28
 categories, 18, 20, 23–39, 42
 cognition, 14, 16, 20, 26, 125–30, 224, 229
 community, 125–26, 130–31, 133, 144, 146, 163, 166, 168, 174–75, 177, 214–15, 226–29
 consciousness, 9, 12, 15–17, 20, 24, 34, 53, 125, 128–33, 167–68, 214, 225–27
 emotion, 20, 127–30
 fallibilism, 43, 126, 171, 177, 227
 interpretation, 20–22, 45–46, 79, 94–95, 142, 166–68, 174
 justification, 124, 177, 224–29
 language, x, 16–17, 23, 27, 30–39, 103, 110
 liberal education, 185
 logic, 15, 17–18, 22, 25, 34, 39–42, 185–86, 224
 meaning, 14–15, 30, 32, 38, 95, 231
 methodeutic, 22, 46, 49, 79, 94–95, 142, 174, 186, 206, 215, 218–22, 231
 object, 11–15, 20, 24–26, 30–31, 34, 126, 128, 144, 179–80, 214, 231
 phenomenology, 23, 26, 39, 42
 pragmatism, 15, 131, 179–80, 222–31
 realism, 3, 15, 22, 30, 33, 124–27, 129–32, 156, 162, 177, 228–29
 representation, 14–15, 26, 131, 135, 162, 181–82, 224, 228
 rhetoric, 22, 46, 186

semiotic, 2–4, 9, 11–18, 23, 25, 39, 127–28, 130–31, 144, 166, 168, 175, 186, 231
sensation, 20, 127–30
truth, 17, 41, 174, 223, 227–29
Pellauer, David, 141
Plato, 7, 54, 75, 135, 181, 193, 204, 209, 216
pleasure, 136, 180
Poirier, Richard, 62
poomse. See form
Pope, Alexander, 171, 217
poststructuralism, 2, 10, 13, 27, 57, 65, 67, 142, 181
pragmatism, 187, 189, 190, 192, 198–99, 202, 204–5, 210, 222–31. *See also* pragmatism under Peirce, Charles Sanders
prescindability, 26
private, 102–3, 116–20, 122, 125, 129, 133, 135, 136, 141, 173, 181–82, 188, 194, 198, 201–19
private language, 113–35, 170, 215, 229
privileging, 139–77
Proust, Marcel, 182, 209–11, 213–14, 217–18

Qualisign, 25

rational, 1, 64, 129–30, 144, 146–48, 151–52, 155–57, 159–60, 162–63, 168, 174, 176–77, 191, 222–29
reader-response criticism, 70
reciprocity, 28, 38
reference, 50, 56–59, 73, 142–43, 145–46, 151–52, 190
Reid, Howard, 105, 111
replica, 30–36, 38, 40, 101, 103, 110
representamen, 12, 26, 30
retroduction, 39, 41
Rheme, 25, 30–31
Ricoeur, Paul, 2–3, 53, 55, 82, 139–77
Robin, Richard S., 124
Romanticism, 59, 68, 142, 145–46, 155, 177
Rorty, Richard, 4, 181–82, 186, 194, 197–219, 222–31
rule, 11, 18, 20–21, 25–26, 30–40, 46, 53, 56–57, 59, 61–62, 74, 79, 82, 84, 97–98, 103, 106–7, 110, 114–31, 136, 170, 212, 215–20

Saussure, Ferdinand de, 6, 7, 10–11, 16–17, 29–38, 82, 110
science, 11, 17, 46, 97–98, 145–46, 149, 153–55, 171, 177, 186, 189–201, 224, 229
scripture, 139–77
Searle, John, 207
Secondness, 20, 23–26, 31, 34–38, 41–42, 128
Shakespeare, William, 76, 183, 185, 193, 225–26
Shklar, Judith, 202
Shotokan, 132–33
sign-ground, 24, 26, 31, 128
signifier, 11, 29, 32–34, 40, 67–68, 136
Sinclair, Upton, 216
Sinn, 142
Sinsign, 25, 30
Sipjin, 106
Smith, John E., 188
societas, 200
Socrates, 52, 90, 204–5, 212
solidarity, 202–5
Song of Songs, 173
stance, 51–56, 70, 108–10
Stein, Gertrude, 158
Stevens, Wallace, 59, 66, 175
structuralism, 2, 6, 10–11, 13, 17, 22, 27, 57, 65, 142, 146, 156, 160, 165, 177
substance, 27–28, 34, 68, 144, 182
syllogism, 41, 127

symbol, 25, 101, 103, 111, 112, 143, 148, 150, 152–53, 155–56, 225
syntagmatic relation, 29, 35–37, 41
systematic philosophy, 206

Taegeuk, 106, 112
taekwondo, 99–137
tao, 100
Taoism, 111–12
testimony, 125, 150–53, 155–56, 175–76
theme, 50, 53–54, 63–64, 77–78
Thirdness, 23–26, 31–32, 37–38, 41–42
Thompson, John, 148
Thompson, Lawrance, 57
truth, 51–52, 57–58, 61, 64, 72, 79, 111, 148, 152–59, 161–62, 174, 176, 181, 193–94, 198, 200–205, 208, 215, 220, 223, 228. *See also* truth under Peirce, Charles Sanders

universitas, 200

Vasari, Giorgio, 76
Veyne, Paul, 162

Welby, Lady Victoria, 26
Williams, Barbara, 120
Wittgenstein, Ludwig, 45, 101, 106–8, 113–25, 129, 131
Wordsworth, William, 59, 61, 62, 65, 166, 174, 193
World Taekwondo Federation, 106

www.ingramcontent.com/pod-product-compliance
Lightning Source LLC
Chambersburg PA
CBHW031548300426
44111CB00006BA/223